Dear Reader,

Thank you for choosing this book as an excellent tool for your computer learning and future desk reference. I have written this book in an attempt to really do just that specific reason; be a serious tool for you to learn and better understand this confusing world of computers.

I think we can all agree that the world of computers is very fast paced and somewhat confusing. Just when you think you have it figured out; everything changes. Hence the reason I decided to write this book... To help you connect the 'confusing dots' when it comes to computers and the technology associated with computers. My desired end result in writing this book is to enable you to have a better understanding of computers (from hardware to software including networking and applications) so that you will not only be able to connect the dots (metaphorically speaking) but also to be able to grasp the full picture of how it all works. Heck along your way of reading this book; your learning and understanding may even allow you to add some shading to the dot-dot picture for some character.

To my Wonderful Wife, Family and most importantly God,

Thank you for always believing in me and being there for me through all the ups and downs of life. Everything I've done over the years has always been for us and the betterment of our lives.

Thank you for our wonderful children, grandchildren and our fantastic relationships with our friends and family. You've always shown me the better side of life and for that I thank you.

I love you all,
-Chris

Understanding Computer Basics

Author:
Christopher P. Anderson

Cover by:
CillyBee

Understanding Computer Basics (Hardware, Software, Networking and more...)
Desk Reference (Edition 1)
By Christopher P. Anderson

All Rights Reserved.

ISBN-13:   978-0-9990325-0-3
ISBN-10:   0-9990325-0-X

Created and printed in the United States of America
Printing: May 2017

Understanding Computer Basics (Hardware, Software, Networking and more...)
Desk Reference (Edition 1)
By Christopher P. Anderson

All Rights Reserved.

Warning and Disclaimer:
This book title is an independent publication not affiliated with any other company or organization. I've taken every effort to make this book as complete and accurate as possible. If I have missed a reference it is purely by accident. Images have been pulled from public domain and are freely available to the public. When referenced; source locations have tried to be included to associate with the originating source. I thank all contributing sources that assisted me with this book.

The information is provided as is and I suggest that as you practice your labs in this book that you always adhere caution, responsibility and best judgement to your practicing to protect your equipment and data. I do not in any way accept any liability nor responsibility to any person or entity with respect to loss or damages which arise from the information in this book.

The example companies, organizations, products, people and events depicted herein are fictitious in nature and used for assisting in education purposes only. I've used common company names to help translate the learning of the material however no association with any real company, organization, product, person or event is intended or should be inferred. In respect to all companies I did not use nor disclose any proprietary information in this book.

ISBN-13:   978-0-9990325-0-3
ISBN-10:   0-9990325-0-X

Created and printed in the United States of America
Printing: May 2017

Table of Contents

1. **Introduction to Computers**

Welcome to the world of computers. In utilizing this manual, I believe you've made a great choice in deciding to inform yourself on how computers work... Better yet – informing yourself how computers should work for you; instead of making you feel frustrated and confused.

Let's start off by explaining the history of and how computers interact with humans and why we need each other. It's a good idea to have a strong overview of this process in order to understand the overall interaction as well as the strengths of each. In this way, you will be able to better understand the symbiotic relationship that humans and computers have with one another and why I say both need each other in order to function. Simply put humans and computers need each other; so I don't see one replacing the other. Humans can think outside of the metaphorical box but are not so good at doing serious repetitive tasks, repeatedly, over and over without any deviations. Whereas computers are just the opposite; a computer can do repetitive tasks repeatedly over and over without any deviations; however, if something goes wrong, a computer will throw an error code which means it cannot figure it out and then stop. Therefore, this creates the symbiotic relationship between the two much like the Yin and the Yang symbol.

If it sounds like I'm referring to computers as sentient beings; they are not. This often seems to be the case when we find ourselves in the midst of wondering how and why computers seem to be doing something that you don't understand. However, for the record I'll clarify this feeling that computers do not live, feel nor think as humans do. They do not have feelings, emotions or revenge whereby they set out to frustrate the end user... They are simply tools which we humans use on a regular basis to help us perform routine tasks. As I previously mentioned, humans usually think and do things and tasks which are referred to as an "out of the box" approach; meaning that humans can think on their own. If a human encounters a problem they can think outside of the box to find a solution. However, computers cannot; computers are just the opposite of humans. Computers operate in a very systematic method and cannot think outside of the box. For example, if you want to add one plus one, a computer will do only that task and provide an answer of 2 and then stop and wait for the next instruction. Likewise, computers cannot think of a good color to apply to the font of the number 2 to go along with the rest of your paper which has this formula (where as a human can determine what color is best for visual representation). Computers cannot think outside the box as to what else needs to be done for your paper... They are dependent on humans to direct them to do certain things. Now looking at humans (in general), humans have the only multi-tasking computer in the world which can truly do multiple things simultaneously without error and that device is called a brain. A brain allows for multiple thoughts (a.k.a: channels) to occur simultaneously such as breathing, painting, listening to music, and thinking of what to have for dinner that night. All these multiple angles occur at the same instance and we come to a conclusion based on given information even though the answer is not a direct result of our suspicions.

If you do something with repetition, it's very difficult for humans to correctly perform that repetition without error more than a few times... For example; think back to elementary school; when someone got in trouble for doing something and the teacher had them write on the chalkboard/whiteboard a sentence that said something like, "I will not do __<fill in this blank>__ " 500 times repeatedly without error. If you remember, the person couldn't do that correctly but more than a few dozen times. Then the writing would become sloppy. You see this is where a computers' strengths outshine humans in that a human could type the first sentence and then copy it 500 times without error very nicely and quickly. The reason here is when a human writes a repetitive sentence and gets to between 25 and 50 sentences the repetitive task becomes a problem, the writing becomes sloppy, becoming slightly skewed and from there progressively going downhill. Now, as I previously mentioned, if you were to use a computer to type that same sentence you would write on the first line "I will not do _____" and then copy it 500 times and the first and the last lines would be without error and without any deviation.

Another thing I want you to think about regarding computers is that a computer is nothing more than a tool. By that I want to use a comparison to help paint a mental picture for you. Just like a spatula is used to cook eggs in a frying pan, a computer is a tool to help you perform a specific task such as writing a resume using a document writer program. A computer is simply a helpful tool. Here's another example. If you had to put a nail into a fence post in order to keep the fence from falling down; what tool would you use? Most likely you would use a hammer, which you would pull from the toolbox and use to insert the nail into the fence post? So just like you use a hammer to insert a nail to perform the task, you would use a computer to perform a given task such as checking email, writing a resume, search the internet or communicate to friends through social media. These tasks are usually repetitive and therefore quicker and easier for us humans to do our jobs. If you keep this in mind as you use a computer, it will make a lot more sense to you. I do not want you to be afraid of the computer; in fact as you go through this book my hopes and intentions are that this book will help eliminate and remove any fears that may arise when you use a computer. You see for the most part you cannot break a computer which is contrary to the fear a lot of folks have. Let's take the older crowd for example who were not brought up on a generation of computers. Breaking a computer is a real fear to them *(Note: in the 25 plus years I have been working with computers as well as teaching computers, I've helped many levels of generations. Working with the generation that was not brought up on computers, they tend to have a feeling of fear when it comes to computers and that's completely understandable. They might be worried that they may delete something or break something and there's no going back. Again, this is a valid feeling and they don't understand it and that's OK - this is why I'm writing this book).*

Even though I say you cannot break a computer there is potential that you can do certain tasks within your daily computer usage which can be devastating such as deleting a document or deleting an email. However, with proper training such as reading this material, you can eliminate or at least reduce the possibilities of these types of mistakes occurring. In other words, if you have certain tools and guidelines to employ as you are using a computer, your computer will operate correctly and it will make your life much easier.

For example, if you are going to use Microsoft Word to write a resume it's a good idea to make a backup copy of the resume prior to you modifying the resume. There are multiple reasons for this. Probably the main reason is if you go in and start changing things around on your resume and you decide that you don't like the modified version; you can delete the modified version and go back to the original resume and start over by making another copy and beginning again.

The main point that I'm trying to establish here is that if you use a computer (which again is only a tool) by using proper techniques; the computer will operate in the correct method without error and your data should be safe.

<u>* Remember it's your responsibility to know how to use a computer *</u>
<u>* and reading this book is a great tool to use as you learn. *</u>

Since I am an instructor I will also suggest taking a class at your local education center, school or college to learn more. Last, if the computer user (a.k.a: operator) such as yourself, is trained to correctly use that tool (computer) then you will also be able to properly direct the computer to do what you choose even as you would any other type of tool.

It's no secret that todays' world is absolutely dependent on computers and networking but at what point did this happen? There are many different perspectives on computers and how they originated and I suppose that depends on which particular company's viewpoint you're looking through as to how computers came about. Computers have been around since 1949 and there are many good links you can find on the internet referring to Eckert and Mauchly and the first computer called ENIAC. In fact here are a few helpful links from doing an open public internet search for which you can follow related specifically to this subject:

1. https://en.wikipedia.org/wiki/ENIAC
2. www.**computer**hope.com/issues/ch000984.htm
3. http://blogs.scientificamerican.com/news-blog/who-built-the-first-computer-2009-09-21/   (Source: Scientific American, By Michael Moyer | September 21, 2009))

I'll focus on the 3rd entry which refers to who built the first computer? Answer: According to John Hauptman, a professor of physics at Iowa State University states that Dr. Atanasoff's (a theoretical physicist) first computer was a 12-bit 2-word machine running at 60 hertz and was created in 1937. Now these terms are something new and may be confusing to you. You may be asking "What does bit, word and hertz mean?"

I'll explain in a moment but first let's cover what a computer or PC actually "is" in today's world. A desktop or laptop computer (also known as: personal computer) combines many internal working parts which I'll discuss further down in this chapter. But quite simply it's just a tool that allows an end user (such as yourself) the versatility and performance to check email, perform work (offline/online), stream information from the internet to any household, company or person. The options that users have today regarding configuration are endless for both off-the-shelf and self-built computer towers. Some of today's off-the-shelf computer manufacturers are Acer, ASUS, Dell, Lenovo, Hewlett Packard (Compaq), IBM, Toshiba and many others. Now another angle would be to self-build your own computer if you know what you're doing. People who choose this option are drawn to the fact that components from one brand can be interchanged with components from another brand due to a wonderful process called "industry-wide standardizations." By this I mean that you can take a hard drive from one tower and move it to another tower and plug it in as either a slave (secondary) hard drive or as a primary hard drive in the new computer *(Note: there may be some hardware & software configurations required to make it a primary harddrive in the new computer)*. Likewise the same is true for a monitor, CD-ROM's, USB devices, etc... With this standardization of interchangeable parts (internal/external) configuration and repairs are less expensive than if there were proprietary parts. Keep in mind that

4

what you want to focus on is compatibility of parts. This is in regards to types of busses, speeds of computer parts, etc.… I'll discuss more of this later.

Let me go back and explain the first computer or better yet let's start from the beginning to better understand this computer thing. What is a bit? You see a bit is a single digit in the computer world and you can think of it as a simple light switch as in image 1 below:

(Image1: Light switch can be thought of the same as binary bit)

The switch is either on or off but nothing in-between. This same concept of the light switch can be applied to this thing called a bit; it's either a 0 (zero) for off or a 1 for on. Now when we add 4 of these bits together (side-by-side) we call that a NIBBLE (meaning 4 bits). If we add another 4 bits to the previous 4 bits for a total of 8 bits then we call that a "BYTE" in the computer hardware & software worlds.

word																Size = 16 bits or 4 Nibbles or 2 Bytes
Byte								Byte								Size = 8 Bits or 2 Nibbles
Nibble				Nibble				Nibble				Nibble				Size = 4 bits
0	0	0	0	0	0	0	0	0	0	0	0	0	0	0	0	Size = 1 bit

(Table 1: correlates bits with nibble and Bytes and word)

So what is this bit, nibble and byte used for? As previously mentioned, these are groupings of data bits which allow data to traverse back and forth inside computers between computer components as well as between computers across a network. These bits travel at extremely fast speeds in order to accomplish tasks. These bits are the lowest level of communication. By this I mean these bits are either a logical 1 (can be a positive 5Volts dc) or a logical 0 (which would be zero Volts dc). Now with me saying this the newer computers are using lower voltages than what I have listed here but the concepts are still the same. If the bit is a 1 then that's like the wire to which the 1 is traversing is powered on; meaning, the wire would have a positive voltage (much like how a house light being on has to have power in its cord in order to operate). Any other computer component that is attached to that same wire (on the circuit board – it's called a trace) will also see that the wire currently has a positive

5

voltage (aka: Logical 1) on that wire/trace and would record or handle that line for that given period of time (called a clock cycles) as a logical 1. When that same line is powered off or no voltage then it would be referred to as a logical 0.

This takes us into what is the called binary. You see computers can only talk in 1 language at a physical machine level and that's by using the binary number system. The binary number system is made up of 1 (ones) and 0 (zeros) and that's it; nothing else. A 1 is a logical high which means on average +5Vdc and a 0 is a logical 0 which is zero Volts DC. So if you have ever heard of machine language or assembly code this binary code was some of the first software which allowed us to program at a low level. Now are there other languages? Absolutely, but I'm not going to go into them here. However, you need to be aware there are other software languages that allow a person to program the computer to do different things... These other languages are used for programmers to write the software code and then it's translated down into binary for the computer to handle it.

So how do all these 1's and 0's speed around the internals of the computer? I think the best way to explain this would be to paint a picture of a local freeway with different cars using the freeway. For this example, imagine you have motorcycles (bits), cars (nibbles), trucks (words) and semi-trucks (double words and larger) all using a freeway at the same time. Now all the vehicles have to follow the posted speed limit... correct? Yes, they sure do. Likewise they have to follow given protocols (more to come later); but you can think at a high level that protocols are rules. The posted speed limit we'll refer to as frequency in the computer world. Well that same communication protocols and frequency rules apply to all the bits, nibbles, words, double words. As previously mentioned frequency is the speed at which data traverses around inside the computer. The blocks of data are broken up into double words, words, nibbles, and bits; again, think of the vehicles I mentioned above being grouped into predetermined sizes. Depending on whether or not the computers bus is 32bits wide or 64bits wide. How many bits of data can go across the wire in a given clock cycle? The system breaks this up or combines the bits, nibbles, words, double words to correctly fit on the 32 or 64bit internal bus structure...

So where does frequency come from within the computer? The frequency comes from an internal clock (called an oscillator). When a dc voltage (also known as: power) is applied to an electronic component called a crystal. The crystal (oscillator) generates a pre-determined, very precise, specific and non-changing electrical clock pattern of waves which we call "frequency". The frequency runs without error until the computer is powered off. For understanding this you can correlate this by imagining ocean waves that are exactly the same and non-changing but extremely redundant without any variation.

Another way of understanding this concept would be to think of this internal clock as the air pump in a fish tank. By this I mean if you have ever had a fish tank you know that you need to pump air into the water for the fish to survive. As soon as you plug in the fish pump, it takes 120Vac voltage and applies it to an internal motor which moves the billow arm up and down. As this billow arm is moving up and down it's causing a very constant rhythm of air to be expelled out the opening to which we connect an air hose and then place it into the water for the fish.

The internal clock (again called: oscillator) uses this same concept but it takes d/c voltage and outputs a very constant non-changing electrical square wave (with some help of circuitry) from which all the internal computer parts operate from. If the above is confusing to you; here's another way to think of this. Think of a marching cadence or music at a night club. It's a beat to which all participants are able to move or dance to in unity... Without it, chaos would ensue and nothing would happen the way it was intended. So you see, in my opinion the clock is probably the most important component second only to actually having proper power applied to the system.

Now regarding the Frequency. We measure frequency in what's called Hertz, this is not referring to the automobile rental company but instead electricity is measured in size and speed. For the size of electricity it's measured in voltage (example: Home PC's and Laptops use 120V Alternating current (ac) and 240Vac for some large Industry Servers. In your home it would be your home dryer and electric oven's that use 240Vac and the speed at which it's delivered across the wire to the device would be referred to as the frequency (Industry term: Hertz). It's called Hertz after the German physicist Heinrich Hertz; one hertz means that an event repeats once per second. A previous name for this unit was cycles per second (cps). For the simplification of this book; let's just say that if your computer is in the United States then all home and office electricity is delivered equally at a constant 60 Hz (hertz). Again, think of hertz as the speed at which the electricity flows (or is delivered to your electronic components. The electric items in the United States all use the same 60 hertz requirements). According to Electricalsafetyfirst.org.uk (http://www.electricalsafetyfirst.org.uk/guides-and-advice/for-travelling/); if it is in the UK region then the electrical waveform is 230Vac running at 50 Hz.

There are different electrical plugs that are needed for both United States verses the UK when it comes to plugging your laptop or computer into power. Never fret though. Most of today's power supplies are auto sensing and auto ranging so they can adjust as needed depending on where you are. So the only thing you really have to worry about is the actual physical plug. Do a search for 'US to UK power adapter' on your favorite search engine for these adapters and you will see a plethora of converters to choose from. Most likely you will see images similar to image 2 below:

(Image 2: Power supply with various country plugs)

Notice that the power converter is still the same power converter. The only difference is in the cord which connects from the Wall (US, AU, EU, UK) to the black box which is the auto-sensing power converter which converts alternating current (A/C) voltage into direct current (D/C) voltage for the laptop.
Likewise, your tower computers have this same setup as well only the A/C to D/C converter is internal to the computer chassis frame and is located in the top rear of the computer cabinet (on most home/office towers) and similar to image 3.

(Image 3: Power Supply includes Power Converter to DC Voltage)

Now that we have the power supplies out of the way we can focus on the internal components of the computer. There are many internal objects that make a computer work of which there are typically no moving parts except for the fans which help expel the heat from the computer running outside of the chassis frame. I've provided a listing of the components inside of the computer:

a) Chassis Frame (metal)	b) Power supply
c) Motherboard (chipset)	d) CPU (processor)
e) RAM	f) Cables (pwr, IDE, Sata)
g) Fans	h) CMOS (BIOS)
i) Input/output devices	j) Operating System (software)

    1. Mouse
    2. Keyboard
    3. Video
    4. USB ports
    5. Sound
    6. Modem/NIC
    7. Floppy disk
    8. Hard drives, DVD, Flash
       (Table 2: internal computer components)

Although each of the above items are inside each computer, what makes each computer different? Well as with anything; as the days pass by there are newer products which are released. These newer versions of the above items in Table 2 may contain fixes or enhancements to the product which makes it perform better, faster, cooler and more effectively than its predecessor.

You see there are 2 main enemies of a computer and they are heat and dust.

Yes some of you may say that water is an enemy of a computer and I'm not negating that but we don't usually subject our computers to water unless you're doing some type of advanced cooling scenario for gaming or graphics. Therefore I'll say that water (and the contaminants inside the water) are a secondary problem to the other 2 enemies of a computer and again those are heat and dust. The reason I say this is that for the average computer system whether home, laptop, tablet, or even small, medium and enterprise systems; if they overheat then the computer system throttles down to protect itself while continuing to operate for the user. You may have witnessed this by placing a laptop on a bed or on your lap in the winter when having a blanket over your lap. When the laptop is placed on top of the blanket; it pulls the ambient air in through the intake ports (typically on bottom or the side of a laptop case) and then across the CPU (which generates heat) and then expels the heated air out the exhaust port at another port located on the side of the case. So if the air inflow port is blocked then the computer is unable to correctly breathe efficiently in order to remove the heat from the laptop case and the thermal design point (TDP) is reached, causing overheating and slowing of the computer to protect itself from heat damage. If this continues the computer may result in shutting down un-expectantly to protect itself. The thermal design point is a predetermined value that computer manufactures calculate which measures the correct air flow for proper removal of heat. The TDP is measured in Watts.

Now regarding dust and why it's an enemy of a computer. The reason that dust is an enemy of a computer is very much similar to that of your car. You see a computer has something similar to your car's radiator which removes the heat. Just like a car, the radiator allows for a cooling liquid to travel into and out of the engine block gathering the heat from the engine while its operating. Then, this heated liquid travels to the radiator in the front of the car where outside air is flowing across the radiator to remove the heat from radiator fins which in turn also cools the liquid and then the liquid returns to the engine to be heated again. This process repeats continually while the engine is operating (provided it's a water cooled engine). If, however, it's an air-cooled engine, this same process occurs, only there is no liquid to travel into and out of the engine block. Instead the engine has air that flows directly over the engine block with external fins that attract the heat away from the engine block to the fins where the outside air flows across the fins to remove heat (Think of a motorcycle engine).

In the same way the motorcycle engine operates to remove heat or an older Volkswagen uses air to remove heat; computers use the same process. Heat is generated by the CPU core and the heat travels away from the core into a device called a heat sync which is mounted directly on top of the CPU with a small amount of heat conducting material called thermal paste. Thermal paste aids in the transfer of heat. For this explanation; you can think of the heat sync similarly to a car radiator or the fins on the side of the motorcycle engine. As the heat travels up the heat sync then there are fans in the computer case to push or pull air through the case which also includes moving air across the heat sync. This is the process that removes heat from a CPU and expels it out the rear of the case. I'll talk more about that later.

Overall, a computer system is a wonderful tool which allows you to perform routine tasks over and over very quickly. You see, we humans are good at thinking outside the box (so to speak) and we think and do tasks all over the spectrum of life. Computers are just the opposite. They cannot think outside the box and are extremely literal. Meaning they have to be told exactly what to do by either the end user or the program to which is running. The computer system will follow each line item of a program code until it's told to stop or an error occurs without deviation. This would have been good to have in the 5th grade when I had to write, on the chalk board, the same sentence 500 times repeatedly without error, for getting into trouble at recess; oh well that's another story.

In summary, I want you to think of a computer as a tool just like a hammer or screwdriver in a toolbox or a spatula or frying pan in a kitchen... a computer is a tool to help you to accomplish your tasks. Also, remember when I say computer, you can replace it with your electronic device such as tablet, laptop, enterprise system, etc....

2. Hardware

Welcome to computer hardware basics. I think I want to start off with asking you to think of as many computer parts as possible and write them down in the table 3 below on the lines (1-12) below in the left column only:

1._____   a._____

2._____   b._____

3._____   c._____

4._____   d._____

5._____   e._____

6._____   f._____

7._____   g._____

8._____   h._____

9._____   i._____

10._____   j._____

11._____   k._____

12._____   l._____

(Table 3: Identify components quiz (Student activity))

Now whether or not you knew all these items, or if you had to look the answers up or ask a friend that's ok. The point is you were able to identify some of the components if not all of them inside a computer. Now, in table 3, I want you to identify the purpose or reason of what each one does in the column on the right labeled (a-l).

Now that you've tested your memory on these items; we'll discuss them in the next section but I'm glad that you attempted to identify these items above (even if you didn't get all of them... you will by the end of this book). I'd also like to tell you that I've provided the answers to table 2 above in table 1 if you would like to go back and check your answers.

Chassis (Frame) & Motherboard.

1. What can I expect from this chapter?
    1. In this chapter you will focus specifically on the metal chassis frame which gives structure to the computer itself as well as the motherboard and what it provides.
    2. After reading this chapter; the reader should have a good understanding of what a computer chassis frame is and what function it serves. The reader will also understand what a motherboard is and why it's important.

2. Explanation
    1. A computer needs a structure in order to correctly house all the electronic components inside of it without the components sliding and moving around in an unwanted fashion. This is much the same as the human body's skeletal system which gives the human body is structure. A computer case looks like Image 4 below. It allows the motherboard to be securely screwed to the case via a number of screws to the goldish colored stand-offs in the image.

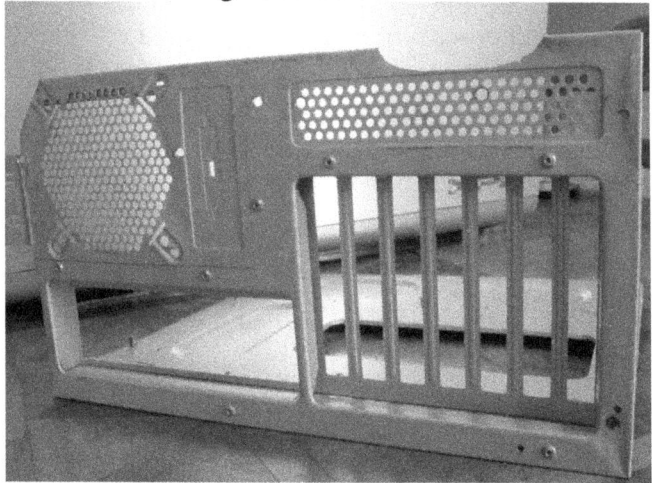

(Image 4: Chassis frame made from sheet metal)

The case also allows for a proper ground plane for the motherboard to correctly operate with voltage that's supplied from the power supply as well as for external drives and other internal components to securely exist. Motherboards come in different sizes and with different objectives for the end uscr. Some motherboards are built for industry servers, others for DVR's (digital video recorders), and others for storage systems. Mainly the average computer case is built for a PC which is similar to that which you have under your desk at work or at home. These are the most common styles of motherboards and case combos and they are referred to as form factors. There are different form factors for cases and motherboards which are AT, ATX, micro ATX, ITX and BTX.

(Image 5:)*Source:* *https://upload.wikimedia.org/wikipedia/commons/1/11/VIA_Mini-ITX_Form_Factor_Comparison.jpg*

Again the most common for home usage is the ATX form factor which houses a full size motherboard and has the dimensions of 12 inches X 9.6 inches (305 mm X 244MM). These motherboards have a built in I/O cluster bulkhead which typically installs smoothly into an ATX case without need for modification. Let's talk about the different types of Motherboards:

AT Motherboard

This motherboard came out in the mid 1980's, and was used until about the time the Pentium 2's came out. The key identifier for the AT system is the I/O bulkhead connectors which were large and bulky and usually absent of color coding or any specific identifiable marks other than the connector type itself as you can see in image 6. This led to some confusion for folks who were new to computers.

(Image 6: Source:
http://www.computersbycampus.com/images/Keyboard_AT.jpg)

The dimensions of the AT Motherboard are 13.8 inches X 12 inches
(351 X 305MM). This form factor is outdated and not typically seen
in today's computer environment. However, I added it to this
material of your history lesson of computers.

*Below is a picture (*Image 7*) of what the AT motherboard looked
like.*

(Image 7: Source: https://en.wikipedia.org/wiki/AT_
(form_factor)#/media/File:IBM_PC_AT_5170_System_Board.JPG

ATX Motherboard

In the mid-1990's Intel came out with a new style of Motherboard which was referred to as Advanced technology extended (aka: ATX) motherboards. ATX motherboards were an improvement over AT motherboards as they were faster and allowed for the interchangeability of the connected parts as well as the physical size was smaller allowing for drive bays to be located correctly in the case. Likewise the ATX motherboards had a keyboard connector (PS2) which was color coded purple and the mouse ps2 connector was color coded a light green to signal where the keyboard and mouse plugged into the motherboard. Again this was for ease of the end user. Lastly the VGA or XVGA 15 pin connector was also color coded blue for end user identification. The ATX Dimensions are 12 inches X 9.6 inches (305 mm X 244MM). You can see the connector bulkhead in the bottom left corner of the Image 8 below.

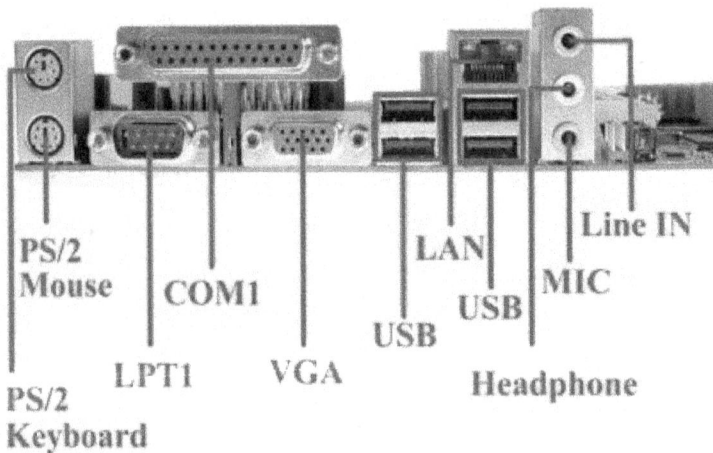

(Image 8: Source: http://usa.chinavasion.com/images/CVFR-H05-12-bbb.jpg)

BTX Motherboard

Balanced Technology extended motherboards (AKA: BTX) were developed to reduce or avoid some of the issues that came up with using newer/latest technologies such as those requiring more power and therefore generating more heat when implemented on motherboards. The ATX standard and the BTX standard, were both originally proposed by Intel. However, in September 2006 the BTX products was were canceled by Intel after the acceptance of Intel's decision to focus again on low-power CPUs after suffering thermal and scaling issues such as scaling and thermal with the Pentium 4. If you were around when the Pentium 4 came out you know that the industry was going faster and faster with the CPU's and of course was generating more and more heat. (Remember that the 2 enemies of a computer are primarily heat and dust primarily and that's because we don't usually have water around computers in normal operations).

The companies that used the BTX were Gateway Inc., Dell, and MPC. However Apple's MacPro uses only some of the elements of the BTX design system but it is not BTX compliant. This type of motherboard has some improvements over previous technologies:

- Low-profile – means a redesigned backplane that shaves inches off the height requirement. This allows for rack mounts or blade servers.

- Thermal design – Remembering that heat is the enemy of computers; The BTX design provides a straighter airflow path which results in better overall cooling capabilities. Instead of a dedicated cooling fan, a large 12 cm case-fan is mounted, that draws its air directly from outside the computer and then cools the CPU through an air duct. Another feature of BTX is the vertical mounting of the motherboard on the left-hand side. This kind of feature results in the graphics card heat sink or fan facing upwards, rather than in the direction of the adjacent expansion card.

- Structural design – The BTX standard specifies distinct locations for hardware mounting points and hence reduces latency between key components. It also reduces the physical strain imposed on the motherboard by heat sinks, capacitors and other components which are dealing with electrical and thermal regulation. Since pressure from installing/removing components can be an issue.

- Dimensions': 12.8 inches X 10.5 Inches (325 mm X 267mm)

Mini ITX Motherboard

The mini ITX motherboard is a low-power motherboard form factor designed by VIA Technologies in 2001 mainly used in small form factor (SFF) computer systems. Think of thin clients. Mini-ITX boards can also be cooled easily because of their low power consumption architecture. Such architecture makes them widely useful for home theater PC systems or systems where fan noise can inhibit the usability of the system. The four mounting holes in a Mini-ITX board line up with the four holes in ATX specification motherboards, and the locations of the back plate and expansion slot are the same although, one of the holes used was optional in earlier versions of the ATX. Hence, Mini-ITX boards can be used in places which are designed for ATX, micro-ATX and other ATX variants if required.

The Mini-ITX form factor has one expansion slot, pertaining to a standard 33 MHz 5V 32-bit PCI slot. However, often case designs use riser cards and some even have two-slot riser cards,

Dimensions: Mini-ITX is a 17 × 17 cm (6.7 × 6.7 in. SQUARE)

For the purposes of this book I won't go any further into the other form factors as they are used for other purposes. Their specifics can be looked up using a simple internet search with your favorite search engine.

So what is a motherboard? A motherboard is the main circuit board to which all the internal components are attached. You can think of the motherboard as being similar to that of a floorplan for a building. With a proper floor plan you can get from one room to another without making an error to get to your destination. Same for a Motherboard (aka: MB). Some of the components which live on the motherboard are the Central Processing Unit (aka: CPU). The Chipset, in older systems the Master Memory Controller (MMC) lived on the motherboard but in the revision of the Intel i3, i5, i7 the MMC had been relocated into the cpu module itself for faster performance. Some other items which live on the motherboard are basic input output systems (AKA: BIOS) and the complementary metal-oxide semiconductor (aka: CMOS). The BIOS is what allows you to control the system when the OS is not running. There are limited resources here and the BIOS does not have the full feature sets as that of an operating system. The CMOS is where the configurations reside on the motherboard. This leads us to the system battery (aka: CR2032) or a super-cap. The battery is what keeps the time on the bios clock when a/c power is not present.

Example: if you unplug your computer and put in the back of a moving van and move from Sacramento, California to New Jersey then you would expect your computer to be off and unplugged for the time it would take to drive back to New Jersey, plus the few days before you were ready to plug the computer back into a/c power. So how does the computer keep the clock correct while there is no power? You got it... the battery is what keeps the CMOS settings alive. So remember that the battery is only used when there is no A/C power applied to the system. If there is A/C power applied then the battery is not being used.

b. Learning Check (Chassis Frame):
1.What does a chassis (frame) do for a computer?

1. _____
   _____
   _____
   _____

2. What is the importance of the chassis?
   1. _____
      _____
   2. _____
      _____

3. What are the different chassis styles?
   1. _____
      _____
      _____
      _____
      _____

CPU (Processor)

What can I expect from this chapter?
1. In this chapter you will learn what a CPU is.
2. What function does the CPU do for the computer as a whole?

1. Central Processing Unit (CPU) Explanation
   I think the best way to explain what the central processing unit (aka: CPU) is; is to start off with asking a question. How do we know which computer is the best for your use? I like to answer this question with a question. My question is: what do you want to do with your PC?
   i.   Surf the web (y/n?)
   ii. Check email (y/n?)
   iii. Shop online (y/n?)

   If you answered yes to questions 1, 2, 3 above then please remember that these are some of the most common tasks performed on a computer and just about any off the shelf computer will work.

   The difference is how fast will your internet searches be?
   Now I have to use full disclaimer here and yes I know it's dependent on many factors such as internet speed and bandwidth as well as load on the PC and many other factors. But for simplification let's

just focus on one area at a time. In this case we'll focus only on the CPU.

Let me give you an analogy that you can use to better understand this principle. It's like this, what kind of car can you use to drive to the grocery store? Can you drive a small 4 door car with 4 cylinders which gets really good gas mileage or a 2 door sports car with a big V-8 engine with Nitrous-oxide or a Mini-van with a V6 engine or a Formula-1 race car to the grocery store? Answer is – they will all drive to and from the grocery store (in theory); however it depends on what you also want to carry to/from the store. If your entire family is going, then the Formula-1 race car is not needed as it only has 1 seat and the 2-door sports car may not easily fit everyone plus groceries. Whereas the small 4 cylinder car or mini-van are better suited for driving to the store and allowing everyone to sit comfortably and still have room for grocery bags. Applying this store analogy to the world of computers. Do you need an old computer or a new computer to do your tasks? The newer computers have multiple cores in them such as a 2 core CPU, 4 core CPU or 8 core CPU. It depends on what your needs demand. If you're a database administrator, graphic artist, musician or an individual who used auto-CAD or are heavy into virtualization, then you need a system with as many cores as possible such as the Intel I-7 CPU or the AMD FX-8350 (in other words a big strong V-8 engine). However, if you are a mild internet surfer, emailer, mild online shopper/researcher then basically any of these systems will work and a smaller CPU such as the Intel I5 or I3 would work just fine.

So let's talk more about what these CPU's do in general. I think the best approach is to go through and explain what a CPU does in general this is the example that I like to use when I teach a class. Since this example has worked multiple times and it always helps my students to be able to correctly visualize what I'm trying to explain; then I think it should do the same for you as you read through manual. So let's begin with the example. Imagine a desk that is completely empty. Sitting at this desk is an individual who has their arms and legs handcuffed – therefore being unable to use their limbs. This person is the ultimate speed reader and the best mathematician available. Therefore, anything that is put in front of this person is able to be read or calculated very quickly enabling results to be returned to whomever needs the information. I will refer to the person in the chair as the central processing unit (CPU). You may be sure that the CPU central processing unit is the ultimate speed reader and the best mathematician available. The problem is that the desktop to which the person (or CPU) is sitting at is a very small desktop. Which means any information that is placed on the desktop must be immediately processed and move it to appropriate location such as L1 cache L2 cache L3 cache ram or externally to a hard drive or RAM or an I/O port.

Let's say, for example, that a book such as "War and Peace" (which is a very large book) is placed in front of the speed reader which in this metaphor is the central processing unit. The CPU will operate at 100% performance to read the book "War and Peace" very quickly. Now when the processor has completed speed reading the book it will return to a zero percentage used. This is very similar to that of an EKG in the medical world which reports a heartbeat – up and down rhythm of the heartbeat. As there are more and more files (think of them as books or calculations) that are placed on the processor to be processed. This generates CPU activity which is reflected in an up and down heartbeat. This can be witnessed in performance monitor or task manager watching the processor. So where does all of the material come from for which the CPU will operate on? This is a good question and the answer is – it depends on the origination location of the data. For example, attached internally to the computer is a hard drive. I will talk more about the hard drive later but for now think of the hard drive as a bookshelf. Just like a normal book shelf you can store multiple books and files and pictures on the bookshelf. With that in mind if we take a book off a bookshelf, carry it across the room and placed it on top of the desktop where the CPU is located then, that is essentially the same thing as copying data from the book shelf or from a hard drive, copying it into ram and then loading it into this central processing unit for processing. When the processor is done doing what it needs to, it will direct the data results back into ram to go wherever it needs to such as a hard drive or possibly out to an external VGA video or maybe to audio as it all depends on multiple avenues. The next thing we have to keep in mind using this example is the processor is ultimately fast whereas a hard drive is actually very slow in comparison to a processor with that said, we have ram that would be the go between. For example, imagine you're the ram and you're running back and forth between the bookshelf on one side of the room and the desktop which is on the other side of the row.

Even though you have two arms and two legs and you can carry two books at the same time back and forth between the two locations you're still not fast enough. If we were going to get all of your friends and family or everybody in the classroom to run between the bookshelf and the desktop each carrying two books at a time or possibly four books at a time; they still would not be fast enough for how fast the CPU operates. With that scenario in mind that's how we need to think of RAM. In other words we have to have a good amount of ram if not a lot of ram (random access media) installed correctly and efficiently providing the operating environment as well as correctly moving data back and forth between all the locations as well as correct allocation to the various applications that are installed in the computer.

Examples:
Some examples of common central processing units (CPU's) that are available in today's market are easily found by doing an internet search on your favorite browser for INTEL or AMD cpu listings. I have to also say that there are two orders of CPU's which are CISC (complex instruction set code) and RISC (Reduced instruction set code) for cpu's. MS Windows must run on a CISC processor platform and UNIX and early versions of Macintosh needed to have RISC platform to correctly operate on. However as time has gone on it seems that the cpu hardware as of the Intel Itanium cpu and on has started to blend these 2 platforms so that either operating system can run on the other. Primarily the CISC environment is now more prevalent allowing UNIX and Apple/Macintosh operating systems to live on it instead of the RISC only platform. So what was the difference? There are many differences here and I'm not going to go into the micro details but at a high level overview the RISC environment was able to operate quicker and faster on what was in essence a reduced instruction set of coding whereas the CISC environment had to have extra commands input into the software to allow for wait states (This is where the cpu would wait for the command to finish. In essence doing nothing until the wait state completed). The CISC environment also had NOP's which were commands input into the code which told the CPU to do nothing until after the NOP was complete. This was good, however it left for some wasted time for the processor and the RISC environment did not incur these built in lags which in turn led to a more effective processing at lower performance levels (i.e.: Frequencies of CPU's). I've noted below the listing of CPU's as I recall them over the years.

CISC (complex Instruction set code)

Intel:

- 4004
- 8008
- 8080 *(note there are a few versions between 8080 and 8086 I've left out on purpose as they were not mainstream processors*
- 8086/8088
- 80186
- 80286
- 80386
- 80486
- Pentium (w/ and w/o MMX)
- Pentium II
- Pentium III
- Celerons
- Intel Core
- Pentium 4
- Xeon
- Itanium (64 bit)
- Itanium2 (64bit)
- *<a few different models here which again didn't make a big splash in the market>*
- Intel Core 2
- Intel Core 2 Duo
- Core i3 (2 core) *
- Core i5 (2 core with hyper threading for 4 logical cpu's)*
- Core i7 (4 core with hyper threading for 8 logical cpu's)*
  (Current Day)

1) * Note: The i3, i5, i7 are common models that Intel uses but what's important is they use the LGA socket set. Likewise each of the models are followed by a dash (-) and then 4 numbers. The first of the 4 numbers is the generation number series of the process and as of April 2016 the current generation number is 6. An example of this would be i3-6###, i5-6###, or i7-6###. There are different Intel sockets such as: LGA-1150, LGA-1151, LGA-1155, LGA-1156, LGA-1366

AMD: (x86 architectures)

- Athlon64 series
- Sempron series
- Opteron series

- Am2+
- AM2
- K5
- K6
- K7
- K8
- K10
- A6-series
- A7-series
- A8-series
- A10-7###
- FX-8### series have 8 cores and use the Zero Insertion Force (ZIF) sockets.
- FX-9### series have 8 cores and use the Zero Insertion Force (ZIF) sockets.
(Current Day)

> **Note:** *There are other CPU's but for the simplification of this AMD listing these are the CPU's I chose to go with. There are different AMD sockets such as: AM2, FM1, FM2, FM2+, FS1,etc..*

RISC (Reduced instruction set code) Processors:

RISC architectures are used on a wide range of platforms spanning from cellphones, tablets, apple/Macintosh products and small, medium and large enterprise servers.

Some of the manufactures of the RISC CPU's are:

- MIPS (Silicon Graphics and ceased in 2006).

- SPARC (Oracle (previously Sun Microsystems) and Fujitsu.

- IBM's Power Architecture, IBM's supercomputers, midrange servers and workstations.

- HP PA-RISC, also known as HP-PA (discontinued at the end of 2008).

- Alpha, used in single-board computers, workstations, servers and supercomputers from Digital Equipment Corporation, Compaq and HP (discontinued as of 2007).

- RISC-V, the open source fifth Berkeley RISC ISA

Learning Check (CPU):

    i.   What does a CPU do for a computer? _____

_____

_____

    ii.   How does the CPU interact with the different components within the computer itself? _____

_____

_____

    iii.   What are the most recent CPU models for each of the CPU manufacturers? _____

_____

_____

    iv.   What are the 2 most common cpu manufactures?

_____

_____

    v.   What does RISC stand for and what OS primarily uses it?

_____

_____

_____

_____

    vi.   What does CISC stand for and what OS primarily uses it?

_____

_____

_____

_____

    vii.   What type of socket set does Intel use in the newer i3,i5,i7 processor family?

_____

_____

    viii.   What type of socket set does AMD use in the newer

_____

_____

RAM (Random Access Memory)

1. What can I expect from this chapter?
    1. In this chapter we will cover what RAM is.
    2. Why is RAM so important?
    3. Examples to better understand RAM.
    4. How RAM interacts with the CPU and chipset

2. Subject Matter:
    1. What is RAM? RAM stands for Random Access Memory and it is the total amount of physical memory installed into the computer. RAM has a finite limit and you cannot exceed this limit unless you physically add more RAM (memory) to the computer. (Disclaimer: Always check with the system configuration, specification sheets and windows operating system to determine what the maximum amount of RAM the PC can hold)

    2. Why is RAM so important? RAM is the actual item that interacts with just about everything in regards to memory pages and how programs operate. More so, RAM directly interacts with the central processing unit (CPU) across the front side bus (FSB). RAM is where the operating system as well as applications are loaded into memory. This is of course once they are retrieved from the hard drive.

    3. Examples
        a. Example 1: You can think of RAM as the genie in the bottle type of thing in that when you power on the computer and the power on self-test (aka: POST) is executing correctly it will count the total amount of physical RAM installed in the machine. Once all the RAM is counted and the operating system files are retrieved from the hard drive then they are loaded into RAM.

        b. Example 2: Another way of thinking about this would be to think of the old nursery rhyme of Humpty Dumpty. As the computer is counting the RAM you can think of that as building a brick wall on which Humpty Dumpty will sit. For this example; in other words each megabit of RAM could be considered equivalent to a masonry brick in the wall. Once the RAM (Wall) is correctly counted and all is present, then we can load the Operating system (Humpty Dumpty) on top of the RAM (Wall).

c. Just as the nursery rhyme states all is fine until something goes wrong and then Humpty Dumpty comes crashing down and breaks into many pieces. Likewise the same adage applies to the operating system. If/when something goes wrong with the operating system (OS) then it crashes (The OS breaks into many pieces as it falls) and the computer has to reboot in order to fix this problem. Upon reboot the pre-stages of the OS loading can auto detect that the operating system was not cleanly shutdown upon last shutdown which means a crash must have happened. Therefore the OS initial loader program will run a recover menu to find all the broken pieces from the previous crash and put them back together again (Just like Humpty Dumpty)... Once all the pieces are put back together then the OS is again reloaded on top of (or more technically = Loaded into RAM) the wall.

4. How Ram interacts with the CPU and chipset
    a. The best way to explain this is what I like to call my theory "T" concept. In my many years of working directly on computers and looking at specification sheets I derived this concept and it has helped me to better understand a computer system as I work on it. I've also shared this theory T concept with many of my colleagues and it has proven helpful for them and the computer systems they work on. So what is it already?

    b. For this example I want you to think of a capital letter T and then look at the diagram (image 10) below for how to apply the capital letter T to the information that I'm presenting.

THE BASIC THEORY LAYOUT OF ALL COMPUTERS

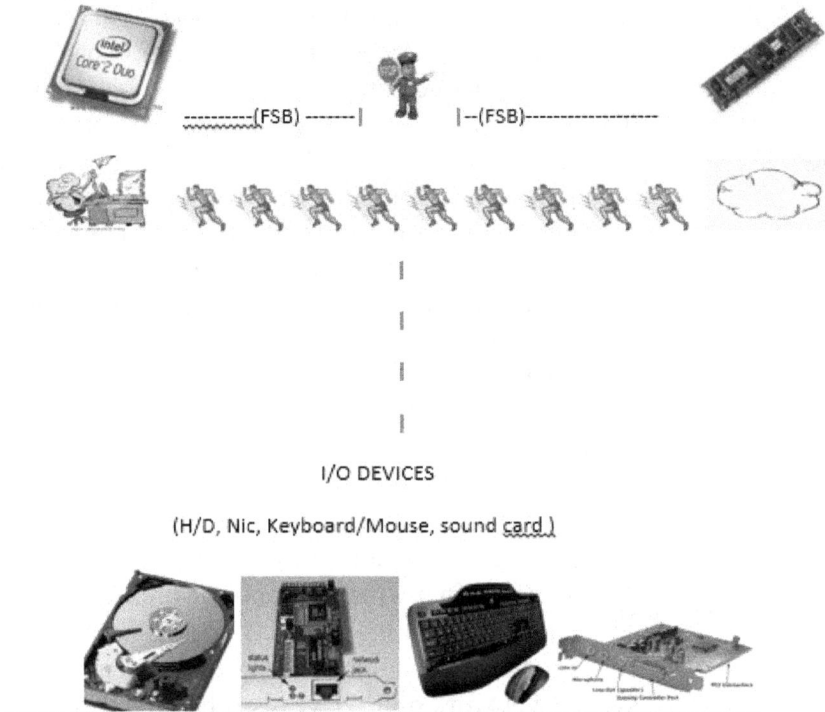

----------(FSB) -------| |--(FSB)------------------

I/O DEVICES

(H/D, Nic, Keyboard/Mouse, sound card)

(Image 10: Theory T Example)

c. As you can see on the top left corner of the capital T is the CPU and likewise the RAM is on the top right of the capital letter T. Between the CPU and the memory is the bus referred to as the Front Side Bus (FSB). The FSB is a high speed dedicated bus usually in a 32 or 64bit bus and I'm sure as time goes on this will increase to 128bit or 256bit dedicated bus between the cpu and memory with the chipset in the middle. Which brings me to the chipset. In the middle of the FSB is the chipset which I have referenced as a traffic cop. The reason I chose to use a traffic cop as the chipset is for the same reason the traffic cop directs traffic in the middle of a busy intersection. Without the direction then vehicles could not safely get to their destinations. Likewise the chipset does the same thing.   The chipset directs data from one point to another inside the computer on the motherboard. At the bottom of the capital letter T is the stem of the T or in my example I'm using it to represent the input and output bus (aka: I/O bus). I'll talk more about the I/O bus in the I/O section.

d. So let's talk more in depth of how memory operates. When you install ram into a computer it's a physical (finite) amount of ram and we cannot go above that limit. For example if we put 4GB of ram into a computer for usable memory then that is the total (maximum) amount of RAM the computer can use. This goes for everything and yes I mean everything that uses ram. By this I mean the operating system uses a certain amount of memory (ram) lets say 1.5GB of the 4GB. Likewise each and every program and application that you have running will also require a given amount of the ram from the 4GB pool of memory. This pool of memory is called contiguous memory and this pool of memory is what the operating system as well as all programs and apps will pull from in order to create small little isolated worlds of memory for the application to operate within.

e. Let's look at an example in real life. When we turn on a computer it counts all the memory installed in the computer. This is done in BIOS and it's a normal operation. When all the memory is counted let's say 4GB of ram (memory) then that creates the memory pool. After BIOS counts the ram then it hands off to the operating system to launch and load. In our case this will be Microsoft Windows. As Windows loads up let's say the Windows uses 1.5GB of RAM for all of its normal features that come with windows. This leaves a remainder amount of 2.5GB of memory left in the memory pool. Next we open a writing program called Microsoft Word to write a letter. In this case Word takes approximately 125MB of memory for it to use (while its operating). This 125MB is pulled from the remaining 2.5GB of free memory. (Note: 1.0GB equals 1000MB which is important as we convert gigabytes of memory into the same measurement of megabytes. With this decoder formula we can now look at this mathematically. This would be 2500MB (a.k.a 2.5GB) of memory subtract 125MB (0.125GB) for word which leaves 2375MB (2.375GB) of memory pool available for other programs and apps to use.

f. When we are done using MS Word program and we save and close our document as well as MS Word then the memory that MS Word was using for its small standalone universe is cleared and released back to the main memory pool... Think the reverse process of what we just explained above. Likewise the above process is very very similar for each program or application you have installed in the computer such as Chrome, solitaire, PDF readers, Office applications, etc....

g. Once the memory is returned to the general memory pool it can be used by other programs as needed and where needed without error.

This leads to the last section of memory which is memory leaks. Memory leaks are when software is not written correctly and the small amount of memory that program needs to run is consumed by the program and that program continues to need or require more and more memory to operate outside its normal operation. If software is created correctly then memory leaks are not a common issue. Memory leaks are usually addressed well before software is released to the public as they are vetted by proper quality and assurance measures. The problem with memory leaks is they continue to consume the memory from the contiguous memory until all the memory is used up. When all the memory is used up and there is no more memory available then the system will typically crash. This can cause system lockups and even blue screens of death (a.k.a: BSOD) which is a term that was more common in earlier versions of Windows. For this book; I mainly wanted you to be aware of them for your sanity in case a program was consuming more memory than needed.

Learning Check (RAM):

1. What does the acronym RAM stand for? _____

   _____

2. Explain how RAM interacts with the CPU and chipset?

   _____
   _____
   _____

3. What is the FSB and why is it important?

   _____
   _____
   _____
   _____

4. Why is RAM so important?

   _____
   _____
   _____
   _____

5. What uses RAM?

   _____
   _____
   _____

6. What programs or applications use memory (a.k.a: RAM)?

   _____
   _____
   _____
   _____

7. Can contiguous memory be reused between operating system and applications; provided that the program was written correctly to release memory when done? Yes/No _____

8. What is a memory leak?

   _____
   _____
   _____
   _____

Input/Output (External Devices)...
What does this mean?

I. Overview: What can I expect from this chapter? In this chapter you will learn:
1. What does input and output mean in reference to the computer?
2. Why so many devices are generically called input and output (I/O)
3. Examples of I/O items such as mouse keyboard, VGA, USB, hard drive, SATA, and Video (ISA, EISA,AGP, PCI, PCI-e)
4. Why we need I/O devices.

II. Explanation:

Let me begin with some of the questions that I've heard my students ask me over the years. Is a mouse an input and output? What about a keyboard? How about video? What about an external USB disk (aka: thumb drive)? Why does input and output get used for so many different items? What does input and output mean in reference to a computer system? Why do so many devices get generically called input and output? Well these are good questions and can be a bit confusing to a newbie.

Let me do some clarifying for you right now. You see that the term input and output is a generic term that is given to a computer part in regards to how it interacts with the computer. So the term input and output can be applied to many different components at the same time. What you have to ask yourself is how does the component you're dealing with interact with the computer.

Let's talk about a keyboard for example. A keyboard is an input device by default (not including some really high tech keyboards). Therefore as you type on a keyboard you're sending information into the computer and thus making the keyboard an input device. Same goes for a mouse.. you move and click a mouse on various items on your computer screen and you're telling the computer to do something. Therefore a mouse is also an input device.

Now in regards to an output device – that would be where data or instructions are coming out of the computer to an external device such as a video display or a printer. Both of these devices are basically output devices. Although I have to admit that due to the invention of the All-in-one printers which means the printers are not only printers but also include a scanner, fax and copier combo device. In this case the all-in-one printer which does all 4 functions such as copy, print, scanner and fax is both an input and output device.

I. Examples (Parts):
  1. Mouse: A mouse is an input device which an end user of a computer uses to command a computer. This is typically done by the user resting their hand on the mouse and then by a series of movements either forward to move the mouse up, backwards to move the mouse down, and left and right to move the mouse either left or right on the screen. The mouse typically comes with 2 buttons on top of the mouse for the user to click on. This is usually how many of the PC mice are by default. However a mouse can come in many configurations from 1 single mouse button (typically this is an Apple style of mouse) to 2, 3, 4, 5, 6 buttons depending on the application. The mice that are used in gaming configurations usually have more mouse buttons due to the more features available in games. Trackballs also fall into this same category as well as touchpads in laptops. You can think of these the same way as you would the mouse. A standard mouse looks like image 11 below:

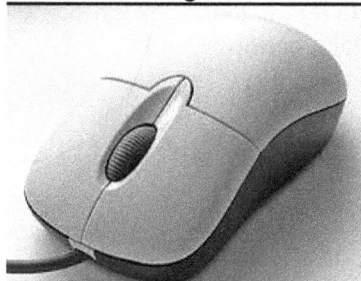

(Image 11: A two button mouse)

Ok so there are 2 buttons on a mouse... What do they do and how do I know that? If you're thinking this, then perfect... you're right where I want you to be. This leads me to what the mouse buttons do. For
many new folks this can be a bit confusing. So the way I like to think of this is:

A) The left mouse button (default) can be used to either single click on an item on the screen which means it will select that item; or the left mouse button can be double clicked on an item in the screen which means it will select it and then take action (such as opening or executing that item).

B) The right mouse button is typically used to show you the contextual menu. Meaning that it will show you the options available for the items on the screen that you're pointing the mouse at. This is good if you want to copy, cut, paste, delete or look at properties of an item. After you right click on an item to display the options available then move your mouse to the item in the new popup menu and then use the left mouse button to select that item and execute it.

C) I've created a general pictorial image (Drawing 1) below to help summarize this left and right mouse button concept.

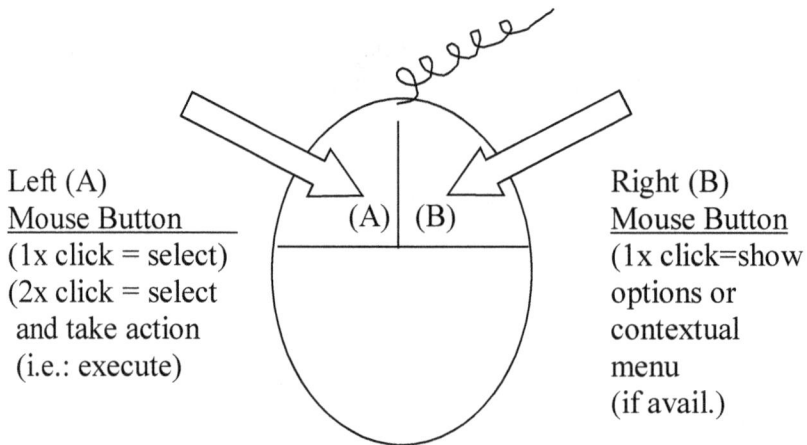

Left (A)
Mouse Button
(1x click = select)
(2x click = select
 and take action
 (i.e.: execute)

(A) | (B)

Right (B)
Mouse Button
(1x click=show
 options or
 contextual
 menu
 (if avail.)

(Drawing 1: Understanding Mouse Diagram)

Here is a picture of a real 2 button mouse for which I created the drawing above:

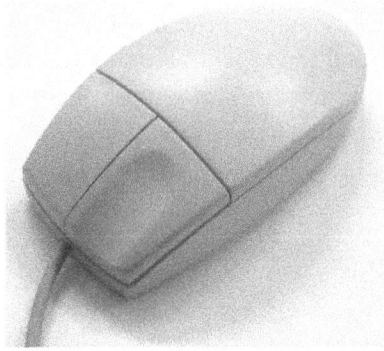

(Image 12: Another two button mouse)

D) Lastly I want to say the above configuration is for a person who is right handed. For a left handed person it's very easy to reverse the left and right mouse buttons by going into Windows control panel and clicking on the mouse configuration icon. You will be able to follow the prompts for reversing the left and the right mouse buttons for a left handed configuration. This will not cause any problems swapping between left and right handed configuration. It's simply a user preference.

2. Keyboard: A PC keyboard is another input device to which the end user is able to type keys on a keyboard to command the computer to type the letters which are pressed. I'm not talking about a piano keyboard silly. This is computer territory and so we are focusing on the computer (PC) keyboard. So what do they look like?

(Image 13: Standard Keyboard)

Remember, this is a very powerful tool in that it allows the end user to write letters, resumes, emails, newsfeeds, updates for online materials, formulas in Excel, or scripts. Basically for any reason a person needs to type a letter or number into a computer the keyboard is the most common method and preferred by many around the world. Keyboards come in many different styles from the standard straight keyboard (above) to ergonomic keyboards (below)

(Image 14: Ergonomic Keyboard)

which help with carpal tunnel or ulnar nerve pain. These are wrist pains that users who type for many long hours a day and for long periods of time may suffer such as I do.

My disclaimer here is that I'm not a medical doctor and if you have any such wrist problems you need to have your doctor check them out. With that said, after I talked with my doctor the best solution for me was to get an ergonomic keyboard which is a miracle to me. I do have to admit that in the beginning there was a learning curve getting use to it but after 20 mins of using it: the pain in my wrists had seriously diminished and I've used one ever since.

Anyhow let's get back to the computer world here... So keyboards are an input device and they come in many styles... Some of these styles include media keyboards, keyboards with touchpads built into them and a variety of other features. I would say that if you don't like the features your keyboard has or the style, you can change to a style that you do like. You see, keyboards are for the most part universal and unless you have some special (out of the norm) configuration they should be an easy replacement for the computer due to the fact they all primarily use USB connections in today's world.

So what is the best way to replace a keyboard? As previously mentioned, the keyboards of today are primarily connected to the computer via USB. I'll cover USB in the next section however, keep in mind that USB means it's hot swappable and you can unplug your old keyboard by just following the cord from the keyboard to the PC tower or laptop. Then when you find the

USB connector, use a firm grip between your thumb and fore finger and pull on the usb plug straight back. This will remove the cord from the computer. Proceed with swapping the keyboards and then reverse the above process for re-inserting the new keyboard USB connector back into that same USB port on the computer. After plugging in the new keyboard you may have to wait a few moments for Windows to be able to detect and assign the correct driver for your keyboard. If it's a non-standard keyboard you may need to install the drivers for it before it will be detected correctly. If this is the case then you will need to look for the installation dvd that came with the keyboard or possibly go to the manufacturer's website and download the proper driver for your version of operating system on your computer.

USB: Now; let's go into the arena of input and output devices at the same time. Yes you got it. We are going into the world of USB devices. Most everything that is externally connected to a computer in today's computers use the most common method possible and that's USB which is short for Universal Serial Bus (aka: USB) connection. When you see the following image (Image 15) it refers to USB:

(Image 15: USB symbol)

So how effective is USB for transferring data? It's probably easiest for me to explain and for you to understand if I put it into a graph such as:

Version:	Rate (Megabits per second):	Referred to as:
1.0	1.5 Mbps	Low
1.1	12 Mbps	Full
2.0	480 Mbps	High
3.0	5.0 Gbps or 5000 Mbps	Super
4.0	10 Gbps/lane (4 lanes)	Thunderbolt

(Table 4: USB versions and Data Transfer rates)

Why did I add the 'referred to' column above? Well if you have ever gone to the store and had to buy an aftermarket USB cable then you probably have already experienced the cables are referred to as low, full, high, super and Thunderbolt. This seems to be the method used to show you how much data can flow through the USB connection (or in other words the speed of that connection).

You would not want to have a USB 2.0 connection which runs as 480 Mbps and then replace the USB cable with a Full cable which is rated at a maximum of 12 Mbps. This could seriously slow down your communication between the 2 USB ports. This is why I added the above chart.

Now, I have to add another disclaimer here. The rates I have listed above are industry rates for that version of USB device. They are best case scenarios under perfect laboratory conditions and not real world data transfer rates. What I've found in real life is that the data transfer rates seem to be about 70% of the rates listed in the chart above. For example on USB 2.0 (Maximum rate of 480Mb/sec) I usually see an approximate transfer rate of 24MB/sec. So how does this happen... Let's do the math.

480Mb/sec * ~70% = 336 Mb/sec
336Mb/sec divided by 8 (8 bits in a byte) = 42 MB/sec
42 MB/sec split between 2 directions (reading & writing) ~ 21 MB/sec.

Now, this is not a hard and fast rule but a generalization of I/O performance to devices. Please remember that reading data from a device is usually faster than writing data back to that device and so the read and writes will fluctuate as you move data back and forth. But for the purposes of this book and to provide you a high level overview, I believe this sets the stage for you to understand how this works.

One last interesting note regarding USB devices which I find equally fascinating to the fast speeds of data transfers which USB devices have by design; is that USB controllers can have a maximum of 127 devices connected to each USB controller at the same time. Now that's a lot of USB devices all connected at the same time and would look something similar to image 16 below.

(Image 16: Multiple USB Devices all connected at once.)

How can that possibly be? Well let me set the stage by saying this is correctly done with USB splitters which are most likely daisy chained to each other. See the picture for better understanding:

With Free
Power Adaptor

(Image 17: A USB Hub/Expander)

The problem that occurs is for that many devices you have to have an additional power supply attached to them to provide the power needed. You see a standard USB connection has only 4 pins as noted below:

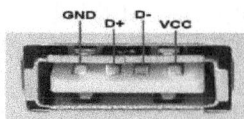

1	VBUS	Red
2	D-	White
3	D+	Green
4	GND	Black
Shell	Shield	Connector Shell

(Image 18: USB Type A Pinout)

The voltage on VCC is +5V dc and it can supply power to a single USB device or even 2 devices. However, if you start going above the 2 device limit then additional power is required in order to verify that all additional USB devices have the correct VCC power that they need. This is a best practice philosophy and a good rule to follow.

There are also different styles of USB connectors such as:

	Type A	Type B	Mini-B	Micro-A	Micro-B
Type A	Yes	No	No	No	No
Type B	No	Yes	No	No	No
Mini-B	No	No	Yes	No	No
Micro-AB	No	No	No	Yes	Yes
Micro-B	No	No	No	No	Yes

(Image 19: USB types and compatibility chart)

NOTE: The Yes means that the 2 connector styles are compatible whereas the No means that they are not compatible and you will need to use a USB converter to change to the other plug. You can pick these USB converters up at your local electronics store or online very easily and they usually plug in without too much problem.

Some of the most common areas where these plugs are found are:
Type A = PC to PC connections
Type B = PC to printer
Mini & Micro connectors = cellphones and tablets.

3. Hard drive

What is a hard drive? A hard drive is a device which can be inside (internal) or outside (external) to the computer. This hard drive device is used for storing data for use by the computer operating system as well as programs. It can also store user data files such as documents, pictures, music, videos, and many other directories and files.

I like to think of a computer hard drive as a book shelf. That's right; think back to when paper files and manila folders were stored in the file cabinets in an office. Now, that's what I like to think of when I hear the word "hard drive."
So if you also think of a hard drive as a book shelf then I have a question for you. Can book shelves come in different sizes, shapes, colors, materials? The answer is "Yes, they sure can." Let me break it down for you:
Are there tall book shelves?
Are there small book shelves?
Are there narrow book shelves?
Are there wide book shelves?
Are there plastic book shelves?
Are there metal book shelves?
Are there wood book shelves?
Are there blue book shelves?
Are there pink book shelves?
The answer to all of the above questions is "YES."

The same goes for hard drives, so if you correlate the word 'hard drive' to mean 'book shelf' and vice-versa then you'll have a pretty good understanding that a hard drive – no matter what size, shape, color or style it is… its purpose is to store data until it's needed. This goes for the different styles of hard drives as listed below:

a. PATA (legacy) – PATA stands for Parallel Advanced Technology Attachment however many of the IT professionals refer to this as Parallel ATA disk drive. Either way this is probably one of the oldest styles of disk drives. This PATA technology was used for communication to hard drives and CD-ROMs. It used a 40 bit bus and typically communicated at 33Mb/sec to 100Mb per second data transfer speeds. However there is one speed which is faster known as EIDE (IDE5 or IDE7) and it used a ground pin between each of the data pins of the 40pin grey data cable. This data cable existed between the hard drive (and carom) and the motherboard. There were 40 ground pins between the 40 data pins for a total of 80 pins all together. This combination along with the EIDE hard drive capabilities enabled the motherboard and bios supported EIDE communications to allow for data transfer speeds up to 133Mb/sec which was extremely fast for pre-2000 years.

Below in image 20 is a picture of the 40pin cable next to the 80 pin cable: (notice the 80 pin has twice as many lines in the ribbon cable and the plastic bulk head is still the same).

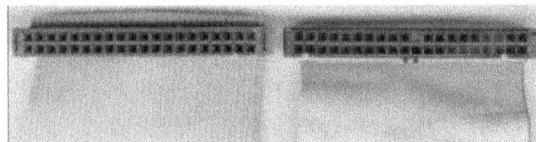

(40pin cable)   (80 pin cable)
(Image 20: IDE Ribbon cables)

Looking at the cable a bit more in depth (see image 21) we see the red line (darker line in image 21) on top which always refers to data pin #1 as well as the two 44 pin connectors. These connectors are used on both the 40pin data cable as well as the 80 pin data cable.

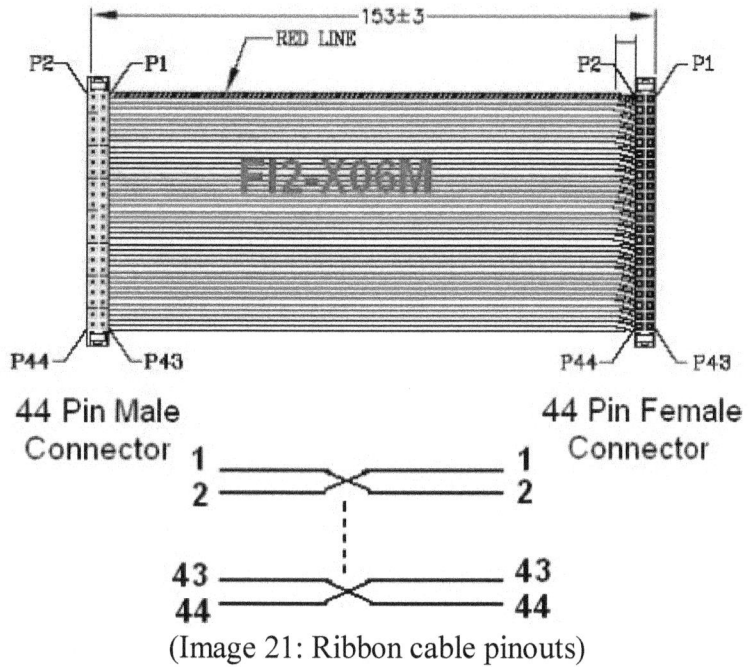

(Image 21: Ribbon cable pinouts)

Now, how do we power on the PATA (aka: IDE) device. To do that we use a connector called the "molex" shown below in image 22:

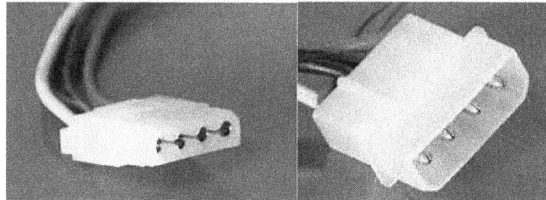

(Image 22: Molex Power connectors)

The pinout for the molex connector is as follows:

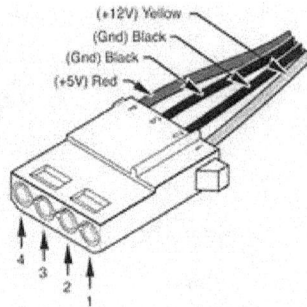

(Image 23: Molex power connector pinouts)

How do the Molex and the 40/80 pin data cables connect to the PATA device? I've shown this in image 24 below:

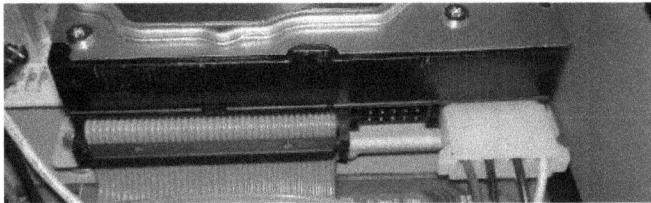

(Image 24: Left is IDE cable and Right is Molex connection)

b. SATA – This is the newer standard for communications with internal disk drives. SATA is the next evolution of data cable standards for hard drives and CDROMS/DVD players and recorders SATA stands for Serial Advanced Technology Attachments. SATA does not have the wide ribbon cable that PATA does (40 and 80 pins) but instead has only 7 data pins.

When you think of SATA I want you to think similarly (generically) to how USB works. Just like USB where there is a power, ground and data+ and data – pins (lines). SATA is similar in that it's like having 2 USB busses together. Look at image 25 for a better understanding of pinout and what it looks like:

SATA Pinout - Plug

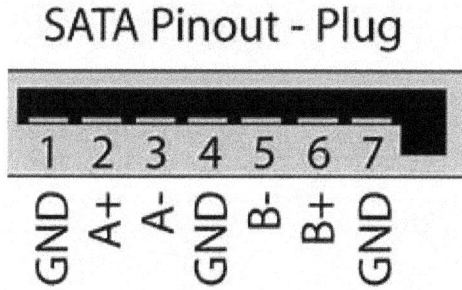

(Image 25: SATA Pinout and cable)

The above example is why I want you to think generically of USB in that there are 2 channels for data to flow (A+ and A-) and (B+ and B-).

So how does this work?

Serial connections (aka: wires) use two lines for sending data in 1 direction and two lines for receiving data in the opposite direction. As noted in the picture above there are 3 lines which are ground wires, which totals up to the seven wires and pins in a standard SATA cable connection. Using SATA connections is a more compact form and more efficient way of transferring data. SATA cables have allowed various types of hardware to continue to get smaller while also getting faster at the same time compared to the legacy parallel systems.

A bit down the history road here but recall my previous section on parallel busses and how the 40 ground pins were added in between the 40 data pins due to interference. Let me continue on this thought here. You see, older parallel systems were replaced because processor speeds increased. As the data speeds continued to increase, interference in the lines also directly increased problems. The fix was to go to serial transmissions which use just one line instead of several parallel lines and then crank up the frequency on that serial line to get the performance that was needed. By doing this interference is minimal.

SATA cables allow for data to be transferred at a higher data clock rate (means the frequency is higher) than the old parallel bus data transfer systems. Please keep in mind that a clock rate is how fast a CPU executes instructions per second. *(note: to convert between frequency and time the formula is $f=1/t$ or $t=1/f$)* Back to the subject here; SATA cables handle faster CPU speeds than parallel cables. SATA lines can transmit data up to 6

gigabytes per second to keep up with newer and faster CPUs.
I've built a table (#5) below to reference the SATA speeds:

SATA Revision (known as)	Bandwidth Speeds (up to:)
SATA 1.0	1.5 Gb/second (1500Mb/sec)
SATA 2	3.0 Gb/second (3000Mb/sec)
SATA 3	6.0 Gb/second (6000Mb/sec)
SATA 4	12 Gb/second (12000Mb/sec)

(Table 5: SATA types and transmission speeds)

Note: the speeds listed in the above table are the best case
scenario efforts under lab environments and are typically not
seen in the real world environments. However since these are
the best case scenario numbers the world is using them so I'll
also use them so you are aware of the numbers.

My findings have shown the real world numbers to be
approximately 70% of what is listed above. In communication
with other instructors and engineers, I have confirmed that using
a 70% mark of best case listed prices for SATA is a good
general rule of thumb. Example: SATA 2 lists at 3.0 Gb/second
(best case scenario in lab environment where everything is
perfect). 70% of 3.0 Gb/sec (3000Mb/sec) equals 2.1 Gb/sec
(2100Mb/sec). To convert this to Bytes per second we divide
this by 8 which equals 26.25MB/sec which is the best case "real
world" numbers you will typically see when transferring data via
USB 3.0 between devices. Now keep in mind this will be the
ceiling for the speed of the transfer but the actual speed of the
transfer will fluctuate under the 26.25MB ceiling until all the
data is transferred correctly so keep in mind that this is 100%
completely normal and expected behavior; nothing is wrong
with this. To witness this behavior in a graph form you can
easily open task manager and then click on disk performance tab

to watch the data transfer. For more details on this you can open the resource monitor from within task manager.

Next, we have the power connector for the SATA device (see image 26) which is a 15 pin power connector which looks like the following along with the pinouts:

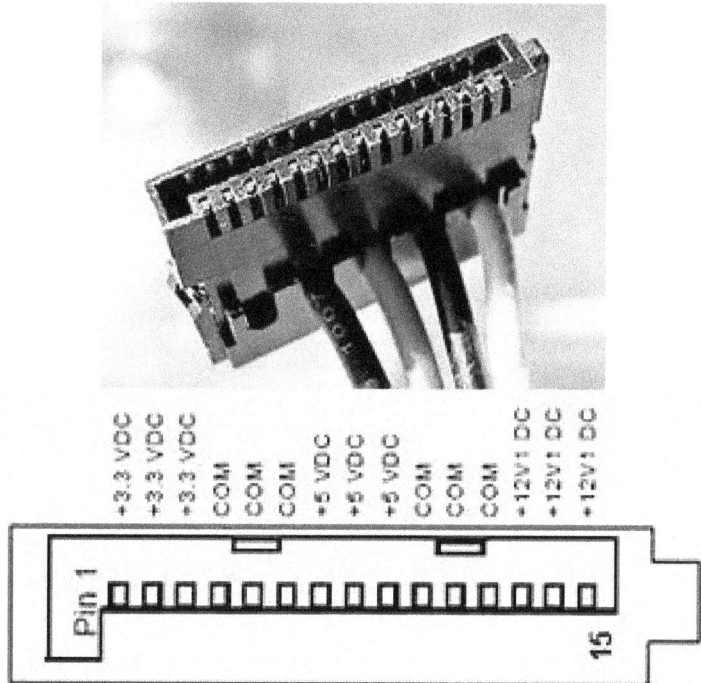

(Image 26: SATA power cable and pinout)

So where and how do these connectors connect to SATA devices. I show this in the following image 27:

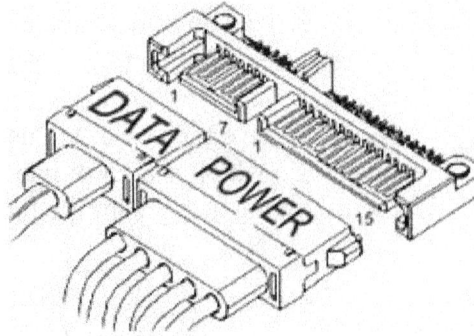

(Image 27: Image of SATA Data and Power connection to harddrive.)

c. SSD – A new type of hard drive has come on the computer playing field called solid state drive (most commonly referred to as SSD). This is a new type of hard drive which has no moving parts inside of it such as its predecessor drives which used platters and arms to move in and out of the platter. The old legacy style drive's internal workings might be compared to how a record player works; like the image below.

(Image 28: Image of record player)

Whereby you would put the record onto the record table and then manually pick up the arm which had the needle attached to the end and then move it out onto the record to hear the music as the table rotated at a specified rotation speed.

(Image 29: Image of pickup arm reading music on record)

Well these old legacy hard drives are just that same concept except instead of using a record we use what's called a platter and we stack 5 platters on top of each other with a spacer of a few millimeters in between each platter.

(Image 30: Hard drive (left) and
internal platters of hard drive on right)

Then we have mechanical arms that move out to place the pickup needle on the top or bottom of the platter to read or write data to that platter. The reason I bring this up in the SSD section is that it takes power (example: 12Volts dc) to power the motor to spin the platters as well as to move the pickup arm in and out on the platter. You can see the inside of a SSD drive below in image 31 and why I say it's similar to that of RAM (memory):

51

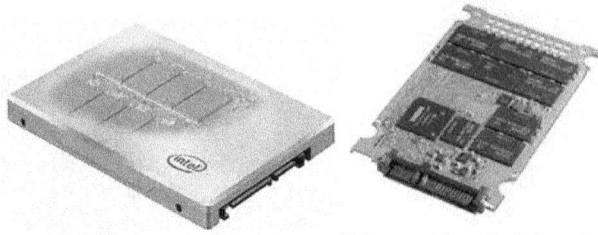

(Image 31: Image of newer solid state hard drives)

In regards to SSD drives there is no platter and no pickup arms so there is no need for 12Volt (dc) power to be applied to the SSD. This reduces the power requirements for the hard drive.

What makes the Solid State Drive the new drive going into the future? Basically you can think of a solid state drive similarly to how RAM memory works except that it's not volatile (meaning when power is removed from the disk it does not lose its memory.. unlike RAM). Just like how RAM is extremely faster than the old hard drive in regards to data bandwidth. The new SSD drives perform in the same way. You may see typical bandwidths of old platter hard drives of 25-50MB/second, whereas with solid state drives you can see, read and write speeds upwards of 450MB/second. See my examples (Image 32) below for copying a 50 MB file to my C:\ drive:

Note: my hard drive is a Hitachi HTS723225A7A364 5400rpm drive in my HP Probook 6460b with 8Gig of RAM.

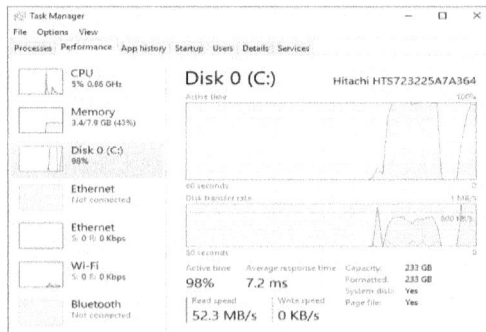

(Image 32: Task Manager Image of C:\ disk)

The testing tool I used was a free program called "CrystalDiskMark. "

See image 33 from testing the C:\ drive below:

(Image 33: Crystal Disk Mark of standard PATA 5400rpm C:\ disk)

Now when I compare this to my wife's computer in image 34; It has a solid state drive you can easily see that the Read and Write speeds drastically increase with the same test:

(Image 34: Crystal Disk Mark of standard SSD hard drive (C:\))

For the record, her hard drive (Image 34) is a Samsung SSD 850 Pro. Her PC is a Samsung core2duo machine with 4 gigs of ram

So what are the pros and cons to a solid state drive?

Basically the solid state drives are faster, quieter, require less power and they can fit in the same size location as the existing hard drives in PC's and laptops. The cons to the SSD is that in the early years of SSD existence there was a finite amount of writes that could be written to the SSD drive. However the reads were unlimited. Now don't panic, this number of writes is extremely large and in fact it's basically in the millions of writes. If I can put it into normal English, the SSD will last the typical user probably over 10-12+ years before it stops allowing writes to be performed and that time line is based on writing data 24 hours a day, 7 days a week (In theory). So what happens after the threshold of writes is reached? Good question and the answer is quite simple. The SSD is still useable as it becomes read only at that point. So you can still read your data from the SSD but you just can't write to it any longer.

So what about the SSD's of today? Modern SSDs will, on average, have a functional life that outlasts their useful life. SSDs have the advantage of not actually doing much unless they're reading and writing, which means that during idle periods they're not going to "wear" like a regular HDD would. There is a memory controller on the SSD which directs data to and from the disk (memory chips). Failure of the memory controller is more likely to happen than actually reaching the max writes of a modern SSD in today's SSD. The memory controller quality is usually what separates the good brands from bad brands. It's been said that Intel has very good ones, among a few other brands.

Overall I'm impressed with the low power consumption that SSD's require as well as the extremely fast input and output they deliver when it comes to storing and recalling data.

d. External – External is a term that is used to refer to any device that is outside of the typical computer (desktop/laptop) case. This includes such items as external hard drives, external webcams, and many other items.

4. Disc's
(CD-ROM, DVD-ROM, BLU-RAY)

a. What is a CD-ROM, DVD-ROM and this thing called a
    Blu-ray disk?
b. Why do I need to know the difference?

As I previously explained in regards to a hard drive being a book
shelf. I want you to also think of the CD-ROM, DVD-ROM and
BLU-RAY the same way. A CD-ROM, DVD-ROM and BLU-RAY
disk are all methods of recording data to a plastic disk much the
same way as a record had music data on it back in the 1970's-80's.
A CD-ROM, DVD-ROM and BLU-RAY all look like:

(Image 35: CD-ROM (left), DVD-ROM (center) and BLU-RAY
(right)

These disks can also store user data files such as documents,
pictures, music, videos, and many other directories and files. There
is no difference in physical size between any of these disks however
the difference between them is in the storage capacity to which each
can contain. This is reflected in the table 6 below:

Media	Storage Capacity	Avg. Movie Length
CD-ROM	740 MB (Single Layer)	Less than 1hr
DVD-ROM	4.7Gb (Single Layer)	2hr standard movie
BLU-RAY	27 GB (Single Layer)	13hours standard/2 HD hours
BLU-RAY	54 GB (Dual Layer)	20hours standard/4.5 HD hours

(Table 6: Disk storage capacities)

These disks are all played in what's called a player and I've provided examples of these players below in images 36-38. Notice that each of them are the same physical size.

(Image 36: CD-ROM player)

(Image 37: DVD-ROM player)

(Image 38: Blu-ray player.)

So what are they? These disks are plastic with a reflective surface made typically of aluminum. The disks are 120mm in diameter.

How do they work? Well, quite simply the plastic disk has a series of microscopic divots called pits. Conversely the areas between the pits are called lands.
A laser is shined at the plastic disk and reads the pits and lands in sequence as the disk is rotated at a pre-calculated speed. Keep in mind the depth of these pits is approximately one-quarter to one-sixth of the wavelength of the laser light used to read the disc, the beam is then reflected off the plastic as shifted light in relation to the incoming beam. This pattern of changing intensity of the reflected beam is converted into binary data which is 1's and 0's. I've provided a graphic representation of this below in image 39:

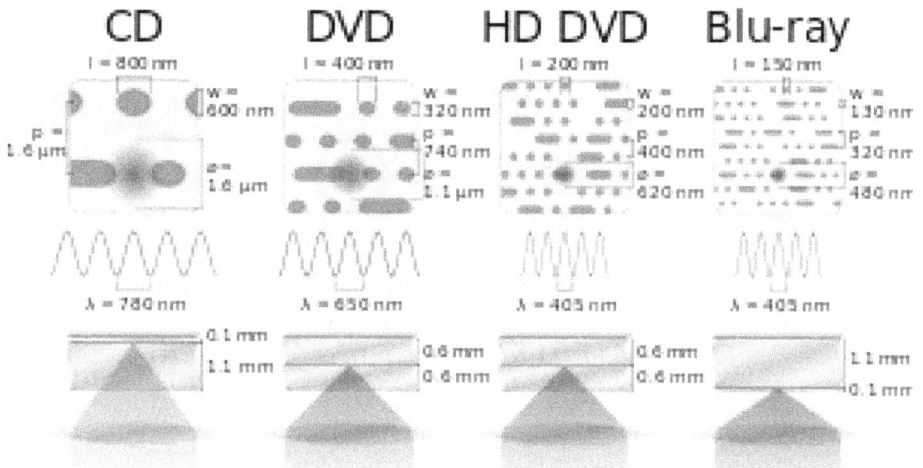

(Image 39: Laser beam sizes for CD, DVD and BLU-RAY)

Notice how big the circle (beam of light) is on the CD. Now compare it to the DVD Beam and then conversely look at the HD-DVD and the Blu-ray beams. As you can see the CD light is the biggest beam followed by the DVD being smaller and then HD-DVD and Blu-ray is the smallest beam of light of the four. Since the beam of light is getting smaller and smaller in the diameter of the light beam then that means that there can be more and more data on the Blu-ray disk itself.

Practice:
Here is another way of thinking about this and in fact let's turn this into a hands-on lab. Grab a standard household flashlight and aim it at a wall across the room (with the room lights off – of course). Notice that the beam is visible on the opposite wall of the room. Now note the size of the beam... let's say its 2 feet in diameter. This would be equivalent to a laser on a CD-ROM. Now walk half way across the room (i.e.: 50% across the room) with the flashlight still aimed at the same spot. Now notice the diameter of the light on the wall. It's now approximately 1 foot in diameter. This would be equivalent to a DVD-ROM. Lastly would be to move the flash light even closer to the wall and have the flashlight approximately 1 inch from the wall. Now look at the light on the wall and it's even smaller than before. It's now the same size as the flashlight since there is no room for expansion on the wall. In this position the light would be equivalent to a Blu-ray laser pointing on a Blu-ray disk.

So why do I need to know the difference? Since each of these types of media can store difference amounts of data then it becomes a customization for the amount of data you want to record or play back at a given time. If you only have music to record or some small files then a CD-ROM will work fine without a lot of wasted space. However if you want to backup one of your HD movies that require 22 GB of storage then you must use a Blu-ray disk as the CD-ROM and DVD-ROMs are not large enough to handle this storage requirement. Lastly this comes down to the cost of the disks. Disks come in different speeds, thicknesses, single verses double layers and these can cost more money.

5. Video – There are a number of different types of video ports that have been used over the year. They stemmed from using the ISA and EISA ports in pre 2000 years to the accelerated graphics port (AGP) followed by Peripheral circuit interface (PCI) and the enhanced version which is, PCI-e. However all of these are old technologies so I'm not going to cover them much as they are no longer used.

In today's world; we use the PCI-e 16x (pronounced 'by-16') slot for graphics buses which is also known as an interconnect. This is the newest graphics port which is directly connected into the CPU and it does not have to go through the chipset as does the smaller

PCI-e slots (below x16) as well as its predecessors listed above did in the old years. By having the PCI-e 16x connected directly to the CPU it eliminates any bottleneck that may occur in the chipset. The graphics controller is what actually resides in the CPU and thus provides a much faster data transfer rate to and from the external video card and monitor. Typically the Graphics port is located in the highest position in the I/O bay which also correlates to PCI-e slot #1 (This will be located closest to the I/O bulkhead on the rear of the computer when the motherboard is installed into the systems metal casing.

You can see the different sizes of PCI-e chart (#40) below:

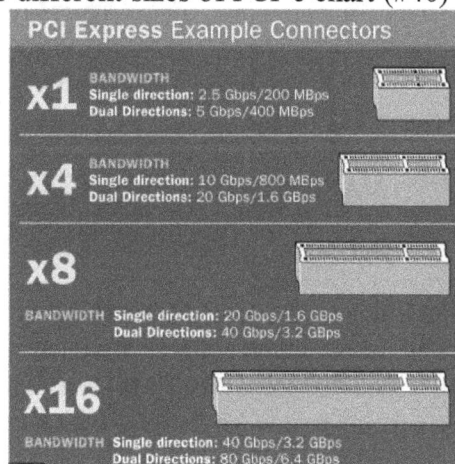

(Image 40: PCI-e chart)

Notice that all the PCI-e slots are oriented the same on the right hand side with the Key marker (white) across the PCI-e slot. You could take a PCI-e x1 card and physically install it into a x4, x8 or x16 slot however you can not go the opposite direction. Meaning that you can not take a PCI-e x16 card and physically install it into a x8, x4 nor x1 slot as these slots are physically smaller and will not accept a longer card in them. However if you do take a x1 card and install it into the bigger slot it will still only perform at a x1 bandwidth due to the card itself is only a x1 card. You can not increase the performance above what it's acutally built for. What do these slots actually look like on a motherboard? See Image 41 below:

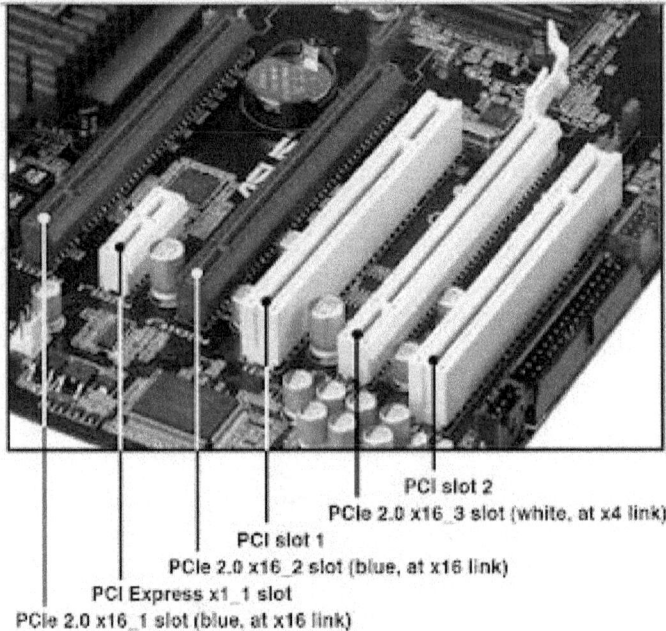

PCI slot 2
PCIe 2.0 x16_3 slot (white, at x4 link)
PCI slot 1
PCIe 2.0 x16_2 slot (blue, at x16 link)
PCI Express x1_1 slot
PCIe 2.0 x16_1 slot (blue, at x16 link)

(Image 41: PCI-e slots)

So what kinds of devices use these interconnects?
Typically the x1 interconnects are used by devices that do not
require as much bandwidth. This may include devices as
soundcards, mice and keyboards which connect to USB cards which
plug into these x1 slots. However where the big bang for the buck
comes into play is for the x16 slots. This is typically used for
graphics cards due to performance level required.

Summary: As you can see it's extremely important to have input
and output devices connected to a computer. By having devices that
connect to the computer which allow us (humans) to give commands
(via an input device) or to read output (via an output device) then we
successfully have an effective communication and control over the
computer. Generally these different input and output devices are
universally grouped into what we call I/O which stands for input and
output devices.

II. Learning Check (Input/Output):

1. What does input and output mean in reference to the computer?

   _____

   _____

   _____

   _____

2. Why so many devices are generically called input and output (I/O)

   _____

   _____

   _____

   _____

3. Classify the device as either input or output and Explain the details of the following I/O items:

   a. Mouse = (Input) - The mouse allows the end user to select items in the computer to perform given tasks.

   b. Keyboard = _____

   _____

   c. VGA = _____

   _____

   d. USB = _____

   _____

   e. Hard drive = _____

   _____

   f. SATA = _____

   _____

   g. Video (PCI-e) = _____

   _____

4. Why do we need I/O devices? _____

   _____

   _____

   _____

   _____

III. Printers

I. What can I expect from this chapter?

    1. The different types of printers that exist.

    2. The pros and cons for each printer type.

    3. Which printer do I need?

II. There are 3 major types of printers that are in use today and these have been around for a number of years. The first of the 3 printers is the oldest (common back in 1970's-1980) and it's called a 'dot-matrix' which is also known as an 'impact' printer and is displayed in image 42

(Image 42: Dot Matrix (Legacy) Printer)

This printer was one of the first common printers that was used during this time frame as a common printer. It printed in a method that was very similar to that of a type writer. It used a print head which would move left and right (back and forth) across the metal guide bar which would guide the printer ribbon across the paper. When a key was needed it would strike the ribbon and impact it; which would transfer the ink of the ribbon onto the paper as shown below:

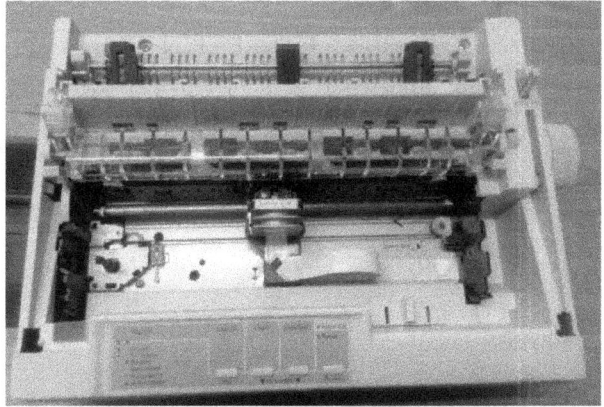

(Image 43: Internal view of Dot-Matrix Printer)

This was effective however it's really effective when it comes to printing on paper which required duplicates such as government forms, medical and also car sales forms. Some of these forms were very long and used a perforated edge that had to be placed just right for proper alignment in order to continuously feed the form into and out of the printer as shown below:

(Image 44: continuous feed of paper through Dot-Matrix Printer)

Typically the dot-matrix (aka: impact) printer was limited to printing 1 or 2 colors depending on the type of ribbon that was used.

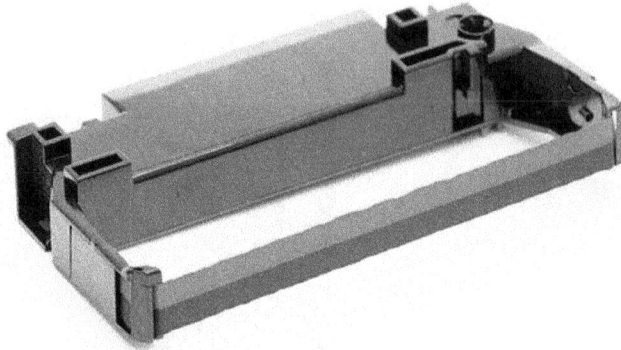

(Image 45: Dot-Matrix Ribbon Cartridge)

However the primary color used on dot-matrix printers was and is still black. It was a slow printing style and communicated via the LPT port on the rear of the computer. A problem with these older impact printers was if the computers bios was not setup correctly for proper communication then the printer might not print correctly. So not only did you have to troubleshoot the printer from the operating system but you also had to troubleshoot the BIOS configuration which took some knowledge and experience to become good at troubleshooting these older printers.

The next printer which came out was called the ink-jet printer. This printer really established itself as a permanent player in the 1990's. It allowed for more colors to be printed on the users' paper. It also allowed for different styles of paper to be used such as plain, glossy, luster and metallic. The colors that it offered were typically a black, red, yellow and blue or in some cases it was black, magenta, yellow and cyan. There are two types of ink-jet printers. These are thermal and piezoelectric. The first is the thermal ink-jet printer.

(Image 46: HP deskjet 710c)

The thermal ink-jet printer uses a print head with print cartridges to produce the image on paper. Notice in the below image how the print head would heat up causing the color in the print head to heat and cause bubbles. As these bubbles would explode they would be minor directional explosions towards the printer paper and would explode the color on to the paper. This was choreographed with the motors in the printer rollers and gears to paint a correct image on the paper.

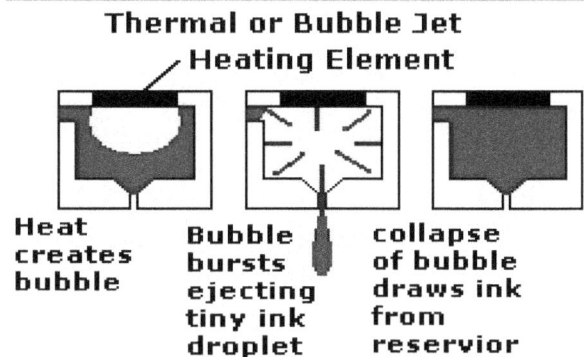

Thermal or Bubble Jet
Heating Element

Heat creates bubble

Bubble bursts ejecting tiny ink droplet

collapse of bubble draws ink from reservior

(Image 47: Thermal compared to Bubble Jet works)

The printers that used this method were Canon, Hewlett-Packard and Lexmark.

The draw backs to thermal printers is the heat can dry out the ink in the print tubes if not used on a regular basis and then you would have to have them cleaned or throw the printer away as the print head was a fixed item to the printer and if it got clogged then it became worthless. What was the best way to clean these tubes? I met an old printer repair man who used steam to clean these tubes. Just the same way as a steam is used at Starbucks for coffee. This same coffee device was used to generate hot steamed air and then applied to the tubes and would blow the pipes clear. This was typically a very messy and dirty process but it did work effectively.

The second type of ink-jet printer is called the piezoelectric.

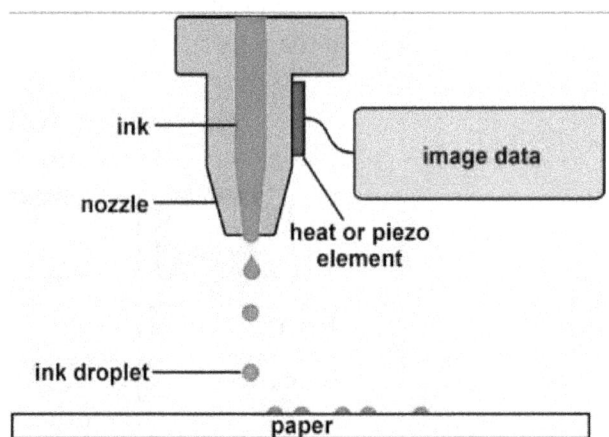

(Image 48: shows how piezoelectric disperses)

The piezoelectric material (element) was used for this method. It did not use heat but instead used electricity in or next to the ink-filled chamber and when voltage was applied the piezoelectric material would change shape (vibrate/resonate) which would cause a pressure pulse in the fluid. This would be the driving factor which would force the color fluid out of the reservoir and towards the paper.

The benefit of this method was the print tubes were not as susceptible to tube drying problems as that of the thermal.

Hewlett Packard did come up with a benefit for their print cartridges which incorporated the print head with the print reservoir so when you replaced your print cartridge you were also replacing the print head. This eliminated the print head from wearing out and smearing colors. It also seemed to eliminate the print color tubes (which went from color reservoir to print head) from filling up and drying with ink in them. This caught on very well in the market and propelled the HP printers into the business world as a desktop item for many employees and managers worldwide.

Finally we get to the third type of printer which is the LaserJet printer. This in my opinion is by far the cleanest of all printers for clean printed documents and pictures. However it's also the most expensive printer to purchase. Advocates and proponents have stated that for the number of print jobs that the printer can print; the cost per print job is significantly lower overall and therefore cost effective. LaserJet printers are capable of printing in black and color. LaserJet printers don't use a ribbon (dot-matrix) nor a liquid ink (ink-jet) but instead they use a dry powder which is kept in a drum inside of the printer.

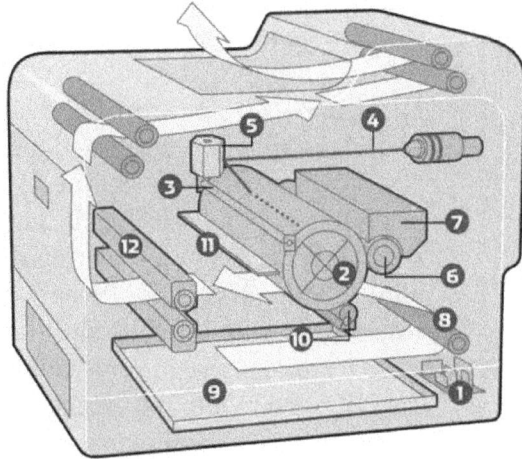

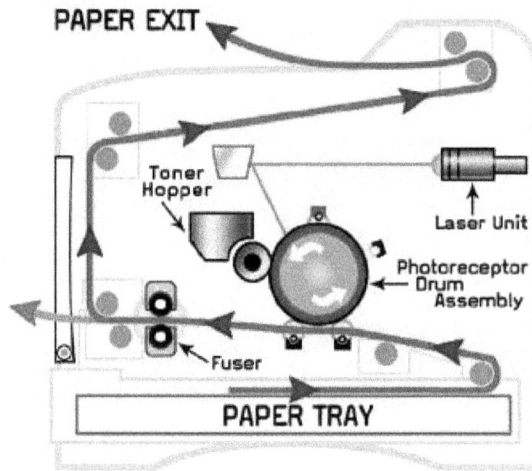

(Image 49: Internal view of Laser printer and operation)

The print drum (hopper) is a replaceable unit and it typically replaced when the dry ink is low. So how does a laser jet printer work? Well there are a few steps to it which I've noted below:

1. Cleaning
2. Charging the drum with -600Volts
3. Write image on to drum
4. Transfer (0 voltage) toner to the Drum
5. Transfer image from drum to paper
6. Fuse image to paper with Heat

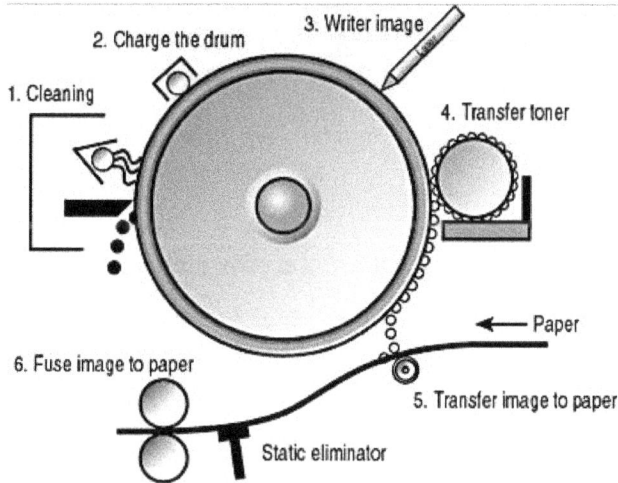

(Image 50: Side view of how laser printer operates)

Another way of looking at this same operation is displayed below in image

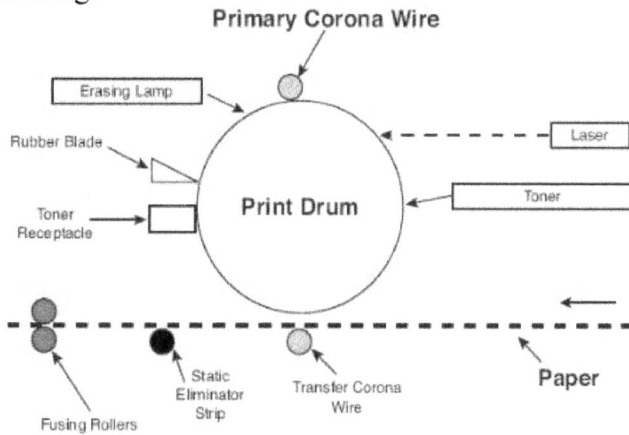

(Image 50: Another way to explain how the laser print process occurs. Please note above are 2 images which describes the same process)

Note: that due to the excessive amount of power that is used with LaserJet printers it's never recommended to plug the LaserJet printer into your uninterrupted power supply (UPS) as it will drain the power faster than any other item.

69

III. **Learning Check - Printers**:

1. What are the different types of printers that exist?

   _____

   _____

   _____

2. What are the pros and cons for each printer type?

   _____

   _____

   _____

   _____

   _____

   _____

   _____

   _____

3. Which printer will you choose and why?

   _____

   _____

   _____

   _____

   _____

   _____

IV.   Summary Check: Hardware

1. Write down all the hardware equipment in the left column and in the right column fill in what it does:

    1._____   a._____
    2._____   b._____
    3._____   c._____
    4._____   d._____
    5._____   e._____
    6._____   f._____
    7._____   g._____
    8._____   h._____
    9._____   i._____
    10._____   j._____
    11._____   k._____
    12._____   l._____

2. What is a computer case and why is it important? _____
    _____
    _____
    _____

3. What is the most common style of motherboard for the home pc?
    _____
    _____
    _____

4. What does the acronym CPU and RAM stand for?
    _____
    _____
    _____

5. Explain how RAM interacts with the CPU and chipset?
    _____
    _____
    _____
    _____

6. What is the FSB and why is it important?

_____

_____

_____

_____

7. Why is RAM so important?

_____

_____

_____

_____

8. What uses RAM?

_____

_____

_____

_____

9. What programs or applications use memory (a.k.a: RAM)?

_____

_____

_____

_____

10. Can contiguous memory be reused between operating system and applications provided that the program was written correctly to release memory when done? Yes/No _____

11. What is a memory leak?

_____

_____

_____

_____

_____

12. What does input and output mean in reference to the computer?

_____

_____

_____

13. Why are so many devices generically called input and output (I/O)

_____

_____
_____
_____

14. Classify the device as either input or output and Explain the details of the following I/O items:
    a. Mouse = (Input) - The mouse allows the end user to select items in the computer to perform given tasks.
    b. Keyboard = _____
       _____
    c. VGA = _____
       _____
    d. USB = _____
       _____
    e. Hard drive = _____
       _____
    f. SATA = _____
       _____
    g. Video (PCI-e) = _____
       _____

15. Why do we need I/O devices?
    _____
    _____

16. What are the 3 different types of printers that exist? _____
    _____
    _____

17. What are the pros and cons for each printer type? _____
    _____
    _____
    _____

18. Which printer will you choose and why? _____
    _____
    _____
    _____

3. Software - Operating Systems

M icrosoft Windows

What can I expect from this chapter?
1.   What is an operating system and why do I need it?
2.   The history of Microsoft Operating Systems
3.   What is the difference between Microsoft Windows and Microsoft Office (Understand this is not MS Office 97, 2000, 2003,2007, 2010, 2013 or 365 (Online version))
4.   How to Power On/Off/Restart the Windows OS.

What is an operating system? An operating system (OS) is pre-written code which is used to run other programs (apps) in. The operating system runs on top of the basic input and output system (aka: bios) and it supports a computer's basic functions during operation and is responsible for managing equipment resources, services and functions. The OS is the first program that is loaded after bios and it's the main software interface that we humans have when it comes to operating the computer. Without the operating system the computer would not be able to operate and we would not be able to perform tasks in the computer.

The history of the Microsoft OS is a bit long but in short there is a wonderful documentary which came out in 1999 called 'pirates of the silicon valley' which helps to explain this. The video covers how the computers came to be; for both Microsoft as well as Apple. For simplification purposes, I'll focus on the timeline of Windows as displayed in image 51 below:

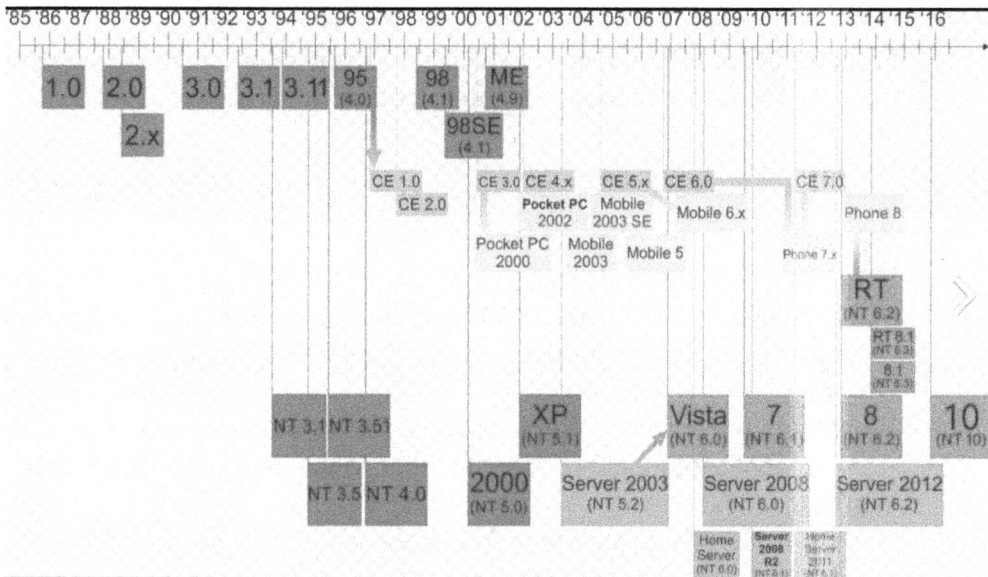

(Image 51: MS Windows release timeline. Source:
https://en.wikipedia.org/wiki/Timeline_of_Microsoft_Windows#/media/File:Windows_Up
dated_Family_Tree.png Document License URL: http://creativecommons.org/licenses/by-
sa/3.0/)

As you can see in the graphic above that Windows did start back in 1986 as version 1.0. I didn't get involved with this until Windows 3.1 came out in 1992. It was nothing like what we have today but instead Windows was an application that had to be installed and executed from the MS-DOS environment. You see the DOS OS was the base underlayment for the computer system which provided a command line interface. If you wanted to run this program called Windows which was a graphical user interface then you had to set the configuration files correctly and then launch it. This was a very exciting time in the computer world and allowed users to use a mouse and have access to programs that were not possible in a command line only environment.

Now in 1995 there was a game changer and all of a sudden this program called Windows had changed from an application to that of the operating system. You no longer needed to boot DOS first and then Windows but instead you could install MS Windows 95 as the OS and when you turned on your computer it would actually boot directly into Windows. The funny part was the DOS environment was still present. However DOS was now an application inside the MS Windows 95 OS. From that point on Windows continues to be the primary OS for home pc as well as office environments for end users and all of the Windows OS have a DOS command prompt application.

From the client OS perspective (which means it's not in a role of a server) these are the major versions of Windows that were released:

Win 1.0

Win 2.0

Win 3.0

Win 3.1

Win 3.11

(Note: Windows Versions1to 3.11 were thought of as an application called Windows which road on top of the DOS operating system)

Win95 – first Version of Windows to be the base OS (instead of an application) and to have the Start Menu in lower left of screen

Win98

WinMe – Short lived version of Windows

WinXP (sp1,2,3) – Probably the best version of Windows 32bit

WinVista

Win7 (SP1,2) – Probably the second best version of Windows 64 bit.

- versions:
- Win7 Starter
- Win7 Home Basic
- Win7 Home Premium
- Win7 Professional (Includes Bit locker)
- Win7 Enterprise (Multi-Activation Keys for deploying operating system to multiple remote systems (i.e.: 500 client machines all being remotely installed but will need their own license once installed)
- Win7 Ultimate = (Same as Enterprise but includes Media Center).

Win8, 8.1 (start menu is back) – Introduced the tile version of Windows to tablets and smart phones but was not user friendly for users who were mouse and 'start menu' oriented.

Win10 – Probably the best version of Windows 64 bit. It incorporates the tile menu from window 8 as well as the start menu from Windows 7 as well as the 64bit backend engine (database) for Windows operation.

Now that we've gone down history lane regarding Windows I want to turn to a more current version of Windows. You guessed it, "MS Windows 10" is the current release of Windows operating system. Windows 10 is a free upgrade from July 29 2015 to July 29 2016 to any person who already has

Windows 7 or Windows 8 or 8.1 currently installed on their PC and their hardware is compatible for the upgrade. The end user can register with Microsoft and do a free upgrade to Windows version 10 either by going to www.microsoft.com/windows10 or by going to the Windows update application inside of Windows 7 or 8 (8.1).

Since we are talking about Windows 10; in my opinion there are some really good features to MS Windows 10. Here is a general list of them that I've noticed since I've upgraded to Windows 10 but keep in mind there are many new features and this is just a list I've found so far:

1) Was a free upgrade which expired July 29 2016
2) Cortana = digital assistant that can be invoked by saying "Hey Cortana".
3) Edge Web browser (replacement for Internet Explorer)
4) Task View (Windows version of multi-desk)
5) Xbox App
6) Halo lens (holographic computer; doesn't require a computer to connect to)
7) Continuum mode (auto detects keyboard add/removed and adjusts between laptop and tablet mode.
8) Start menu is a combination of application menu and the tile menu (Windows 8.x) not to mention there is a secret menu option (right click).
9) Tile menu has many different items such as pictures, edge, stocks and weather.

As I've already mentioned Windows10 is a free upgrade (until July 29 2016)

Second is the creation or adaptation of Windows assistant called Cortana. Cortana is the Windows 10 digital assistant that can be invoked by saying "Hey Cortana". This has been very helpful when using voice commands to open programs, issue commands, or to perform local file searches or internet searches. This leads me to a fun fact that you can do with Cortana. Cortana listens for the words "Hey Cortana" and doesn't care who says it. This leads me to my funny practical joke for the computer world. It's in regards to my son just after we installed Windows 10 on his laptop for the first time. He was working on a document and in the back ground I yelled, "Hey Cortana – Find me funny pictures on the internet". Of course Cortana heard my voice and did as it was told… Right in the middle of my son's writing Cortana opened an internet window and looked for funny pictures… I thought this was funny and proceeded to repeat this a few more times throughout the evening at the most awkward moment I could find… My son didn't like the interruption too much but I found some humor in it… (I think some parents might agree with me).

Anyhow Cortana seems to be a really good program for voice recognition and so far I've been impressed with how it responds to my voice whether using the laptop when travelling or when I have my laptop on my docking station. Cortana is able to easily pick up my voice and so far has had a really good recognition of my voice to text features.

The next feature for Windows 10 is the new web browser called "Edge". Edge is the replacement web browser for Internet Explorer. That's right, Microsoft had decided not to continue the Internet Explorer line of web browsers but instead to start a new product line of web browser which still incorporates the basics of Internet Explorer plus new options such as Cortana, writing on the web and importing your favorites. When you open Edge for the first time you will see the Edge browser welcome screen which looks like image 52:

(Image 52: Edge and Cortana welcome screen)

Edge has all the standard features that Internet Explorer has including the options' window which is noted by the 3 horizontal dots in the top right corner of the screen.

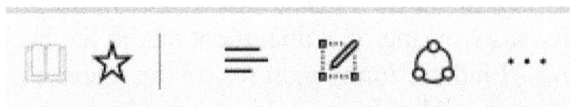

(Image 53: control options from within Edge)

From left to right you have the following buttons available. (Reading View, Favorites, The Hub, Make a Web Note, Share a web note and then options for Edge Browser).When you press the 3 dots button; the options window will drop down revealing the different options you can do with the Edge browser. Notice that from the Edge browser you can still open up the Internet Explorer window for the folks who are comfortable using Internet Explorer as noted below in image 53:

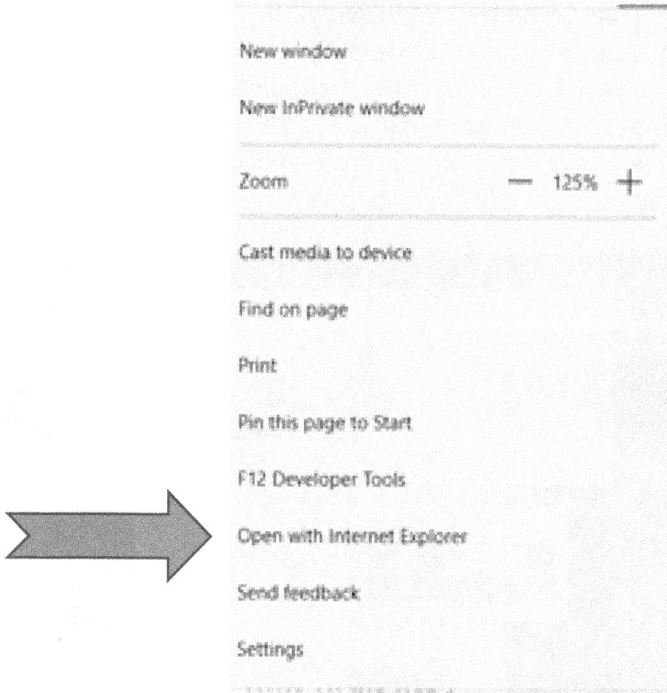

New window

New InPrivate window

Zoom   —   125%   +

Cast media to device

Find on page

Print

Pin this page to Start

F12 Developer Tools

Open with Internet Explorer

Send feedback

Settings

(Image 53: How to open Internet Explorer from within Edge Browser)

I feel that it's only appropriate that I add in that Yes Internet Explorer is present in windows10 but you have to turn it on. To do this perform the following steps:

1. Right-click the Windows (Start) menu icon
2. Select Programs and Features
3. On the left, click Turn Windows features on or off.
4. In the list of check boxes, check Internet Explorer 11
5. Click OK and when prompted, restart your PC.

PRACTICE: Now is a good time to practice the above steps as it will help to re-inforce this new information that I've just covered.

Next is the new Task View. In my opinion Task View is the Windows version of a multi-desk environment. For those who are familiar with this option in other environments such as Linux and standalone apps. Task

(Image: 54)

View allows the end user to click this button (see image 54) near the start menu and be able to see all the different running apps which are running on the computer at that given time. Then the user can easily change to other applications quickly and easily. This is good if you have many windows open at the same time and you require quick access as well as repeated access. What does Task View look like? See Image 55 for an example.

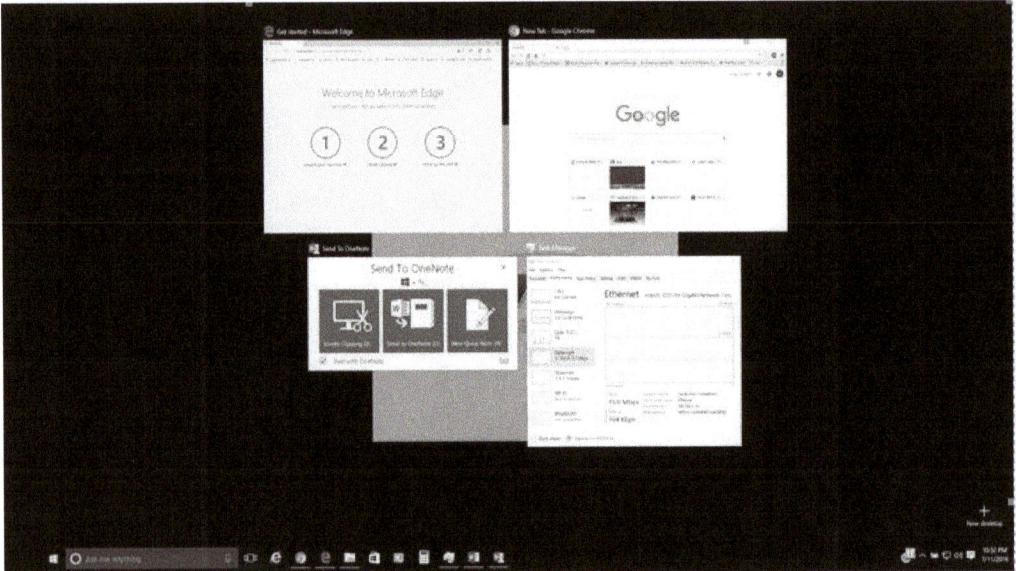
(Image 55: Windows 10 desktop with Task View option)

PRACTICE: Now is a good time to practice the above steps as it will help to re-inforce this new information that I've just covered.

Next in the list of items that Microsoft has rolled out in Windows 10 is the Xbox Application. This is not a new item to the Xbox world of gaming however it's new to the operating system world. You see Microsoft has merged the 2 worlds into 1 by adding the Xbox Application into Microsoft Windows 10. How do you start the Xbox application? As with any of the windows programs you can open them by using the start menu followed by clicking on their respective icon name or you can type their name into the

Cortana search window and let Cortana find it for you. In this case I clicked on the 'Start menu' followed by 'all apps', followed by 'Xbox' and it opened a screen such as that shown below in image 56:

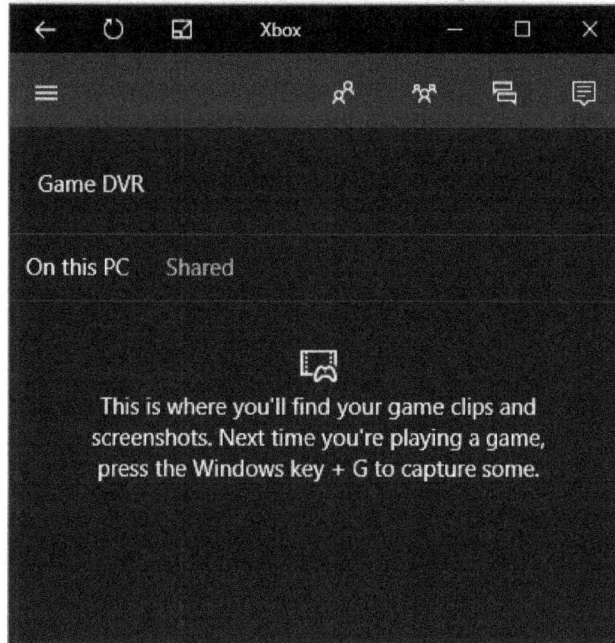

(Image 56: Xbox Live image)

So what does the Xbox application do? To the best of my knowledge the Xbox application is a portal into the gaming arena from the Windows 10 environment. Mainly the Xbox app will allow you to stream and record console games as well as create small video clips of gaming sessions which has become very popular recently. It's this later option which makes is strengh in Windows 10 as you can also record more than just games. The Xbox application can record basically any running application which can prove helpful when trying to show someone else what you're doing when that other person is a long distance away from you. The recorded video can be sent to them and displayed for their review. This would be helpful in troubleshooting computer problems, programs, etc..

So how do you use this feature? If you have ever logged into Xbox app, the Game DVR is ready. If however you have not then start the app and login then follow these steps to record:

1. Press Windows key+G to open the Game Bar.

2. If you see a box asking if this app is a game, click the checkbox next to "Yes, this is a game."

3. Click the red circle to start recording.

   Note: you may not be able to record if the red dot is not enabled. If this is the case then please follow the link for assistance. I did follow the link and found for my specific laptop the following: What hardware do I need to record Xbox game clips on my PC?

   Your PC needs to have one of these video cards:
   - AMD: AMD Radeon HD 7700 series, HD 7700M series, HD 8500 series, HD 8500M series, R9 series, and R7 series or later.

   - NVIDIA: GeForce 600 series or later, GeForce 800M series or later, Quadro Kxxx series or later.

4. When you're done, press Win+G again and click the red circle to end the recording.

Lastly regarding the Xbox Application, the 'Win+Alt+R' combination of keys allows you to start and stop recording, as long you've previously told the Xbox app that a given application is a game. When finished recording, you'll get a notification in the Action Center (Win+A). To go to the Game DVR section of the Xbox app; click this notification and find your clips. Here you can trim the clips and jump to the folder where the files are contained.

PRACTICE: Now is a good time to practice the above steps as it will help to re-inforce this new information that I've just covered.

Ok so the next item that is new to the Windows 10 environment is the Halo lens (holographic computer; doesn't require a computer to connect to). The Holographic computer is basically Windows virtualization to imagery. A user will use goggles and can create a drawing or object in thin air based on the Holographic basis. Then when done the image or subject can also be printed on standard or 3D printers.

The Continuum mode is a really cool feature that auto detects keyboard add/removed and adjusts between laptop and tablet modes. This is important for users who have laptops that are convertible between laptop mode and tablet mode. The Continuum mode can adjust accordingly with ease for the end user.

The Tile menu has many different items such as pictures, edge, stocks and weather which all are live tiles and may be adjusted on the fly to provide the user up to date information. Most likely you're already asking yourself, "What does the start menu with the tiles look like?" See image 57 for details.

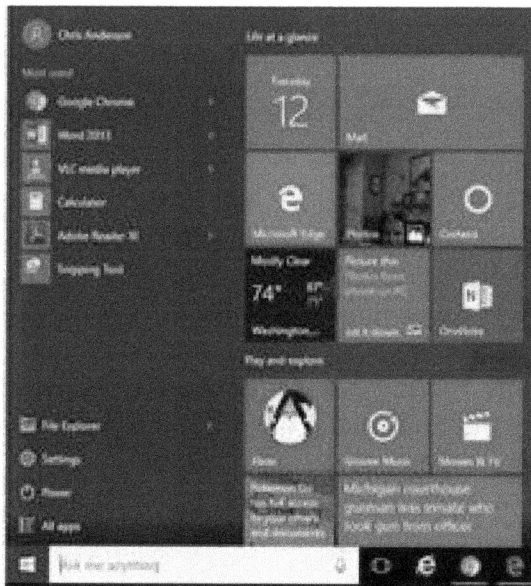

(Image 57: Windows 10 Start menu with tiles)

This brings me to the Start menu which is a combination of the application menu (windows 7) and the tile menu (windows 8.x) not to mention there is a secret menu option (right click). Let's talk more about this new 'Secret Menu' (you can also think of it as the 'options' menu for the start menu). To access the 'secret' Start menu; right-click the Windows icon (Start) button which will divulge a variety of administrative tools, as well as shutdown options, desktop link as noted below:

```
Programs and Features
Power Options
Event Viewer
System
Device Manager
Network Connections
Disk Management
Computer Management
Command Prompt
Command Prompt (Admin)

Task Manager
Control Panel
File Explorer
Search
Run

Shut down or sign out        >
Desktop
```

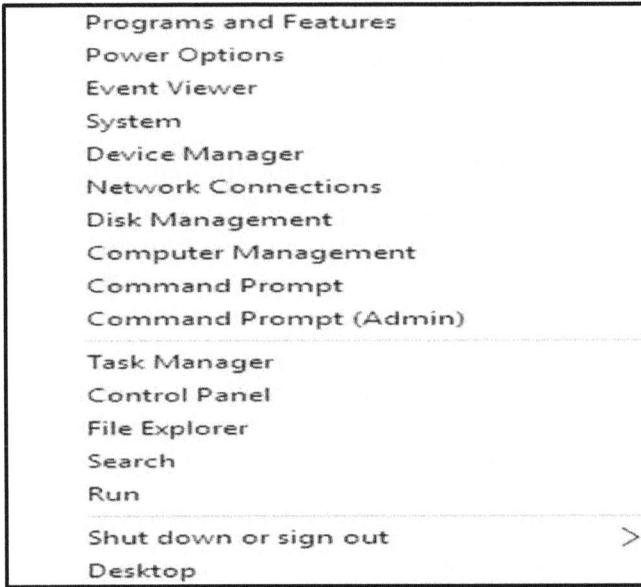

(Image 58:
Windows 10
secondary "aka:
hidden" menu
source :

http://www.cnet.com/how-to/windows-10s-secret-start-menu/?ftag=CAD3c77551&bhid=2648192150855024776803693099005)

If you're using a touchscreen you can access this menu by tapping and continue holding the start menu button for a few seconds. This hidden 'secret' startup menu bar is a true benefit of the new Windows10 operating system as it allows you access to tools that would normally take you multiple mouse clicks and navigation turns to get to. Let me give you an example. If you want to look at the event viewer you would normally have to click on Start > All apps > Windows Administrative Tools> Event Viewer. If you were accessing the command prompt, control panel and task manager would be accessed from the Start > All apps > Windows System menu item. Instead, the 'secret' start menu puts all of these tools into one single right click. This is much more system administrative easier to access.

How to Power On/Off/Restart Windows:
    a. Powering on the computer will usually allow MS Windows to correctly and fully boot up to a full running OS level.
    b. To power off the computer you usually press the Start (Menu/Orb) and then click on shutdown.
    c. To restart the operating system it's the same process as shutting down only instead of clicking shutdown you will click on the small triangle on the right of the shutdown key and from the options menu press the 'restart' option as

noted below in image#

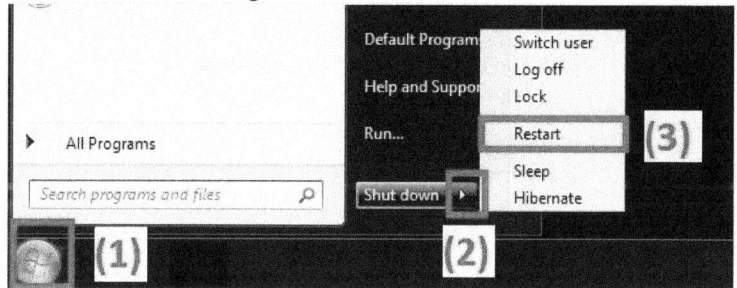

(Image 59: Windows shutdown and restart)

2. What are Windows Hotkeys? Windows Hotkeys are shortcut key stroke combinations which perform the same given task as using the Microsoft Ribbon or navigation menus. The hotkey format is noted as CTRL+<Key>. This means that the end user will press and hold the control key (CTRL) and at the same time will then press the option key to do a specific task. The most common hotkeys are listed in table 7:

a.	Copy	b.	= CTRL+C
c.	Cut	d.	= CTRL+X
e.	Paste	f.	= CTRL+V
g.	Print	h.	= CTRL+P
i.	Bold	j.	= CTRL+B
k.	Italicize	l.	= CTRL+I
m.	Underline	n.	= CTRL+U

(Table 7: common hotkey in Microsoft)

Note: these control keys are universal throughout the Microsoft environment so once you've learned them you can use them anytime you're inside of a Microsoft environment (OS, office, application). I have to also say that even some webpages are incorporating these hotkeys as well which is even better for the end user.

3. Is there a difference between the Microsoft Operating System and Microsoft Office? The answer is a whopping yes. These are probably the most confused 2 items for newbies to the Microsoft environment and it's mainly due to the names of the products. However in functionality these two are completely separate. As I've already previously mentioned what an operating system (os)

is and for review I'll say it again. The os is the first program to load after the bios runs which provides the basis for the end user to interact with the computer and the applications inside the computer (including webpages and emails). So what is this Microsoft Office program? It's an office suite that is produced by Microsoft to allow end users to write word documents such as resumes and letters via the Word program. There are actually a few programs that are part of the office suite which are MS Word (document), MS Excel (spreadsheet), MS PowerPoint (presentations), MS Outlook (Email and calendar), and MS Access (database). Just like there are different versions of Windows there are different versions of MS Office and they were released with the version number being the year they were released. However in recent years that's changed.

ii. Learning Check (MS Windows):

1. What is an operating system and why do I need it?

_____
_____
_____
_____

2. Explain the history of Microsoft Operating systems: ____

_____
_____
_____

3. List 3 of the new features of Windows 10 and their significance to each:

_____
_____
_____
_____
_____

4. What are hotkeys? Provide an example of one?

_____
_____
_____
_____

5. What is the difference between Microsoft Windows and Microsoft Office (Understand this is not MS Office 97, 2000, 2003, 2007, 2010, 2013 or 365 (Online version)): _____

_____
_____
_____
_____
_____

Bonus: How do you Power On/Off/Restart the Windows OS?

_____
_____
_____

1. Apple OS

1. What can I expect from this chapter?
    1. In this chapter you will learn the basis of the Macintosh computer as well as its history and why it's as powerful as it is.
    2. We will also cover the released versions of the Macintosh OS.
2. Explanation
    1. This chapter will provide some comparisons of Macintosh versus computers and provide examples.
3. Learning Check:

PC or Macintosh (iMAC)

2. What can I expect from this chapter?
    1. What is the difference between OS X and Windows? Although there has been a rivalry between Apple/Macintosh and Microsoft Windows for a number of years as to which is better. I'm not going to jump on either side and fly my support flag. Likewise will I negate the fact that for a number of years there has been animosity between the 2 Operating Systems; No I won't do that. If you want to watch a nice documentary on this rivalry you can watch a movie called "Pirates of the Silicon Valley" which does a nice job depicting how it all began back in the 1970's (*https://www.timetoast.com/timelines/pirates-of-silicon-valley*). Instead I want to speak from what I can say and that is both of the platforms definitely have secured their point in todays environment and in my opinion have satisfactory proven their own worthiness. For purposes of this book and this section I'm going to refer to IOS (Mac OS) and Windows as Clients and not as servers. As I write this I think it will help the beginner to keep focus of their end machine as a network client which will pull its information from servers on a network or internet. Using the perspective of both IOS and Windows as client machines will simplify the learning objective here.

    So what is a Client? A Client is simply any device connected via wire or wireless to a computer network which gets its affiliation from another computer (Server) on that same network.

So are both Macintosh 10.10.1 (Yosemite) and Windows (7, 8 and 10) all Clients? Yes, in just about all counts we can think of both of these OS'es as clients.

2. What hardware requirements are needed for OS X (10.10)? Now this is interesting because for a number of years Macintosh has been run using a Motorola chipset starting with the 68000 back in 1983. The 68000 CPU was a 16bit CPU with double registers which did give it some 32bit characteristics. In 1987 Macintosh moved to the MC68020 (32bit processor) and was followed by the MC68030 in 1988 where they incorporated the Memory management into the CPU itself. In 1991 the MC68040 was used which included the floating point.

The hardware changed in 1994 when the PowerPC 601 Processor came out for the Macintosh and was followed by the PowerPC processor models 603 [e/ev], 604 [e/ev], 750 [CX/CXe], 755, 750FX. In 1999 the PowerPC 7400 series (7400, 7410, 7450, 7455, 7447, 7447a came out for the G4 product line. Included the AltiVec vector Processing Unit. In 2003 The G5 product line rolled out and included the PowerPC processor 970 [FX/MP]. The importance here is that this was the first duel-core processor and the first to be implemented into a quad core configuration.

In parallel to the 68000 product line increasing, Intel's x86 product line was increasing just the same. In 2006 Intel had made many strides in their processors enough so that Macintosh migrated to the world of Intel Inside and started using the Core Duo (aka: Yonah), Core 2 Duo (aka:Merom & Penryn) But in my opinion I think the big move was when the i3 (aka:Clarkdale),i5 (aka: Clarkdale/Arrandale) and i7 (aka:Arrandale) processor lines were introduced to Macintosh. These newer CPU's were introduced starting in October 2009 and have been the go forward model. These models have allowed the following features such as simultaneous multithreading (Hyper-threading), SSE4 instruction sets to be used as well as Intel Turbo Boost,

Integrated memory controllers and multi-core on a single chip to be used.

Enough with the history of the CPU's although that is very important. The hardware that is typically needed to run the Macintosh operating system is typically Macintosh proprietary and therefore you must have a Macintosh to run the OS. With that said you can visit your local Apple/Macintosh store to purchase a new computer or you can do a simple internet search for resale of Macintosh devices.

3. Examples (src: http://www.ebay.com/gds/iMac-Vs-PC-/10000000177844116/g.html)

In my opinion; the iMac and the desktop PC (windows) are both known for providing high quality performance as well as extra features, whether creating documents for school, work, gaming (local or online) or streaming media. Both types share many of the same hardware components, capabilities, functions and features just with a different spin on some of them per the OS. When comparing iMac to PC's we can see the following:

Features	iMac	PC
Price	Few price points	Multiple price points
Operating system	OS X (standard) Windows, Ubuntu,, Linux (optional with parallels)	Windows, Linux (Various Distributions)
Monitor	Built-in	Built-in or external
Display size	21.5" or 27"	Varies with external monitor choices
Processor	i5 or i7 Intel	Intel or AMD
Graphics	NVIDIA GeForce	NVIDIA GeForce, AMD Radeon
Hard drive	3TB (Max)	Multiple Vendors
Memory	32 GB (Max)	Multiple Vendors
Wireless connectivity	Built-in 802.11 and Bluetooth	Multiple Vendors and options
Camera	Built-in HD camera	Multiple Vendors
Peripherals	Wired/wireless	Wired/wireless

(Table 8: Hardware comparisons between iMac and PC)

It's been said in the industry that the iMac is Apple/Macintosh's addition to the desktop computer world. One great selling point of the iMac is how Macintosh has combined the screen and internal components into one entity (the case). This includes the cpu (core2duo, i5 or i7 processor), memory (32GigByte Maximum) and a 3TB maximum hard drive as well as the peripherals such as an HD FaceTime webcam, speakers, and microphone with built-in USB and firewire ports on the back side of the unit which makes it effortless to add the proprietary Apple keyboard and magic trackpad. Virtually all other keyboards and mice connect via USB or wirelessly and work immediately upon introduction.

If a repair/replacement is needed, a combination of company storefronts (called Apple Stores), stock virtually all the necessary parts required to ensure compatibility with the brand's proprietary systems. Macintosh also has other offerings such as the MacBook, iPad, iPod, and iPhone as well online sites, applications, and programs.

I've had it asked of me what the differences are between the PC and the iMAC and it wasn't until I took a class on iMac's to really determine the difference between these 2 worlds. In short one could say the differences are in the operating systems, software integration, and compatibility issues.

The standard operating system that comes with all iMac computers today is Apple OS X (Version 10.10.x as of this writing) as compared to most off-the-shelf PC's (desktops, laptops, tablets) of today which come with some flavor of Windows such as Windows 7, Windows 8 (8.1) or now Windows 10.

I do want to make a point that with additional software installed on your base OS installation on either your iMAC or PC you can also run other operating systems in a virtual environment (think of it as a second OS running piggy-back on top of the first (base) OS. For example; on the iMAC if you use the "parallels" program, the Mac can also run Windows, Linux, or Ubuntu to accommodate needs such as business, gaming, or personal programs (apps). Likewise from the PC side of the market if you install 3rd party programs such as Microsoft virtual machine, Oracle VM Virtual Box or VMware you can create virtual machines for which you can install Macintosh OS.

Regarding software applications and games, it seems virtually all software sold today is built primarily for PCs (windows environments), but will run without instance on an iMac in most cases. There is a bit of a Rubik's cube to software applications working with operating systems. By that I mean you have to make sure the program you're trying to install and use is compatible with your running operating system. Note, you may need to get additional custom versions of that same program to run on the iMac but once you do then there should be little to no differences. However with that said, there are still some programs that are incompatible with Mac and the company may or may not offer a Mac version. If they do offer a MAC only version I've seen it where it is sometimes substandard to the options offered to PC users. Again you will have to try your software with both PC's and MAC to determine your specific scenario. I'm only trying to enlighten you on this potential software to the OS puzzle.

Is OSX 10.X.x Downloadable?

Yes if you already have an iMAC then you can go to the Apple/Mac Store and download a copy from there to the newer version provided you have a newer system. This is a really good feature that Apple/Macintosh provides to their customers.

Versions:

By doing a simple internet search you can find all of the versions that have been created for the Apple/Macintosh software. For purposes of this book (keep in mind that there are previous versions that were released). I'll focus on a more recent perspective or roadmap of the OSX (aka: Version 10) releases here:

Version	Name	Date Released (finals)	Processor
• Version 10.0: "Cheetah"		March 24, 2001	Intel Core 2 Duo
• Version 10.1: "Puma"		September 25, 2001	Intel Core 2 Duo
• Version 10.2: "Jaguar"		August 23, 2002	Intel Core 2 Duo
• Version 10.3: "Panther"		October 24, 2003	Intel Core 2 Duo
• Version 10.4: "Tiger"		April 29, 2005	Intel Core 2 Duo
• Version 10.5: "Leopard"		October 26, 2007	Intel Core 2 Duo
• Version 10.6: "Snow Leopard"		August 28, 2009	Intel Core 2 Duo
• Version 10.7: "Lion"		July 20, 2011	Intel Core 2 Duo
• Version 10.8: "Mountain Lion"		July 25, 2012	Intel Core 2 Duo
• Version 10.9: "Mavericks"		October 22, 2013	Intel Core 2 Duo
• Version 10.10: "Yosemite"		October 16, 2014	Intel Core 2 Duo
• Version 10.11: "El Capitan"		September 30, 2015	Intel I5, I7
• Version 10.12: "Sierra"		September 30, 2016	Intel I5, I7

(Table 9: OSX releases, dates and processors.)

IMac Summary:

Remembering that Apple/Macintosh produces one flavor of desktop PC called the "iMac"; there is not a lot of changes that can be done to it. You can order small variations in RAM, hard drive capacity, display size, and price, but the common look and feel as well as functionality will all be the same such as image 60 below:

(Image 60: iMac)

4. Learning Check (Apple OS-X):

a. What is the difference between OS X and Windows?

_____

_____

b. What hardware requirements are needed for OS X (10.10)? _____

_____

_____

_____

c. Can OS X (10.10) be run on an i5 (greater) CPU in PC?_____

_____

_____

_____

Linux/Unix

1. What can I expect from this chapter?
    1. What is Linux?
    2. The history of Unix/Linux
    3. Why it's an important operating system in todays world.
    4. What is open source code verses closed source or private code.

What is Linux? Linux is an operating system which runs on a computer (personal computer (aka: pc)) similar to that of Microsoft Windows and Apple/Macintosh operating system. Now I'm sure that I've offended some folks by including these operating systems in the same sentence; however that's not my intension. My intension is to draw a comparison for the newbies to computers so that can relate what Linux is. Taking it one step further Linux has many different distributions (aka: flavors) to it as represented in table 10.

These distributions include versions of Linux such as:

RPM based flavors	Redhat, CentOS, Fedora, openSUSE, Slackware, Turbo,
Debian based flavors	Knoppix, Mint, Ubuntu, Caldera, Stampede,
Note: These are only a handful of distributions and a simple internet search can easily provide you with a current list of Linux distributions.	

(Table 10: Linux versions)

One could think of these distributions roughly equivalent to the different versions of Windows such as Windows XP, Vista, 7,8,10. However I only say that in the context to help the new person in understanding.

These Linux distributions are different in each flavor of the Linux however they all use the same Linux kernel, which is open source and free to everyone in the world under the GNU license. You see these different flavors are created by different people or companies who wrap their software packages around the "free" Linux kernel. Then these companies take that free kernel and build their specific OS shell around them. Thus making the different distributions (aka:

flavors) of Linux. Keep in mind that each distribution of Linux may have the same kernel but it's intensions for operation can vary widely depending on the software requirements and the company or person who is directing that distribution thus making it very versatile.

The history of Unix/Linux (high level overview):
Ok so that helps but I still don't understand what Linux is. So again what is Linux? Linux is an operating system that was created by Linus Torvald back in the mid 1990's as a way to incorporate the UNIX environment into the Intel i386 based hardware world. More accurately, Linus created the kernel for this new operating system and applied it to the GNU license. Some of the people who are strong Linux based mindset refer to this as GNU/Linux but for the mass of the world; they usually just call it Linux. Linux has progressed in a positive fashion and migrated into the various distributions we have today. So how did the name Linux come about? It's actually a combination of Linus + UNIX.

Why is Linux so important in today's world. Please excuse my reference here, but as with anything, there usually ends up being a few crème's of the crop that rise to the top in most situations. In this case these software companies that have risen to the top are Microsoft, Apple/Macintosh and Linux

(Note: Order of presentation does not reflect which order of preference nor reliability is better than another. There is no specific order chosen here relative to which one is better than another.)

All of these above companies want to rule the software world and they are trying their best by creating as much product to fit every little niche out there. However in reality each of them generically have their own strengths over each other and this really works well for the world in my own opinion. For example; they all have an operating system to which can load on to a computer/laptop. However for basic end user functionality Microsoft Windows and the Apple OS are probably a better fit visually for the person new to the usage of computers.

(Image 61: Windows 7 Desktop with Startmenu)

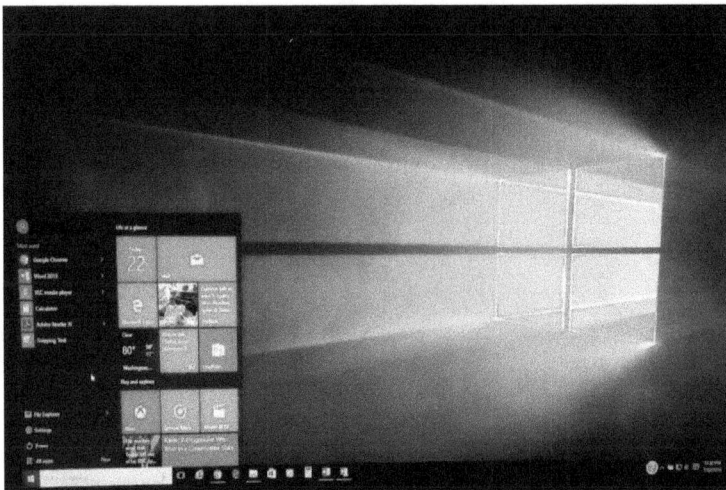

(Image 62: Windows 10 Desktop with Startmenu)

(Image 63: OSX Desktop (version: yosemite))

Reason, Microsoft Windows is used in a strong majority of businesses which range from small to large businesses around the world. Therefore most people are somewhat already exposed to some flavor of Windows as an end user environment through their work place. Likewise the Apple OS is very strong in the graphic rendering environment and as an end user (client) operating system the Apple Macintosh OSX is highly regarded as perfect for end user graphic rendering.

For the newbie, Linux is more of a command line based interaction operating system (OS) and not super strong on the graphics and friendli-ness as compared to Windows and Apple OS. Now I know that hit a nerve somewhere for some folks but again this is in reference to the new person who is trying to understand the computer for the first time. I think we would all agree that Linux is probably not the best operating system to start out with for the beginner. Per the images below (image 64 and 65) of some of the common versions of Linux; one can see how it's not as friendly as Windows or OSX:

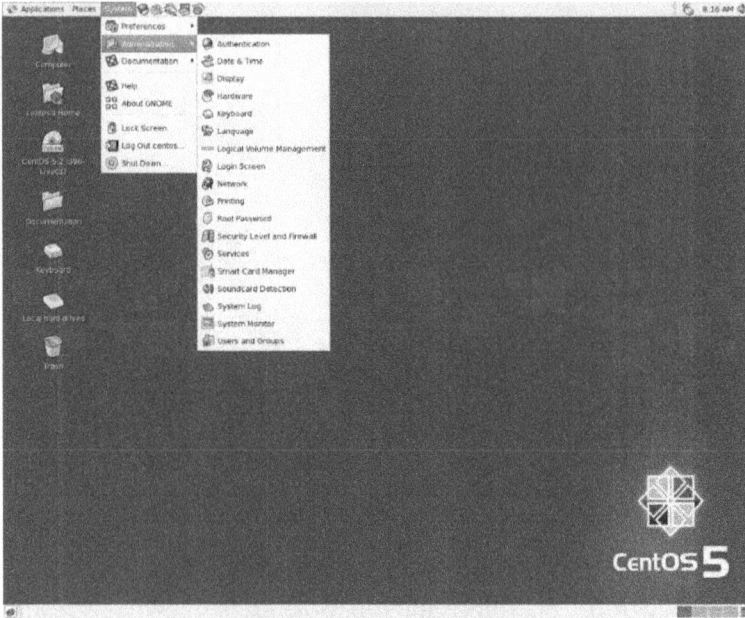

(Image 64: CentOS5 desktop with no running apps)

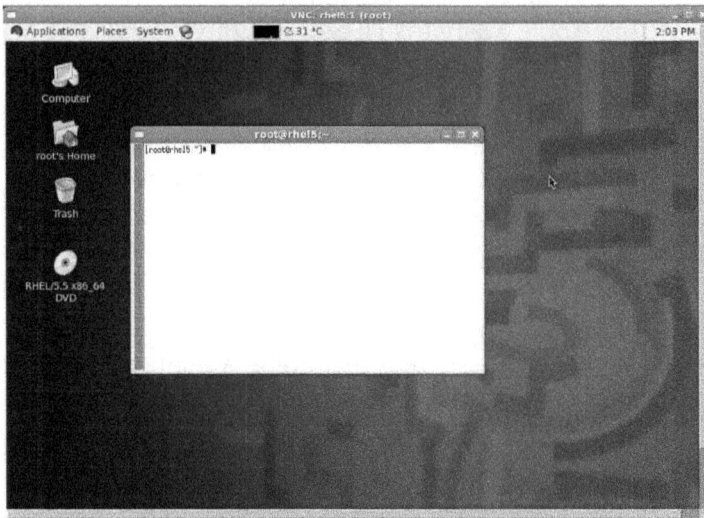

(Image 65: RHEL5 desktop with command prompt window)

Ok so Linux may be weak in the friendli-ness and ease of operation when it comes to the newbie starting to use it. However for a backend server functionality; Linux and Microsoft both soar to successful realms here. With that said, I have to say yes there are some computer shops that have Microsoft only for their OS's and servers. Likewise there are other computer/IT shops that are only

Linux shops. Again both are good and I think it comes down to what will work best for that specific system. I've even noticed it since 2000 that many shops are running both Microsoft and Linux for their various servers and include Apple in their company where needed; such as in the graphics department, but Apple/Macintosh's can be used for more than just graphical use. They are actually very versatile as well and can duplicate many of the features that the latest version of Microsoft Windows delivers. The point that I'm trying to deliver here is that all of these operating systems are very good and strong. I've used them all and yes there are specific niche's where one is better than another and yes I also agree that you can use one to do the same thing as another... I'm not saying that isn't possible. I'm trying to make the newbie aware of what these are and allow them to better understand the difference.

The Linux kernel is written in a programming language called C and this Linux kernel is licensed under the GNU license which also is incorporated into the open source world. What is open source code verses closed source or private code? Open source code is where anyone in the world can download the source code and then modify it as they choose. Whereas closed source or single source code is owned by a person or company and they do not give out the source code. Both have their benefits. However if you talk to anyone in the Linux world they will just about always state that open source code is always better than closed code for this given reason.. 'Anyone can access it' ... including you who are reading this material right now.. yes you!

There is also a benefit to Linux being written in open source and that is the number of technical people around the world who are various degrees of programmers (beginners to professionals) all get to look at the source code and verify its validity and correct-ness. If something is wrong it's not very long before the bugs have been identified and the entire world of programmers are jumping on this code problem and working to correct it. This number of open source programmers who are looking at the code can range from thousands to tens of thousands or even more.

Let's talk about the opposite of open source for context. The opposite of open source is closed source which is also referred to proprietary code or I've even heard it referred to as 'single code'. As I previously mentioned above, this proprietary code is code that is written and controlled by a single entity which can be a person, group or company. Probably the most popular company with closed proprietary code is Microsoft and Apple/Macintosh is a close second when it comes to software operating systems. Microsoft controls their own code and does not release their source code to the outside world. This gives them the control and power to modify and correct problems as they come about. However they do it by themselves without the help of the worlds various degree of programmers as is done for the Linux environment. Microsoft has been successful in controlling their operating system source code as well as all the software programs they distribute but again they have to do it by themselves by utilizing a finite amount of programmers (which is much smaller than that of open world's programmers).

Lastly let's talk about the Penguin. You see many new folks to Linux stumble across the penguin at some point and think that it's referring to their specific distribution of Linux. This is a false assumption. The penguin is referred to as "Tux" and was Linux Torvalds sympathetic way to associate to Linux. He liked an idea of a slightly fat penguin sitting down after a great meal as Tux the penguin. Tux the penguin is an open-source image to help promote the Linux related platform. Since Tux is part of the open-source environment Tux is free for anyone to use without cost. Tux is shown below:

(Image 66: "TUX" the Linux Penguin image)

If Linux is a command line operating system then what makes it so powerful? The mere fact that Linux is a command line operating system makes it extremely powerful. For example, in using a graphical user interface (aka: GUI) to perform a function then you can only click on the buttons that were provided in the GUI window. If the programmer did not include the function that you wanted into that GUI, then you cannot click on it. However in a command line environment you don't have this limitation. All you need to do is type the command followed by the options you want to include for that command and provided you followed the correct syntax needed.. ala-walla-presto.. it's done. How do you know what features are available for that command? You can type the word 'man' in front of the command and it will list the description, options and how to use it (provided there is a man (manual) page for that command). An example might be, #man ls <enter>. What this command would do would be to list the man page for the ls command. The result would show this command lists the content of the current directory the user resides in if no other options are available. In some versions of Linux you can also add the '/?' After the command and it will do something very similar.

When I teach Unix/Linux classes there is usually a common question I get every time and that is, "What are the most common command line instructions?" This depends on the distribution of Linux that you're using as well as keeping in mind there are commands as well as options that are included with those commands. If you were to use the commands and the options available there could easily be thousands of command combinations available in Linux (not including the custom created commands by individuals/companies). Instead of trying to memorize all of the various commands and their options, I have found that I regularly use a handful of commands most regularly in administering Linux. Here is a list of commands that I use on a regular basis but keep in mind there are many more:

Command	Description (What it does):
pwd	Display the current working directory you reside in.
whoami	Display the username you're currently logged in as.
ls -al	List the contents of the directory you're in
df –a	Disk free –a(all)
du –a	List disk usage
cat <filename>	Concatenate <filename>
cd <dir. name>	Change directory to <directory name>
mkdir <dir. name>	Make directory called <directory name>
rmdir <directory name>	Remove directory name (note you can't reside in directory when you remove it)
cp <file1> <file2>	Copies <file1> to <file2> (makes duplicate file)
grep –i <searchword> <file1>	Will search for a word in a file.
ps	Display your current active processes
top	Display all running processes
date	List current time and date of system in CLI window
uptime	List how long server has been running
man <command>	List the man page for a given command
uname –a	List kernel information (version)
ping <host/ip addr>	Ping another host/server's name or ipaddress to see if that computer is active on a given network.
dig <domain>	Get DNS information for a domain
ifconfig <eth0>	Display the interface information for Ethernet 0 interface.
Iwconfig <eth1>	Display the interface information for wireless 1 interface.
Traceroute <FQDN/IP addr>	Provide the route across routers from your current location to a given domain name or IP address.
Tar –cvf <filename>	Creates a tarball file called <filename> of the current directory unless otherwise given.
Tar –xvf <filename>	Extracts a tarball file called <filename> of the current directory unless otherwise given.

(Table 11: a short list of common Linux commands)

5. Learning Check (Linux):

1. What is Linux?

   _____

   _____

   _____

   _____

2. What is the history of Unix/Linux?

   _____

   _____

   _____

   _____

3. Why is Linux an important operating system in today's world.

   _____

   _____

   _____

   _____

4. What is open source code versus closed source or private code.

   _____

   _____

   _____

   _____

5. Who is the person who is responsible for starting the Linux movement? _____

6. Can you do the same thing in Windows as you can do in Linux? (If so explain to what degree. If not explain to what degree)

   _____

   _____

   _____

7. What animal is associated with Linux? _____

• Software Summary Check: Operating Systems

- What did I learn from the Windows, Macintosh and Linux Operating systems? _____
  _____
  _____
  _____
  _____

- What is the difference between OS X and Windows? _____
  _____
  _____
  _____
  _____

- What hardware requirements are needed for OS X (10.10)? _____
  _____
  _____
  _____
  _____

- Can OS X (10.10) be run on a i5 (greater) cpu in PC? _____
  _____
  _____
  _____

- What is Linux?
  _____
  _____
  _____
  _____

- What do I know about the history of Unix/Linux
  _____
  _____
  _____
  _____
  _____

- Why is Linux an important operating system in today's world.
  _____
  _____
  _____
  _____

- What is open source code versus closed source or private code.

  _____
  _____
  _____
  _____

- Who is responsible for starting the Linux movement?

  _____
  _____
  _____
  _____

- Can you do the same thing in Windows as you can do in Linux? (If so explain to what degree, If not explain to what degree)

  _____
  _____
  _____
  _____
  _____

- What animal is associated with Linux?

  _____
  _____

4. Networking

History of the Network: To best understand what networking is we will begin a journey down a path where we will need absolute concentration in order to not get lost. So let's jump right into it and ask ourselves what is networking? According to Microsoft, networking is the communication between computers and if we go way back to prior educational material for MCSE 4.0 certification, Microsoft said a network consisted of 3 or more computers all talking on the same network/segment. So why does it have to be 3 or more computers to create a network? Again, Microsoft said if there were only 2 systems on a network they would be communicating in a peer-to-peer network which is not a true network per se. Instead it's more like you are talking to a friend on a phone call which would be a peer-to-peer conversation. However if you conference in a third person into your phone call allowing the 3 of you to be on the same call, then you can think of that roughly as a network that the 3 of you are conversing on.

But let's back up here and try to better understand where or why the network/internet came about... To do this we need to look back and give thanks to the Cold War and actually even prior to that. Wait one minute... Are you telling me the internet has been around since the 1960's...? Well yes... kind of... It got its start back in the 1958 and 1960's as a result of the Cold War. Side note: You see, America was so excited about sending a man to the moon that it overshadowed the beginning growth of the internet and so the beginning growth of the internet was pretty much a mute subject except for the people who knew about it.

Getting back to the birth of the internet; In 1958 President Eisenhower requested funds to create ARPA which was approved as a line item in an Air Force appropriations bill. Between 1961 to 1965 there were many papers written on packet switching, internet concepts and distributed communications networks. However it was in 1966 when the ARPA project officially began and became alive. The reason for this was the United States Military was very interested in having redundancy between military sites and duplicating data in case one or multiple military facilities were destroyed from enemy attack. Beginning in September of 1969, The U.S. military partnered with many universities (UCLA, Stanford, UC Santa Barbara, University of Utah, Cambridge and University of

Hawaii over a 10 month period) to establish a network system to share files quickly between locations. Their effort was successful. This network system had to be a mesh style network to ensure data redundancy for protection. In 1972 the first email was successfully sent by Ray Tomlinson at BBN for the ARPANET project. In fact the ARPA-NET project was later called the ARPANET which in turn ended up being called what we know today as the internet.

Looking at image #67 below shows us the internet's birth certificate which states:

"Birth of the Internet"

THE ARCHITECTURE OF THE INTERNET AND THE DESIGN OF THE CORE INTERNETWORKING PROTOCOL TCP (WHICH LATER BECAME TCP/IP) WERE CONCEIVED BY VENTON G. CERF AND ROBERT E. KAHN DURING 1973 WHILE CERF WAS AT STANFORD'S DIGITAL SYSTEMS LABORATORY AND KAHN WAS AT ARPA (LATER DARPA). In the summer of 1976, Cerf left Stanford to manage the program with Kahn at ARPA.

Their work became known in September, 1973 at a networking conference in England. Cerf and Kahn's seminal paper was published in May 1974.

Cerf, Yogen K. Dalal, and Carl Sunshine wrote the first full TCP specification in December 1974. With the support of Darpa, Early implementations of TCP (and IP later) were tested by Bolt Beranek and Newman (BBN) Stanford, and University College London During 1975.

BBN built the first internet gateway, now known as a router, to link networks together. In subsequent years, researchers at MIT and USC-ISI among many others, played key roles in the development of the set of internet protocols.

BIRTH OF THE INTERNET

THE ARCHITECTURE OF THE INTERNET AND THE DESIGN OF
THE CORE INTERNETWORKING PROTOCOL TCP (WHICH LATER BECAME TCP/IP)
WERE CONCEIVED BY VINTON G. CERF AND ROBERT E. KAHN DURING 1973
WHILE CERF WAS AT STANFORD'S DIGITAL SYSTEMS LABORATORY AND
KAHN WAS AT ARPA (LATER DARPA). IN THE SUMMER OF 1976, CERF LEFT STANFORD
TO MANAGE THE PROGRAM WITH KAHN AT ARPA.

THEIR WORK BECAME KNOWN IN SEPTEMBER 1973 AT A NETWORKING CONFERENCE IN ENGLAND.
CERF AND KAHN'S SEMINAL PAPER WAS PUBLISHED IN MAY 1974.

CERF, YOGEN K. DALAL, AND CARL SUNSHINE
WROTE THE FIRST FULL TCP SPECIFICATION IN DECEMBER 1974,
WITH THE SUPPORT OF DARPA, EARLY IMPLEMENTATIONS OF TCP (AND IP LATER)
WERE TESTED BY BOLT BERANEK AND NEWMAN (BBN),
STANFORD, AND UNIVERSITY COLLEGE LONDON DURING 1975.

BBN BUILT THE FIRST INTERNET GATEWAY, NOW KNOWN AS A ROUTER, TO LINK NETWORKS TOGETHER.
IN SUBSEQUENT YEARS, RESEARCHERS AT MIT AND USC-ISI, AMONG MANY OTHERS,
PLAYED KEY ROLES IN THE DEVELOPMENT OF THE SET OF INTERNET PROTOCOLS.

KEY STANFORD RESEARCH ASSOCIATES AND FOREIGN VISITORS
VINTON CERF

DAG BELSNES	JAMES MATHIS
RONALD CRANE	BOB METCALFE
YOGEN DALAL	DARRYL RUBIN
JUDITH ESTRIN	JOHN SHOCH
RICHARD KARP	CARL SUNSHINE
GERALD LE LANN	KUNINOBU TANNO

DARPA
ROBERT KAHN

COLLABORATING GROUPS

BOLT BERANEK AND NEWMAN
WILLIAM PLUMMER · GINNY STRAZISAR · RAY TOMLINSON

MIT
NOEL CHIAPPA · DAVID CLARK · STEPHEN KENT · DAVID P. REED

NDRE
YNGVAR LUNDH · PAAL SPILLING

UNIVERSITY COLLEGE LONDON
FRANK DEIGNAN · MARTINE GALLAND · PETER HIGGINSON
ANDREW HINCHLEY · PETER KIRSTEIN · ADRIAN STOKES

USC-ISI
ROBERT BRADEN · DANNY COHEN · DANIEL LYNCH · JON POSTEL

ULTIMATELY, THOUSANDS IF NOT TENS TO HUNDREDS OF THOUSANDS
HAVE CONTRIBUTED THEIR EXPERTISE TO THE EVOLUTION OF THE INTERNET.

DEDICATED JULY 28, 2005

(Image 67: William Gates Computer Science Building (Stanford University))

2. Networking Devices:

What can I expect from this chapter?

1. In this chapter you will be introduced to the equipment that allows communication to occur between computers. This will include NIC, hub, switches, routers and bridges

Network Interface Card (aka: NIC)	A printed circuit board that is installed into a computer peripheral slot to allow communication to a remote device via a network connection.
Hub	A hub operates at layer 2 and deals with the MAC addresses. It's a device that allows multiple computers to connect via this single device. All devices can hear and communicate with all other devices in this device. This is where broadcasts can occur and cause storms to occur. This is older technology and is replaced with switches
Switches	This is a device much similar to a hub and operates at layer 2. However a switch is smarter than a hub in that it can memorize the machine address code (aka: MAC address) of the NIC in the remote computer. This is important as it can connect a single computer to another single computer without disruption to any other computer plugged into the switch.
Bridges	A bridge is a device that operates at the layer 2 level and separates broadcast domains. This can be helpful if you have a network where you have a lot of traffic and you need to calm it down.
Routers	A router is like a switch however it operates at the Network layer of the OSI model. A router does exactly what the name implies in that it routes a connection from one network (a) to another network (b).

(Table 12: Listing of devices and short summary of functionality)

(Image 68: Network interface card (aka: NIC) Source:
http://4.bp.blogspot.com/_Svwa4PMZAQc/TRxdB7qv-
TI/AAAAAAAAAQk/LPyzVlqqcYc/s1600/nic+card.jpg Feb 2017)

(Image 69: Hub Source: www.ebay.com Feb 2017)

(Image 70: Switch Source: http://brain-
images.cdn.dixons.com/6/2/00939526/l_00939526.jpg Feb 2017)

(Image 71: Bridge
Source: http://3.bp.blogspot.com/--
QHFyMSnwnM/T6P9dt1r8II/AAAAAAAAAF0/L4B_gqWabfo/s1600/brid
ge.jpg Feb 2017)

(Image 72: Router Source:
https://www.netgear.com/images/Products/Networking/WirelessRouters/WNR1000/header-wnr1000-hero-photo-large.png Feb 2017)

(Image 73: Router Source:
http://www.netgear.com/images/Products/Networking/WirelessRouters/R7500/header-r7500-hero-photo-large.png Feb. 2017.

3. Understanding Binary

1. What can I expect from this chapter?
    1. In this chapter you will be introduced to the Binary system which we also covered in PC hardware.
    2. You will also learn how to convert an IP address into Binary format.

2. Explanation: The Binary system is a very simple system to understand and it's the system that is used in computers for internal communication as well as communication across a network. You see the Binary system only has 2 numbers and that is a one (1) or a zero (0) and that is it. Now, it is how or where the 1 and 0 are located that will allow you to build up a number.

   First off let me go off on a tangent and explain a concept which I've found to be very true in the computer world. It's a simple concept which I've found repeated in many different angles and quite simply it's this, "If one is better, then double it and make it two" or another way of saying it is, "If one is good then two is better and if two is good then four is better and this repeats." There is actually a word for this and it's called the power of 2. You see, if you take the number 1 and double it you get 2. Likewise if we double 2 we get 4 and double that we get 8 followed by doubling again to get 16.

   If we repeat the process we can see the following numbers in table 13 below:

(lsb)   (msb)

1	2	4	8	16	32	64	128	256	512	1024	2048	4096	etc...

(Table 13: power of 2's listing starting at number 1)

   (Note: lsb means least significant bit and msb means most significant bit)

   Now, this is easy to follow as it's just doubling the numbers and since we read from left to right the numbers in the chart are left to right with the smallest number being on the left. The smallest number – we'll call it the least significant bit (lsb) and the largest number on the right – we'll call that the most significant bit (msb).

The problem here is the chart works good for humans but when we are using it for IP address decoding we have to flip it 180 degrees, so the most significant bit is on the left and the least significant bit is on the right as in the example below:

(msb)   (lsb)

4096	2048	1024	512	256	128	64	32	16	8	4	2	1

(Table 14: power of 2's list reversed & ready to count binary from Right to Left)

Now that we have the order laid out correctly we have to trim some of the spaces off the msb side as we only have 8 characters to make up an octet which is what is used in the version4 IP address scheme for networking. Therefore, we end up with a chart that looks like:

(msb)   (lsb)

256	128	64	32	16	8	4	2	1

(Table 15: Binary chart)

We can now use this chart as a value holder in which we can place a #1 to enable that value. Let's call it a Binary chart for reference. Here is a hint which might help you to better understand this concept. Think of a light switch in your house.

If the light switch (image 74) is down ↓ then the lights are off. Since the lights are off; this would be equivalent to a logical zero (0v DC) I'll reference this in this example as the direction of the light switch being in the down direction ↓.

Image: 74

Conversely, if the light switch is flipped up ↑ or on then that would be equivalent to a logical 1 (i.e.: +5v DC). So hopefully you can now see how a light switch can be off (0) or on (1) the same way or have the correlated mindset of each bit location in the binary chart being turned on (enabled) or off (disabled). Let's look at some examples:

Example 1:

(msb) (lsb)

256	128	64	32	16	8	4	2	1	Value
↓	↑	↓	↑	↓	↓	↓	↓	↓	160
0	1	0	1	0	0	0	0	0	160

Example 2:

(msb) (lsb)

256	128	64	32	16	8	4	2	1	Value
↓	↑	↑	↓	↓	↓	↓	↓	↓	192
0	1	1	0	0	0	0	0	0	192

You see you only count the place holder when the arrow is pointing up (just like the light switch example) or when there is a value of 1 present. If it's a zero we don't count it. In example 1 the only value setting with 1's were 128 and 32 which when added together equal 160. In Example 2 the only 2 value holders that have up arrows (which are equivalent to 1's) is the 128 and 64 place holder which when these are added together equals 192. Now these 8 place holders make up what we call an octet which consists of 8 bits in the octet. In a standard IP version 4 address there are 4 octets and the notation is referenced as ###.###.###.###
A common IP address would be 192.168.1.1.

Let's do one more example here and work on a very common IPv4 IP address of 192.168.1.1. What would the binary conversion look like for that? In Example 3, fill in the fields below with your thoughts as to which place holders are turned on and off to correctly make the successful combination to equal the number on the right under Value:

256	128	64	32	16	8	4	2	1	Value
↓									192
0									192

(msb)   (lsb)

256	128	64	32	16	8	4	2	1	Value
									168
									168

(msb)   (lsb)

256	128	64	32	16	8	4	2	1	Value
									1
									1

(msb)   (lsb)

256	128	64	32	16	8	4	2	1	Value
									1
									1

Now that you've been shown the long way on how to convert IP to binary and vice-versa, let's look at the short cut way. There is a simple and fast way to understand binary values and that's using the powers of exponents. When we look at numbers with exponents we have to remember the first number is the base number and the smaller number to the upper right (immediately following the base number) is the exponent. The exponent is the number of times that the base will be multiplied against itself. Remembering that any number raised to 1 is its own value, then any number raised to a power of 2 is basically doubled the original value. After that the exponents increment synchronously but the results change dramatically. Let's take a look at the table for the 8 bits in the octet:

$$2^0 = 1$$
$$2^1 = 2$$
$$2^2 = 4$$
$$2^3 = 8$$
$$2^4 = 16$$
$$2^5 = 32$$
$$2^6 = 64$$
$$2^7 = 128$$
$$2^8 = 256$$

(Note: if you look at the value of the exponent it matches with the place holder in the above example and therefore you can also determine the value needed for that location)

I have provided this powers table in the hope that it will help some folks to better convert place holders to binary values. Overall, converting IP addresses into binary is fairly simple once you understand the process as we did above in example 3. You can plug any IP address into the Value filled for each octet and decode it just as you did in example 3.

3. Learning Check (binary):

1. What numbers are used in binary?

   _____

2. What is the msb and lsb of an octet?

   _____

   _____

   _____

   _____

3. How many bits are in an octet?

   _____

4. How many octets are in an IPv4 address?

   _____

5. What is the maximum number for an octet if all bits are enabled?

   _____

4. **IPv4 address, Mask, Gateway, Broadcast - Are they important?** What can

I expect from this chapter?
1. Does Binary work with IP Addresses?
2. What is an IP addresses (version 4), Subnet mask, Gateway, Broadcast Address
3. The different configurations of networks such as LAN, MAN, WAN and Wan's and the public internet.
4. Lastly, You will also learn about the internet version 1 (aka: people's network)

5. Does Binary work with IP Addresses? This is a good question which many folks who are new to computers and especially IP addresses ask. The short answer in is, "Yes binary and IP addresses absolutely work together" – in fact so much so that they are the same thing. By this statement it's very similar to looking at a quarter. Just like a quarter has 2 sides (heads and tails); IP addressing can be viewed in two methods.

In fact if you remember back to the section on binary, what was a binary number? It's a combination of either 1's or 0's which when combined together equals a value the computer can and does understand. Think of this equivalently as looking at the side of the quarter with heads on it. As for the other side of the quarter (tails); we humans don't tend to communicate in binary format (as well as a computer does) so we like to convert that binary number into a decimal number which is 0-9. Not only do we like to use the decimal numbers we will even group them together into groups of 3 which will stop when we reach a predefined limit of 255. In networking this grouping is called an Octet.

Let's talk about this thing called an octet number. I said in the previous chapter that an octet was a group of single bits totaling 8 bits which is true. However an IP address is made up of 32 bits total. When 32 bits is divided by 8bits (per octet) it leaves us with 4 groups (aka: octets) for an IP address. That is how we come up with an IP address which fits into the following format ###.###.###.###. Keep in mind that each octet can individually range from any decimal number between 0-255. So a valid IP address could read 1.1.1.1, 1.1.1.2, 1.1.1.3 and range all the way up to 255.255.255.255 (In theory – however we don't use 255.255.255.255 as that is a network broadcast address and therefore unusable to all). Some common IP addresses for home and private networks are 192.168.1.1, 192.168.X.X (where X is a reference number which can be any number between 0-255). A golden rule here is you can't use the first IP address of the network as that is reserved for the network wire itself (think of this first number as defining that network). Likewise you cannot use the last IP address of that network as it is the broadcast IP address for that network. So the simple rule here is you can't use the first and you can't use the last IP address of a given network but all the IP addresses in between are valid for host use. Overall this is a great beginning to start with for beginners and a refresher for professionals. But what defines a network? How many networks can we have? I'll discuss this more in detail here shortly. For now, I want to conclude in an overview summary that the binary number format is how the computer reads and writes the computer internet address and we humans convert that binary number into decimal and read in 4 octets.

6. What is an IP address (version 4), Subnet mask, Gateway, Broadcast Address? As I've previously mentioned and I'll continue here with more detail about an IP address. An Internet Protocol (IP) address is a series of binary bits that when put together in a given layout represent a computer network along with the host of that network. Look at image 74 to better understand:

Network Portion			Host Portion
192	168	1	1
1 1 0 0 0 0 0 0 .	1 0 1 0 1 0 0 0 .	0 0 0 0 0 0 0 1	0 0 0 0 0 0 0 1
255	255	255	0
1 1 1 1 1 1 1 1 .	1 1 1 1 1 1 1 1 .	1 1 1 1 1 1 1 1	0 0 0 0 0 0 0 0
1st Octet	2nd Octet	3rd Octet	4th Octet

192	168	1	0
1 1 0 0 0 0 0 0 .	1 0 1 0 1 0 0 0 .	0 0 0 0 0 0 0 1 .	0 0 0 0 0 0 0 0
Network Address (host portion of IP all zeros)			

192	168	1	255
1 1 0 0 0 0 0 0 .	1 0 1 0 1 0 0 0 .	0 0 0 0 0 0 0 1 .	1 1 1 1 1 1 1 1
Broadcast Address (host portion of IP all ones)			

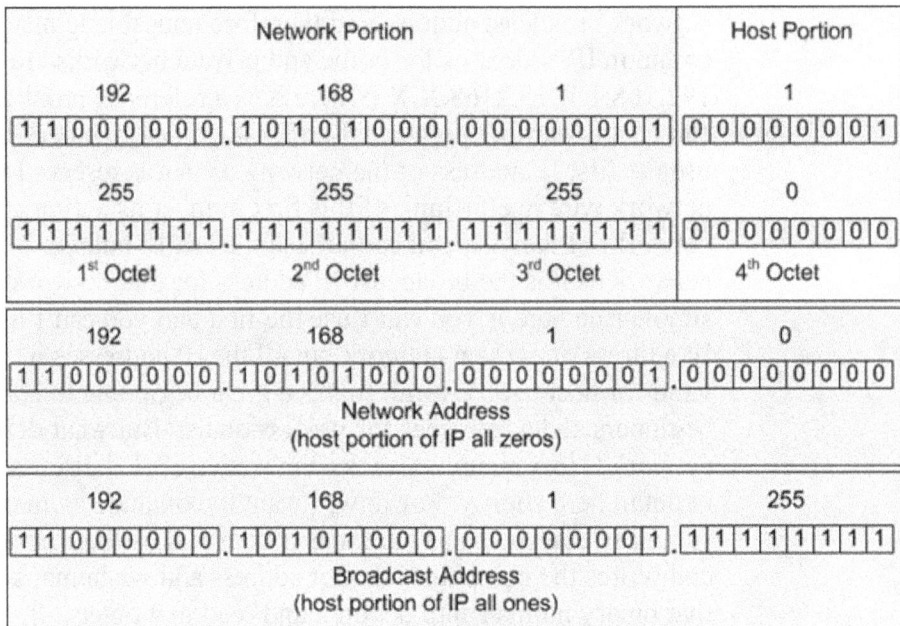

(Image 74: Network to Host relationship)

Notice when you look at that 192.168.1.1 IP address I previously talked about, you can see how it's broken down into parts. The top left green section is the part of the IP address that creates/refers to the given network which is called "192.168.1" Notice the last octet is left off. The reason it's left off or in the yellow square is because that is the octet of the host itself. Meaning that we could potentially have 255 devices (subtract 2 for the first and the last IP address, resulting in 253 devices) on the 192.168.1 network. If this is confusing then let me say it a different way. Instead of calling the network "192.168.1" we could have called it the bananas network and on the bananas network we could have 253 devices. So if we replace the word bananas with a different word such as apples then everything stays the same. So far so good? Ok so let's take this one step further...what if we have both the bananas' network and the apples' network. Each network can have 253 hosts per each network and we can have the bananas' network and the apples' network both operational at the same time. Hopefully this still makes sense? Ok, so again since we are using computers; computers do not like words but instead numbers and therefore we replace the word bananas with an IP address of the network such as 192.168.1 and for apples we would replace that name with an IP address of 192.168.2.

So what determines the split between the network and the number of hosts? Well the vertical line between the green and yellow box in image 74 above. This vertical bar is a visual line break for us humans. However we really don't use that for anything other than training. In reality that line is determined by a subnet mask. What is a subnet mask? A subnet mask is a set of 1's followed by 0's which is applied to the IP address to cover out the network.

But before we dig deeper into this; I think I would like to provide you a IPv4 subnet address compass. Look at the below cheat sheet "IPv4 subnet address compass" to better understand how it's all laid out and how you can easily recreate. Study this table 16 and in time you'll have this entire sheet in your head for memory... Trust me... you will.

2^7	2^6	2^5	2^4	2^3	2^2	2^1	2^0	Step1: List your 'Bits' locations	(Hint: think 2 to the what power)
128	64	32	16	8	4	2	1	Step2: List the total number of 'Hosts' _Remember to minus 2 as you can't use the first (network address) and you can't use the last (network broadcast)_	(Hint: start with #1 and then double it until all 8 bit locations are full and we count from right to left)
128	192	224	240	248	252	254	255	Step3: List the decimal version of the Subnet Mask for the place value	(Hint: add 128 + 64=192 from step 2 above (repeat across)
2	4	8	16	32	64	128	n/a	Step4: List the # of networks available out of the 256 available (for 8 bits)	(Hint: Out of 256 networks divide the # of hosts from step 2 into it. This will give you the subnet number(ie:256 / 32 =4 networks.
/25	/26	/27	/28	/29	/30	/31	/32	CIDR notation	(Hint: Class C subnet mask has the first 3 octets all turned on which uses 8 bit's/octet which means 24 bits are turned on. So just continue into the last octet by borrowing a bit and adding to the 24. This gives you the decimal values listed to the left.)

(Table 16: IPv4 Network Compass to figure out IP address, Mask, # of Nets & Hosts.)

Look at the example image 75 on the next page for a full overview explanation:

# of bits in IP Address (32)	32	31	30	29	28	27	26	25	24	23	22	21	20	19	18	17	16	15	14	13	12	11	10	9	8	7	6	5	4	3	2	1
Row A	32	31	30	29	28	27	26	25	24	23	22	21	20	19	18	17	16	15	14	13	12	11	10	9	8	7	6	5	4	3	2	1
Row B twos complement Place Value	2147483648	1073741824	536870912	268435456	134217728	6.7E+07	33554432	16777216	8388608	4194304	2097152	1048576	524288	262144	131072	65536	32768	16384	8192	4096	2048	1024	512	256	127	64	32	16	8	4	2	1
Row C 192.168.1.1 (IP address)	192								168								1								1							
Row D Octet Bit Value	128	64	32	16	8	4	2	1	128	64	32	16	8	4	2	1	128	64	32	16	8	4	2	1	128	64	32	16	8	4	2	1
Row E Bit On/Off	1	1	0	0	0	0	0	0	1	0	1	0	1	0	0	0	0	0	0	0	0	0	0	1	0	0	0	0	0	0	0	1
Row F Class C Subnet (Binary form)	1	1	1	1	1	1	1	1	1	1	1	1	1	1	1	1	1	1	1	1	1	1	1	1	0	0	0	0	0	0	0	0
Row G Class C Subnet (Decimal form)	255								255								255								0							
Row H Final Result on Subnet for host	X	X	X	X	X	X	X	X	X	X	X	X	X	X	X	X	X	X	X	X	X	X	X	X	0	0	0	0	0	0	0	1

(Image: 75)

125

Lets look at this one octet at a time to better understand what I'm trying to cover. I'll start with the first octed which is 192.

Row A	32	31	30	29	28	27	26	25
Row B	2147483648	1073741824	536870912	268435456	134217728	67108864	33554432	16777216
Row C	192							
Row D	128	64	32	16	8	4	2	1
Row E	1	1	0	0	0	0	0	0
Row F	1	1	1	1	1	1	1	1
Row G	255							
Row H	X	X	X	X	X	X	X	X

# of bits in IP Address (32)

twos complement Place Value

192.168.1.1 (IP address)

Octet Bit Value

Bit On/Off

Class C Subnet (Binary form)

Class C Subnet (Decimal form)

Final Result on Subnet for host

(Table 16: Break down of first octet)

In case there is still any confusion, I'll explain each of the rows above.

Starting with RowA - This is the location bit of the total number of bits used in a full IP address. It's only used for reference for the newbie to show the newbie how many bits are being used in a IPv4 address.

RowB - Shows the two's complement place value for that bit location in the IPv4 address. However more importantly it shows if that bit location is turned on then that location represents the number of hosts that could be used for that location. (Again, let me clarify due to RIP1 and RIP2 rules you can't use the first IP address of a network as it's reserved for that network (defines that network) and secondly you can't use the last IP address of a given network as it's reserved for the broadcast address for that given network. Hint:

subtract 2 from any given network to cover this first and last issue and you can use all the IP addresses in between freely as you choose.) Think of an Oreo cookie, all the free IP addresses are like the white good stuff in the middle.. so the first and last IP address would be like the cookie edges. (although with Oreos we love all of the oreo.. Ok who's ready for dessert?

RowC - This is the decimal number we humans like to use for a given octet. Also referred to as dotted-decimal notation.

RowD - This is the octet bit location value. It also represents the number of hosts available.

RowE - I'm trying to show you what the binary representation of the 192 looks like. This is also what is done when you convert 192 to binary. A process which is also called the 'binary calculator'

RowF - The binary form of a subnet mask of 255 which means that all bits are turned on.

RowG - Same as RowF only in decimal form which we humans work better with.

RowH - When you use a mathematical function called 'or-ing' (see below for explanation) together between rows E and F you get a result as in RowH. Quite simply this 'or-ing' truth table says any 1 gives a 1.

If we apply this to subnetting, this is true as well as if both inputs are a 1 that gives a result of a 1 with a carry to the next most significant bit. Another way of understanding this is the subnet mask simply covers the network portion of the IP address and leaves only the host IP information. In the examples I've used if you see an X; it basically means "don't care," however, to be truly correct here, binary is only a 1 or zero so the X in this case is instead truly 1's. Let's take a look at this truth table which is called an "OR truth table" below in image 76.

A	B	out
0	0	0
0	1	1
1	0	1
1	1	1

(Image 76: "OR" Truth Table)

Now how do we correlate the A and B to an IP address and subnet mask? Quite simply replace the A with <IP address bit> and the B with the <subnet mask bit> to get the end result which is also known as the output or end result... So if the rule for this 'or' table is any 1 gives a result of 1 and if there are two 1's then the result is a 1 with a carry to the next bit. If the next bit is a 0 add it to the carried 1 and the result is now a 1 for this next bit. So when we work on subnet masks this process starts with the least significant bit 2^0 and then works its way across the subnet mask list and binary IP address to the most significant bit side of the listing; See below:

(Example 4: **OR truth table example**)
IP address = 192.168.1.1
Binary address   =
11000000.10101000.00000001.00000001
Binary subnet mask   =
11111111.11111111.11111111.00000000 (decimal=255.255.255.0)

Subnetted addr. result =
11111111.11111111.11111111.00000001
(Aka: Or-ed address)

Notice if you read the above subnetted address result fields in Example 4; that when reading it from left to right it starts with 1's and it continues until it reaches the first zero and then it changes to read the IP address. This is why you can only have certain valid subnet masks that are valid as listed below:

I've seen way too many people try to use other number (invalid)

128	192	224	240	248	252	254	255

128

subnet masks than what is listed to the left. By not understanding this rule, their efforts resulted in incorrect subnet masks with serious wonky network problems.

Now with the information that we've covered. Let's review. Between Rows A to H; I'll repeat this same concept for the next 3 octets below. This way you can see how it all plays out – but again this is all shown in its entirety in the previous page.

24	23	22	21	20	19	18	17
8388608	4194304	2097152	1048576	524288	262144	131072	65536
168							
128	64	32	16	8	4	2	1
1	0	1	0	1	0	0	0
1	1	1	1	1	1	1	1
255							
1	1	1	1	1	1	1	1

# of bits in IP Address (32)

twos complement Place Value

192.168.1.1 (IP address)

Octet Bit Value

Bit On/Off

Class C Subnet (Binary form)

Class C Subnet (Decimal form)

Final Result on Subnet for host

16	15	14	13	12	11	10	9
32768	16384	8192	4096	2048	1024	512	256
1							
128	64	32	16	8	4	2	1
0	0	0	0	0	0	0	1
1	1	1	1	1	1	1	1
255							
1	1	1	1	1	1	1	1

# of bits in IP Address (32)

twos complement Place Value

192.168.1.1 (IP address)

Octet Bit Value

Bit On/Off

Class C Subnet (Binary form)

Class C Subnet (Decimal form)

Final Result on Subnet for host

8	7	6	5	4	3	2	1
127	64	32	16	8	4	2	1
1							
128	64	32	16	8	4	2	1
O	O	O	O	O	O	O	1
O	O	O	O	O	O	O	O
O							
O	O	O	O	O	O	O	1

# of bits in IP Address (32)

twos complement Place Value

192.168.1.1 (IP address)

Octet Bit Value

Bit On/Off

Class C Subnet (Binary form)

Class C Subnet (Decimal form)

Final Result on Subnet for host

(Image 77: 2nd, 3rd and 4th Octets explained)

Now let's talk about classes of IP addresses. There are 3 main classes of IP addresses that the open public gets to use provided they want to pay for them. These classes are Class A, Class B and Class C. Full disclaimer here, there is also a Class D and E but they are reserved for government and special research projects use and so the open public really doesn't get to use them and therefore I won't cover them. I will however talk more about the Class A, B and C IP addresses. You see in table 17, these classes are defined by the value of the first octet.

IP Address Class	First Octed Binary Value	Possible # of Networks	Possible Number of Hosts	First Octet Decimal Value	Default Subnet Mask
Class A	1-126	128	16,777,214	00000001 to 011111110	255.0.0.0
class B	128-191	16384	65,534	10000000 to 10111111	255.255.0.0
Class C	192-223	2097150	254	11000000 to 11011111	255.255.255.0

NOTE: Class A 127.0.0.0 - 127.255.255.255 cannot be used and is for Loopback and diags.

(Table 17: IPv4 Classes, # of networks, hosts and masks)

The private NON-ROUTABLE IP addresses are:

10.x.x.x	Class A non-routable address
127.x.x.x	Class B non-routable address (Used for Loopback testing purposes)
192.168.x.x	Class C non-routable addresses
169.254.x.x = APIPA Address which mean that DHCP addressing did not occur correctly.	Automatic Private IP Addressing (APIPA). APIPA is a network process when DHCP services are not available on the network but the client devices are configured to use a DHCP server to obtain their IP addresses. This means the client did not successfully obtain a valid IP address.

(Table 18: Non-routable IP addresses)

5.   The different configurations of networks such as LAN, MAN, WAN and Wan's and the public internet.

So what do these different acronyms mean? Well they are different references for the size of the networks. These sizes range between small to medium to large network configurations. You see a LAN stands for Local Area Network which means it's a local network usually inside of a small office, home or a network which consists of approximately 250 computers/servers or less. The next largest size of a network is called a MAN which stands for Metropolitan Area

Network. A MAN usually covers multiple LAN's but can cover an area such as a business complex or hospital complex. This includes up to multiple buildings across a college campus or a business that is startled across a city or in multiple cities which are close in proximity.

The third measurement of a network is called a WAN which stands for Wide Area Network. A WAN is the next size larger than a MAN and it usually consists of multiple MAN's. A WAN usually startles long distances and we typically think of WAN's as across a state or country.
A WAN can be used by a large company which does business across multiple states within a country and possibly around the world and needs network access to all locations.

There is also a Wi-Fi-LAN which is also referred to as a WAN. This can be somewhat confusing for the newbie because there are 2 meanings for the term WAN; but there are two different meaning for this. As I've previously mentioned this is a Wi-Fi Local Area Network and it usually exists within a Local Area Network. A Wi-Fi-Lan (aka: WAN) is what is usually available for mobile devices in homes, offices and businesses. A person can easily find a WAN in most public areas, malls, airports, etc..

Ok, let's move on to talk about the internet. We can call it version 1 (aka: people's network) and why we call it internet version 1.0. Quite simply the explanation for the internet 1.0 is connecting people to people. In other words we can call it the "People's internet" due to the fact it did just what it was supposed to and that is it connected all people to the internet. It did this with the Internet protocol version 4.0 which is what you learned above with the format of XXX.XXX.XXX.XXX for an IP address. Now moving on to the next version of the internet is what we call internet version 2.0 or also known as the internet of things (aka: IOT). The primary purpose here is to connect devices to devices. As it's easy to see we have many more devices now than we did 5, 10 or even 20 years ago. Since we have so many more devices all of which need access to the internet then we need a new structure to support this. This is where the internet protocol version 6.0 comes into play. We won't cover version 5.0 as it never got a strong foothold. Back to Internet protocol version 6.0 and the format used to identify it is quite simply 4 bits to a hextet and there are 8 hextet or in other words this allows for 2^{128} or 340,282,266,920,938,463,463,374,607,431,768,211,456 devices connected using the IPv6 method. What does this look like? I'll cover this in the upcoming chapters but for now I just want you to be aware of it.

1. Learning Check: (IP Version 4)

2. Q: What is an IPv4 address?

    _____
    _____
    _____
    _____

3. Q: What is a subnet and why is it important?

    _____
    _____
    _____
    _____
    _____

    Q: What are the different classes of IP Addresses (List all
    classes, number of networks and number of hosts)?

    _____
    _____
    _____
    _____
    _____
    _____
    _____
    _____

4. Q: What are the different sizes of a network? (Not classes)

    _____
    _____
    _____
    _____

-   Q: Which is best for home or small office use and why?

    _____
    _____
    _____
    _____
    _____

-   Q: Is there a difference between a Wi-Fi-Lan (aka: WAN)
    and a wide area lan (aka: WAN)? If so explain:

    _____
    _____
    _____

_____

_____

- Q: Convert the following IP address (192.168.29.57) to binary: _____

  _____

  _____

  _____

  _____

- Q: Apply the correct subnet mask to the above IP address answer you provided to net out the correct IP address when the subnet mask is active.

  _____

  _____

  _____

  _____

- Q: Convert the following binary address to decimal: 11000000.10101000.01100011.01101001

  _____

Internet Protocol Version 6.0

2. What can I expect from this chapter?
    1. History of IPv4 and IPv6
    2. # of devices that can connect to IPv4 vs IPv6
    3. Looking at IPv6 Address
    4. IPv6 Header (think train, payload and caboose in the back)

History of IPv4 compared to IPv6:

As I previously mentioned there is a new version of the internet called IPv6 which has been in the works for many years. Actually IPv4 was a 32bit (OSI Layer protocol) and was created in 1980 and allowed for 2^{32} which equals 4,294,967,295 total addresses (just under 4.3 billion addresses). However in 1999 it was evident that this IPv4 methodology would not be sufficient into the future and therefore a new version of Internet device addressing was created. This was called Internet protocol (IP) version 6 which is also known as IPv6. IPv6 is 128 bits long and is 2^{128} = 340,282,366,920,938,463,436,374,607,431,768,211,456 addresses. This should work for many years to come for connecting various devices to the internet (hence the term "internet of things"). However to put full light on how fast the new IPv6 is progressing in the world wide web, around the mid 2015 year approx. 97% of the world wide web is still using IPv4 and 3% is using the new IPv6 scheme. So you can see that since 1980 to 1999 and now up to 2015 this is a slow progression but still a constant one. As with time and the demand increasing in recent years, this progression may occur at an increased pace. I've provided a table below to help understand what we've talked about in the above paragraphs:

	IPv4	IPv6
Released	1980	1999
# of bits in address	32-bits (uses IP class ranges)	128-bits (does not use IP class ranges)
Format	dotted decimal 192.168.001.001	Hex: fe80::f114:36e0:f87e:e259
Addresses	2^{32} = 4,294,967,296	2^{128} = 3.40282366920938463463374607431768211177e+38

(Table 19: Comparison between IPv4 and IPv6)

Which devices can be connected to the internet? Everything you can imagine including computers, servers, switches, routers, mobile devices, websites, televisions, security cameras, refrigerators, stop lights, street cameras, temperature thermostats in home and office, wearable exercise equipment, and the list continues.

3. Let's look at the IPv6 address:
   There are different IPv6 addresses which are referred to by the first hextet value such as:

Global Unicast		
Global Prefix	Subnet	Interface ID
48 bit	16 bit	64 bit
1st Hextet Values Examples: 2001: (Teredo Tunneling=gives full IPv6 connectivity to IPv6 capable devices running on IPv4 network connectivity) 2002 (6to4 = converts IPv6 to/from IPv4 Addressing) 1080: Unicast Address		

(Table 20: Global Unicast)

Link-Local Unicast	
FE80::1/64	Interface ID
64 bit	64 bit
1st Hextet Values: Fe80::1/64	

(Table 21: Link-Local Unicast)

Multicast			
FF##	Flags	Scope	GroupID
8 bit	4 bit	4 bit	112 bit
1st Hextet Values: FF01::1/64			

(Table 22: Multicast)

Others:
FC## = Non-Routable (equivalent to IPv4 Non-routable)
::1 = Loopback address
:: = Unspecified address

(Table 23: Others)

Let's looks at some terms before we get too deep:

Link-Local Unicast	*Similar to ARP or broadcast on the local network.*
Uni-cast	*one-to-one communication*
Multi-cast	*one-to-many communication*
Any-cast	*An single device address configured in multiple locations for it to connect to or an interface that is assigned to a pre-set range of addresses for it to connect to. This address range can vary and therefore there is no pre-defined any-cast range.*

(Table 24: IPv6 general terms you need to know and understand)

Let's start off with Global Unicast. You see the Global Unicast addresses are made up of 8 blocks of 4 hexadecimal digits (nibbles) separated by colons (:). Remember that a hexadecimal digit means any number or letter between 0-9 plus a,b,c,d,e and f. I've listed this out for your reference in the following numbers below:

0,1,2,3,4,5,6,7,8,9,a,b,c,d,e,f and then it repeats starting at
10,11,12,13,14,15,16,17,18,19,1a,1b,1c,1d,1e,1f,
20,21,22,23,24,25,26,27,28,29,2a,2b,2c,2d,2e,2f,
30,31,32,33,34,35,36,37,38,39,3a,3b,3c,3d,3e,3f
<This process continues>

Notice that it's different than our normal decimal system which is 0-9 and then repeats in the 10's-19, 20-29, 30-39, etc. Therefore you can also see that a hexadecimal number system provides more numbers for use.

Let's look and see what this looks like for an IPv6 address. I'll use a lowercase "h" to represent one of the hexadecimal digits in the 4 digit (nibble) block below:

hhhh:hhhh:hhhh:hhhh:hhhh:hhhh:hhhh:hhhh	
Network portion (64bits)	Host portion (64 bits)

When we use a hexadecimal numbering system for each of the 4 hexadecimal blocks (aka: nibble) replace the above 'h' with any number between 0-f which is a total of 15 actual possibilities. If we use one of the blocks of hhhh above and dive more into detail we can see that it starts at

0000 and ends in FFFF. The total number of possibilities for this single 4-digit block is 65,535 devices if viewing in decimal. This is only for 1 of the 8 blocks of hexadecimal numbers. Now you can see why we say that IPv6 is $2^{128} = 340,282,366,920,938,463,436,374,607,431,768,211,456$ devices or addresses. We need to remember that IPv4 and IPv6 are both layer 3 protocols and both use TCP/UDP ports.

There are a couple of rules to an IPv6 address and they are:

A) *All zero groups can be omitted and :: can represent the place holder (aka: Zero compression) Rule: you can only do this once per IPv6 address even if there is another block later in the IPv6 address with zero's. You can only do the :: for one of the blocks of zero's.*

B) *(not trailing zeros)aka: Zero suppression)*

If I use the previous example and replace the h's with numbers you'll see my example reduced down to simplest notation below:

hhhh:hhhh:hhhh:hhhh:hhhh:hhhh:hhhh:hhhh
||
V
fe80:*0000:0000:0000*:fl14:36e0:*00*7e:e259
||
V
fe80*::*fl14:36e0:7e:e259

4. Does IPv6 still use subnet masks? Are they important? The simple answer here is yes. However there is some difference and I'll cover this lightly. You see the new IPv6 address is how many bits long? If you said 128bits then you are correct and you're paying attention which is good.

The first 48 bits are the global routing prefix (aka: The network portion). The next 16 bits which are bits 49-64 are for the subnet ID (aka: These bits define the subnet – if being used). If the subnet is not being used then these bits are used with the global routing prefix for a total of 64 bits and it's Classless Inter Domain Routing (aka:CIDR) notation is /64.
However if we do want to subnet our IPv6 network (meaning we want to cut it up into smaller networks) then we must use the subnet bits of the 4th nibble and this is noted below as (S).

Let me show you another way of looking at this concept to help solidify the concept. Using the IPv6 image from before I'll focus into the Network portion only (not the host portion) and identify the network portion with (N) and subnet portion with (S).

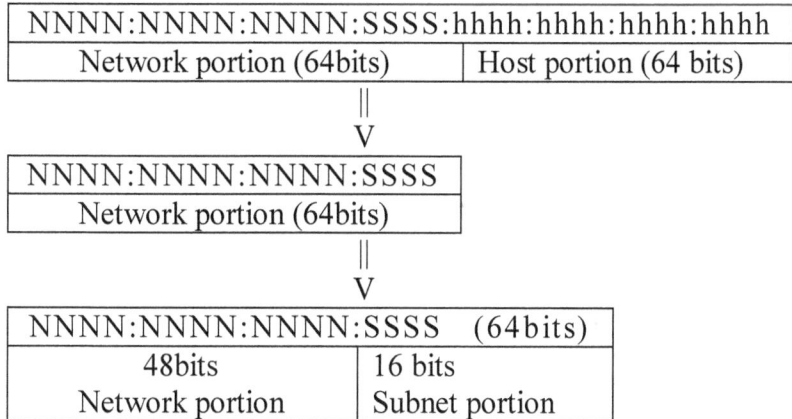

NNNN:NNNN:NNNN:SSSS:hhhh:hhhh:hhhh:hhhh	
Network portion (64bits)	Host portion (64 bits)

$$\parallel$$
$$V$$

NNNN:NNNN:NNNN:SSSS
Network portion (64bits)

$$\parallel$$
$$V$$

NNNN:NNNN:NNNN:SSSS (64bits)	
48bits	16 bits
Network portion	Subnet portion

The key to IPv6 subnetting is if no subnet is used then the CIDR notations would be /64 to represent that all 64 bits are being used for the network portion. However if we are using any of the 16 bits in the fourth nibble (subnet portion) then our CIDR notation would be the network portion which would be a value of 48 + the number of bits to borrow or add to our 48 for the network. Let me show you what I mean here:

<48bit network address> + <SSSS =16 bits for subnet>
$$\parallel$$
$$V$$
<NNNN:NNNN:NNNN> + SSSS

Focusing only on the fourth nibble which I identify as SSSS; If we look at the farthest right 'S' and count it as a hexadecimal value between 0 to F that gives us a total of 15 possible values. Likewise if we do this same thing for each of the S's then we can see there are a lot of values that can be generated. We will do this for all 4 place holders 'S' of the 4 nibble (subnet). Walking through this process; break the 4 SSSS into binary to better understand table 25 on the next page.

S S S S	
0000 0000 0000 0000	(*IPv6 Hex Value to be used*=0000)
0000 0000 0000 0001	(*IPv6 Hex Value to be used* =0001)
0000 0000 0000 0010	(*IPv6 Hex Value to be used* =0002)
0000 0000 0000 0011	(*IPv6 Hex Value to be used* =0003)

‖
V

0000 0000 0000 1110	(*IPv6 Hex Value to be used* =000E)
0000 0000 0000 1111	(*IPv6 Hex Value to be used* =000F)

‖
V

0000 0000 0001 0000	(*IPv6 Hex Value to be used* =0010)
0000 0000 0001 0001	(*IPv6 Hex Value to be used* =0011)
0000 0000 0001 0010	(*IPv6 Hex Value to be used* =0012)
0000 0000 0001 0011	(*IPv6 Hex Value to be used* =0013)

‖
V

0000 0000 0001 1110	(*IPv6 Hex Value to be used* =001E)
0000 0000 0001 1111	(*IPv6 Hex Value to be used* =001F)

‖
V

0000 0000 0002 0000	(*IPv6 Hex Value to be used* =0020)
0000 0000 0002 0001	(*IPv6 Hex Value to be used* =0021)
0000 0000 0002 0010	(*IPv6 Hex Value to be used* =0022)
0000 0000 0002 0011	(*IPv6 Hex Value to be used* =0023)

‖
V

0000 0000 0002 1110	(*IPv6 Hex Value to be used* =002E)
0000 0000 0002 1111	(*IPv6 Hex Value to be used* =002F)

‖
V

1111 1111 1111 0000	(*IPv6 Hex Value to be used* =FFF0)
1111 1111 1111 0001	(*IPv6 Hex Value to be used* =FFF1)
1111 1111 1111 0010	(*IPv6 Hex Value to be used* =FFF2)
1111 1111 1111 0011	(*IPv6 Hex Value to be used* =FFF3)

‖
V

1111 1111 1111 1110	(*IPv6 Hex Value to be used* =FFFE)
1111 1111 1111 1111	(*IPv6 Hex Value to be used* =FFFF)

(Table 25: The Hex Value (0-F) is what we use in the IPv6 address.)

Now that we understand how the fourth nibble is able to be broken down into binary, let's look at the place holder locations for subnetting which will help us to determine the CIDR notation that we will use. Remembering that the global routing prefix is 48 bits long then we can add each of the converted binary positions (IE: 0100 0100 0000 0000) as the next sequential value above the 48. This would look like:

Binary subnet	0 1 0 0	0 1 0 0	0 0 0 0	0 0 0 0
/Place value	49 50 51 52	53 54 55 56	57 58 59 60	61 62 63 64

The thing we have to remember is that if we are using a subnet of /56 then that means that the first 8 bits of the subnetting nibble above 0100 0100 will be combined with the global routing prefix (aka: the network) to become that network. Likewise the remaining 8 bits (0000 0000) will be the number of hosts available. In this case that's 2^8=256 hosts available for this subnet.

This is some heavy understanding and I hope that you're still with me. Let's continue: How do we identify what subnet is being used. This is simple and I can best explain it by using the following IP address: 2001:ACAD:9876:<u>4400</u>::1/56
Taking the 4400 decimal notation of the hexadecimal value we convert it to binary in table 26 below:

2001:ABCD:9876:4400::1/56	
Network portion (64bits)	*Host portion (64 bits)*
2001:ABCD:9876:4400	::1
4400 *(subnet bits)*	<< focusing on subnet bits only
0100 0100 0000 0000	Subnet bits converted to binary
49 50 51 52 53 54 55 56 57 58 59 60 61 62 63 64	Place value for binary bits
<u>Bold & Underline shows CIDR notation as well as these bits will be joined with the network.</u> The 8 bits on the right (not bolded nor underlined) will be the number of hosts available on the network.	<empty>

(Table 26: Identifying which subnet is being used)

The point to subnetting is that we have to remember we are taking a large network and cutting it up into smaller networks. Think of an apple pie and cutting it up into smaller pieces. Sometimes the pieces are equal and other times they are not. Subnetting is the same way and so one must ask themselves how many devices do I want on my IPv6 network. Once this is identified then IPv6 subnetting can commence.

IPv6 Host addresses:

Ok so now that we've talked about IPv6 networks and subnets; let's talk about host addresses and how they map out. I found this to be one of the most important and interesting sections of learning the IPv6 address. I mean really, this is some important and highly technical information and I have to give props to all the folks who came up with these ingenious concepts. Ok with that said let's dive into the IPv6 host address decoding. Let's look at the previous example of:

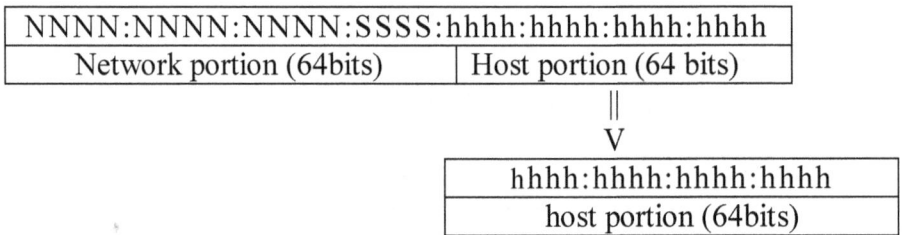

NNNN:NNNN:NNNN:SSSS:hhhh:hhhh:hhhh:hhhh	
Network portion (64bits)	Host portion (64 bits)

||
V

hhhh:hhhh:hhhh:hhhh
host portion (64bits)

Ok so if you're looking at the above example and seeing that the IPv6 host address is 64 bits long and thinking back to IPv4 MAC addresses as only 48 bits long and having a problem with this, then you're exactly where I want you... You may be asking yourself; Why does this not match up? Hang on and I'll explain.

You are correct that the standard burned in MAC address (aka: BIA) is only 48 bits long and that is still correct. So why does the IPv6 have 64 bits? Well we take the 48 bits and we add padding to it as shown below:

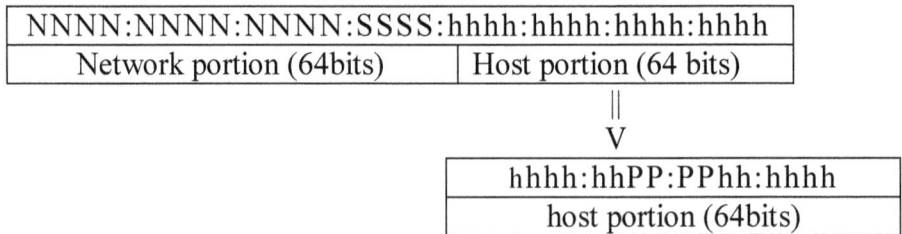

NNNN:NNNN:NNNN:SSSS:hhhh:hhhh:hhhh:hhhh	
Network portion (64bits)	Host portion (64 bits)

||
V

hhhh:hhPP:PPhh:hhhh
host portion (64bits)

As you can see above the P is the position of the padding that we are adding to the 48bit MAC Address. For the padding we add in the middle of the 48 bit address the following hex addresses: 0xff and 0xfe to look like:

hhhh:hhff:fehh:hhhh
host portion (64bits)

This turns the 48 bit MAC address into a 64 bit MAC address which answers your question as to how this maps from a 48 bit MAC address to a 64 bit MAC address and we refer to this as the 'EUI-64' (Extended Unique Identifier -64bit). In fact if you run an ipconfig /all command from a windows command window you will even see the 'EUI-64' notation behind the IPv6 address. When you see this type of notation; you can also think of this as the padded (modified) 48bit MAC Address. However we are not done. There is another step we need to cover and that is the 7bit also known as the 'U' (Universal/Local) bit. This bit is in the first hextet of the EUI-64 (host address) and is reflected below in table 27:

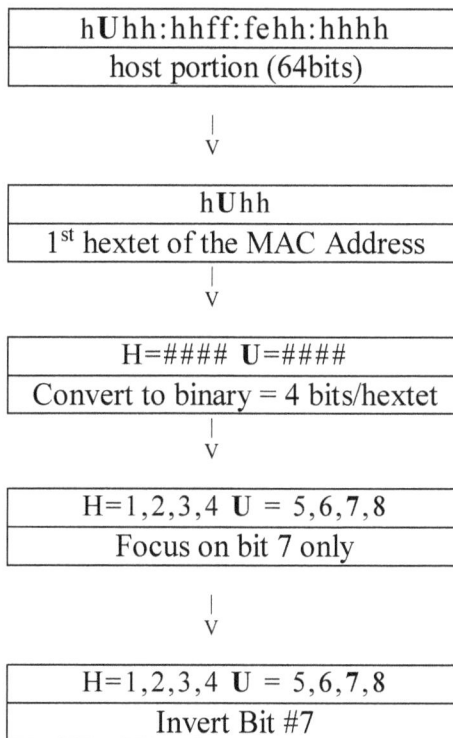

hUhh:hhff:fehh:hhhh
host portion (64bits)

|
V

hUhh
1st hextet of the MAC Address

|
V

H=#### U=####
Convert to binary = 4 bits/hextet

|
V

H=1,2,3,4 U = 5,6,7,8
Focus on bit 7 only

|
V

H=1,2,3,4 U = 5,6,7,8
Invert Bit #7

(Table 27)

Example only shows how to flip the 7th bit of a EUI-64 address:

FE80::3C4B:26:BA3A:0922	IPv6 address

|
v

3C4B:26:BA3A:0922
host portion (64bits)

|
v

3C4B	1st hextet of the EUI-64 Address

|
v

3=0011 C=1100	Convert to binary = 4 bits/hextet

|
v

3=0011 C=1100	Bit locations: focus on bit **7** only
1st Hextet=0011 2nd Hextet=1100	3=1,2,3,4 U = 5,6,7,8

|
v

3=0011 **C=1100**	H=1,2,3,4 **U** = 5,6,7,8
Invert Bit #7	
3=0011 **C=1110**	

|
v

3=0011 **C=1110**	Convert binary back to Hexadecimal
0011=3 1110=e	This converted value returned to IPv6 address as locally modified by Mfg/Local admin

|
v

*FE80::*3**E**4b:26:BA3A:0922	IPv6 address with 7th bit flipped

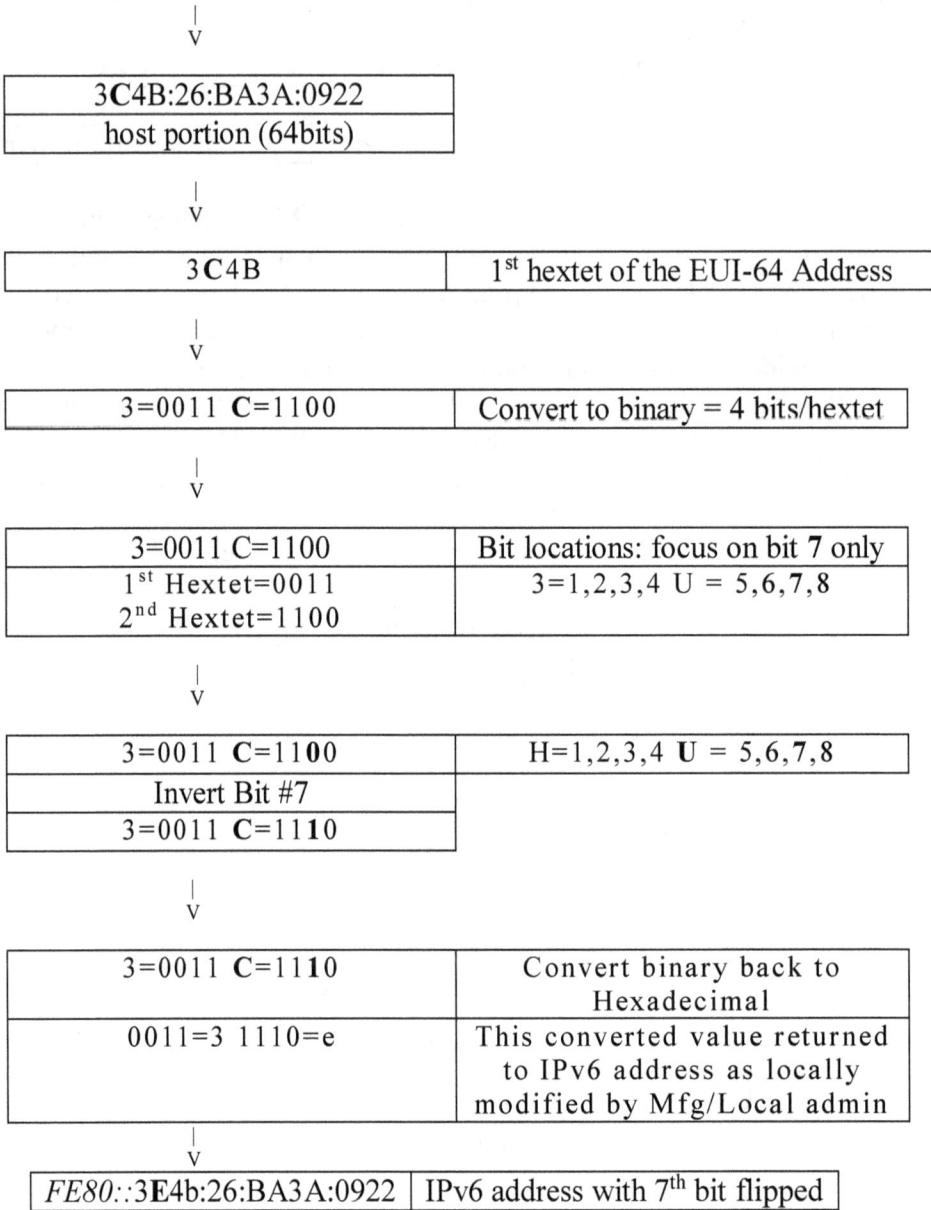

(Table 28: Duplication of table 27 but with real IPv6 address)

Ok so what does this mean in English? Well you see the 7th bit (also known as the Universally or locally assigned bit refers to whether the IP address was created from a MAC address which was created (or granted) by either Internet Assigned Numbers Authority group (URL:www.iana.org) or from a manufacturer which got the MAC address from Internet Assigned Numbers Authority group and is allowed to burn that MAC address into their network devices PROM chip which is referred to as the Burned in Address. The Burned in Address (aka BIA) is a one time permanent burn and is unchangeable.

The next question you might have is why do we have to invert the 7th bit. Well this is a good question and a question which I too had when I was learning this material. You see the 7th bit means the MAC address was assigned globally (aka: universally) or by a Local administrator (aka: by manufacturer or by a local site administrator; usually the latter). So why do we have to worry about this if this is the MAC address. Well this comes into play for a security reason and provides you anonymity. You see your MAC address is permanent and now that you know how to convert between 48 bit and 64 bit, it's somewhat traceable across the internet (aka: globe).

With the IPv6 being the new go forward model of Internet and providing the new internet version 2.0 this is referred to as the internet of things. Again meaning that every individual thing can have its own dedicated specific IP address. This is a good thing and also a bad thing. Good in that, for example, you can connect to your home thermostat and change your house temperature. This can be a wonderful thing especially in the hot summer months or in the cold winter months when you're not at home. You can easily change the temperature before you get there. This same concept can be used for recording your favorite shows, etc.… However this can also be bad in that your MAC address can be traceable across the internet (globe). Whether you are in San Francisco, Dallas, New York, Paris or Tokyo. Based on the information above you can see that your BIA is still static no matter what network you connect to. This allows you to be tracked across the network/internet which removes the ability to have ambiguity on the network. Therefore another method has been created to provide you ambiguity with your MAC address. It's called 'Random Generated Machine Address'. How does this work:
1) It uses your stable storage (data that has been written to your hard drive (aka: C:\ on a laptop)) and runs a MD5 checksum on this entire data. This generates a unique random MD5 checksum HASH value.

2) Next, it uses that left most 64 bits of the MD5 checksum (which are always random based on the data on your stable storage) and applies them as the 64bits of the MAC address. This generates the random value every time and is applied to the MAC address cloaking the original burned in MAC address with this new randomly generated MD5 Hash 64 bit value. This is why the BIA MAC address will not match the random MAC address. (NOTE: this is what provided you ambiguity across the internet)
3) It will use this new ambiguous MAC address to apply to the IPv6 host device section which will provide you security.

Lastly, according to ietf.org (https://tools.ietf.org/html/rfc2373#section-2.5.1 dated: 12/28/2015) there are some rules that need to be followed and I've listed them below:

Text Representation of Address Prefixes:
The text representation of IPv6 address prefixes is similar to The way IPv4 addresses prefixes are written in CIDR notation. An IPv6 address prefix is represented by the notation:

ipv6-address/prefix-length

- where ipv6-address is an IPv6 address in any of the notations listed in section 2.2.

- prefix-length is a decimal value specifying how many of the leftmost contiguous bits of the address comprise the prefix.

For example, the following are legal representations of the 60-bit prefix 12AB00000000CD3 (hexadecimal):

- 12AB:0000:0000:CD30:0000:0000:0000:0000/60
- 12AB::CD30:0:0:0:0/60
- 12AB:0:0:CD30::/60

The following are NOT legal representations of the above prefix:

- 12AB:0:0:CD3/60   may drop leading zeros, but not trailing zeros, within any 16-bit chunk of the address

- 12AB::CD30/60   address to left of "/" expands to 12AB:0000:0000:0000:0000:000:0000:CD30

- 12AB::CD3/60   address to left of "/" expands to 12AB:0000:0000:0000:0000:000:0000:0CD3

When writing both a node address and a prefix of that node address (e.g., the node's subnet prefix), the two can combined as follows:

the node address   12AB:0:0:CD30:123:4567:89AB:CDEF
and its subnet number 12AB:0:0:CD30::/60

can be abbreviated as 12AB:0:0:CD30:123:4567:89AB:CDEF/60

This is some deep information and I'll summarize it here before we continue. Since IPv6 addressing is based on network, mask and machine (host) address if it's given from IANA or the MFG then the 7th bit will be a 0 which means it's been universally assigned. However if a network admin needs to modify it such as padding the 48 bit MAC address and converting it into a 64 bit MAC address then the 7th bit of the first hextet will be inverted to reflect that it is locally administered. Secondly since IPv6 is large enough to provide an individual specific 'static' IP address to everything on the internet, this means that everything is more secure but at the same time still vulnerable. So IANA fixed this vulnerability with IPv6 by using a random generated MAC address which is based off of the stable storage of your local system. This provides you ambiguity and in turn security for the device you're on. This is more-so with the Windows environments and not with the Unix/Linux nor Apple iOS. They do not use the Random Generated MAC address and instead use the flipping of the 7th bit combined with the burned in address (BIA). This is why some people say that Windows might be better for surfing the internet using IPv6 due to the ambiguity built into the IPv6 address. Most of the time you don't surf the web or do a heavy amount of internet traffic using a Unix/Linux or major server. If you were to do that you would use your client workstation which again brings you back to the built in ambiguity of the IPv6 Random Generated MAC.

To provide full disclaimer here regarding IPv6, I've only scratched the surface of IPv6 and how it works here. If you're interested in diving more into the world of IPv6 please contact your local educational institution or do an internet search for more details.

IPv6 and GATEWAYS:

What about Gateways in IPv6; are those used too? Yes we use gateways in IPv6 addressing. In fact any device that has IPv6 enabled can point to a gateway. Here is an example you can find in MS Windows10 Ethernet IPv6 properties regarding IPv6 addressing, subnet prefix length and a default gateway below:

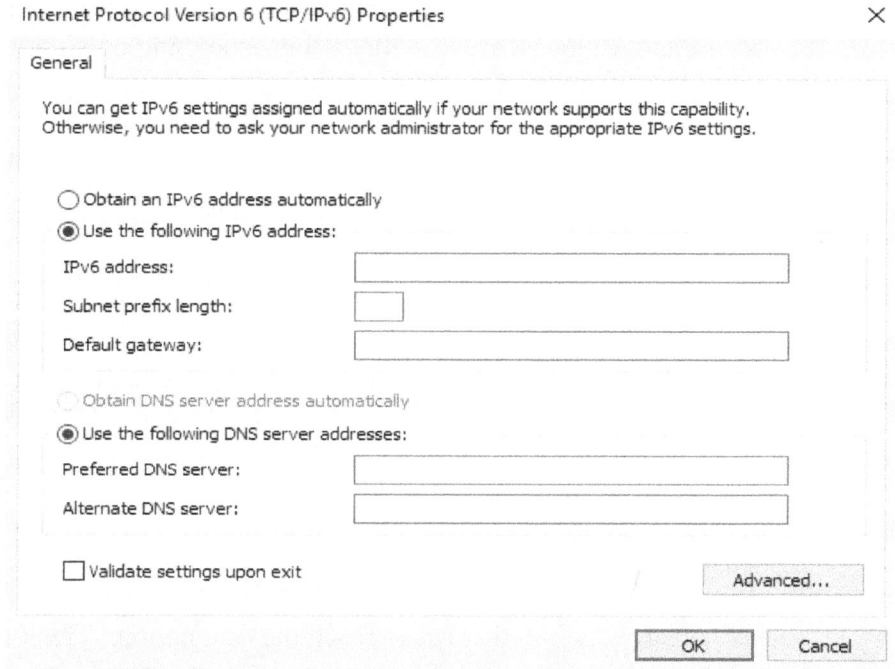

Internet Protocol Version 6 (TCP/IPv6) Properties   ✕

General

You can get IPv6 settings assigned automatically if your network supports this capability. Otherwise, you need to ask your network administrator for the appropriate IPv6 settings.

○ Obtain an IPv6 address automatically
◉ Use the following IPv6 address:

IPv6 address:

Subnet prefix length:

Default gateway:

○ Obtain DNS server address automatically
◉ Use the following DNS server addresses:

Preferred DNS server:

Alternate DNS server:

☐ Validate settings upon exit   Advanced...

OK   Cancel

(Image 78: Windows10 TCP/IP v6 properties window)

Do we use broadcast addresses in IPv6? Not as you once thought of broadcast. Instead we now use what we call a Link-Local address. What is a Link-Local address? This is an IPv6 address that only operates on the local network link and is great for discovering other systems on the common network wire. Think of this as the local broadcast. It starts with FE80: and it will reach out to any other device on this network only but keep in mind that a link-local address is NON-ROUTABLE. Think of the link-local address's main function is to replace the Address Resolution Protocol (ARP) for when a network interface comes online. It will only exist and converse with items on the same network. If you wanted to think of this as a broadcast address in IPv4 I suppose you could roughly correlate these 2 together for ease of your educational purposes.

What is the take away from this paragraph?
1) Know what a Link-Local Address looks like: starts with FE80:
2) Connects only with other IPv6 interfaces on the local wire.
3) Replaces the ARP when interface comes online.

Next we have what is called Multicast and Anycast which is similar to broadcasting but better. Multicast can connect your one device to multiple other devices and Anycast works great for the Wi-Fi concept. For example: Broadcast and Multicast are essentially the same thing only multicast is supposed to be for a larger number of devices and allow for less network bus contention. Cellphones like to use anycast as they are always reaching for a "Any" connection to link to as they move around a neighborhood, city, etc...

Overall I think we should now have a pretty good understanding of what IPv6 is and how it differs from IPv4. However I still don't think we have as good of understanding as we can have for IPv6. I think it would be good to look at the IPv6 header to better understand what we are dealing with here. So with that thought in mind let's get a bit deeper here. Please don't freak out here... I'll keep it simplistic for this book.

What is an IP header? Simply put it's the source and destination IP information that will traverse the network between locations A to location B. Along with this IP information there is a payload, which is your data packet you are sending, that has to reach the destination. Think of sending a letter through the post office. You write a letter to a family member or friend on the other side of the country. To send that letter you fold up the paper(s), insert it into an envelope and then what do you do? That's right, you put your returning address along with the sending to address on the front of the envelope so the postal service knows where to send it to. Likewise in case of any error your return address is on the envelope so the post office can return it to you. Well for this book; you can correlate the IP header information to the envelope concept. Likewise correlate the writing on the envelope such as the from address and the to address fields to that of the source header information and the destination header information. For clarification in the IP header; we call that source (from) and destination (to) addresses and the payload would be your data you're sending or in the letter analogy it would be equivalent to your paper letter you inserted into the envelope.

Going a bit deeper into this concept. when you send data across the internet it doesn't go as 1 full letter. No, in fact it goes down the OSI Model from

Level 7 to level 1 and then traverses across the wire in binary form (1's and 0's) to the destination and then travels back up the OSI model from level 1 to level 7 by being reassembled into a full packet. Think of this process as writing a letter and then putting it into a shredder that cuts it up into 100 pieces. You're full letter (prior to shredding) was at layer 7 and at layer 1 is 100 smaller cut up pieces. Each of these layers puts its header information on it for the destination to read and then sends it to the next layer below it. So following the OSI model we can see there is a full IP header of information (completely filled in with all source and destination information for each layer) which is attached to each of the smaller 100 pieces to be sent across the wire to the intended destination machine. When the information reaches the destination it is then received and the header information is stripped off of the datagram and sent to the next OSI layer above it. In essence reattaching all 100 pieces back together to recreate the letter (think taping the letter back together at the destination). I hope this is not too confusing and I said I would keep it fairly light but I'm sure as you can imagine there is a lot of detail here.

When we are looking at how IPv4 or IPv6 works; I like to think of this like a train. Yes I know the metaphors I use are somewhat silly but seriously they work. So think of a Train and what is in the front of every train? That's right an engine (sometimes many). Then we have box cars in the middle of the train and in early years there was a caboose at the end. So how does that this train concept apply to the internet? Well I think this will probably shock you on how closely these two concepts are to each other. Let's take a look at my simplistic table 29 below to see what I'm talking about.

Front	Middle	Rear
Train Engine(s)	Box Car	Caboose
IP Header & Info.	Payload	Frame Check/Footer

(Table 29: Comparison IP Header to Train)

With this train concept in mind you need to be able to attach it to something. Well that something is how the information traverses the internet or even your local network. That's right I want you right now to think of the network wire (i.e.: Ethernet wire which is called Category 3,5,5e,6 or 6a) between your computer and the local switch, hub or router. Imagine if you will on that network wire a train with box car moving from your computer to the switch/router. What's in the front? You guessed it; the train engine (aka: IP header) followed by the box car (Payload which has only 1 of the 100 pieces of paper we talked about above.). There may or may not be a frame check/footer for that data. Now repeat this process including the header and payload for each of our other 99 pieces of paper we previously metaphorically shredded and you have imagined how this process works. Quickly let's talk about the caboose or Check. Why was a caboose present? In case something fell off of the train and to have a validity check point (eyes) on the train from the rear of the train in case something went wrong. Well guess what the Check is that same concept. Let's go back to our 100 pieces of paper example. Let's say that piece 44 never made it to the destination. Can we fully reassemble the letter with only 99 pieces? No we cannot. So this is addressed by the destination sending information back to the source stating that it never received piece 44 and to resend it or all of the data again. This continues and can get quite deep into this concept but for simplistic terms I want you to be aware that the source can send only piece 44 or if needed can fully resent all 100 pieces. I won't go into the details of this here but I mainly want you to be aware of it.

So what does this look like in a picture format? See Image 79 on the next page:

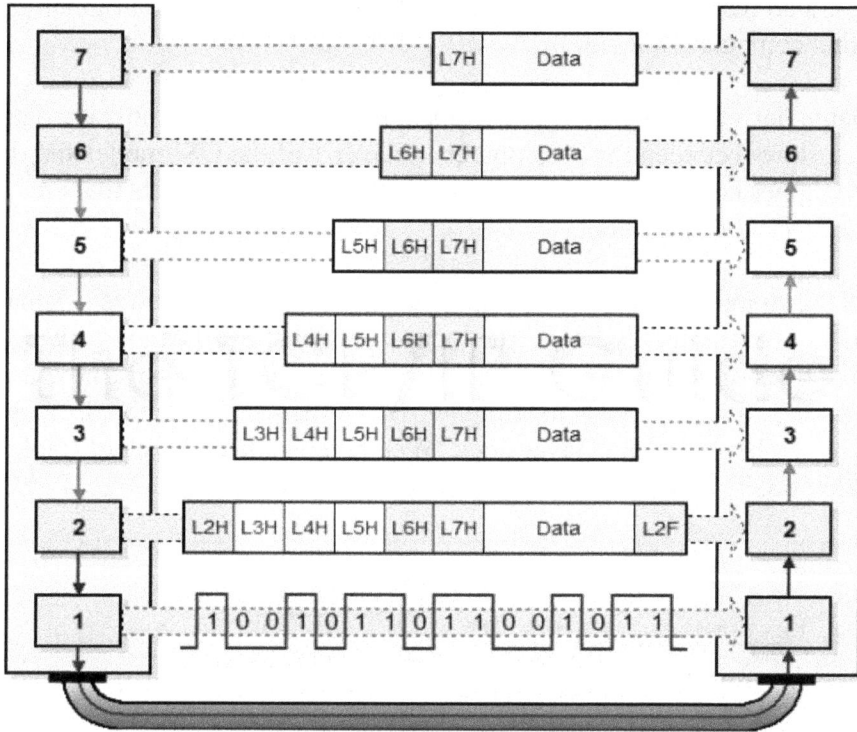

(Image 79: 7-Layer OSI Model with each layer header attached accordingly.

Source: http://i.stack.imgur.com/JkC1I.png)

We can see in the image above that as data moves down the OSI model
from the sending computer (left side) the header for that layer of the OSI
model is attached to the data packet and then sent down to the next layer.
This continues from layer 7 down to layer 6 where the next header
information is added to the packet and then sent down to layer 5 where layer
5 adds its header. This continues until it gets down to layer 1 which is the
physical wire that connects the 2 devices which has the binary data traverse
the wire. Remember the only thing that can exist on a wire is power and it's
either on or off (hence binary 1 or 0).

When the data reaches the other computer (right side of image) at layer 1
the information (data plus all the headers) is picked up by the computer,
read and understands the information is meant for this computer and it starts
to read the data and strips off the header(s). Then the information
progresses up each layer of the OSI model on the receiving computer. Each
level will remove its header and then send it up to the next level above it

until it's all reassembled into the proper form as it was on the original sending computer (left side).

So again, let's look at the train reference, the train would be how the data packet flows between the 2 computers at layer 1 of the OSI model and the train engines could be thought of as each of the header packets that are added in front of the data.

Let's take a moment and talk more about this OSI Model. It was originally for IPv4 but still mainly holds true today. Obviously you can already see it's the rules of how data is broken down into smaller pieces and how it traverses from computer A to computer B and then is reassembled. So how do I remember what each layer does? Well here is a friendly chart (table 30) to help you:

Layer	Description	Protocols	Devices	Encapsulation	Layer #
Applications	User interface, communication partner Identification.	HTTP, Telnet, FTP, TFTP, SNMP		Data	7
Presentation	Date format/exchange. Encrypt, translation, compression	JPEG, BMP, TIF, MPEG, WMV, AVI, ASCII, EBCDIC, MIDI, WAV		Data	6
Session	Setup, maintain and tear down communication session. Keeps data streams separate.	SQL, RPC		Data	5
Transport	Reliable/unreliable connection. End-to-end flow control, port/socket numbers. Segmentation.	TCP, UDP		Segments	4
Network	Logical address; path determination; route packets here.	IP, IPX, AppleTalk, DECNET	Routers and L3 Switches	Packets	3
Data Link (LLC + MAC)	Convert bits to bytes and bytes into frames; MAC address; flow control: ACK, Buffering, Windowing; parity/CRC	802.2(LLC), 802.3 (Ether), 802.5(Token), 802.11(wifi); WAN HDLC, PPP, Frame-Relay, ATM, ISDN	Nics, Switches, Bridges	Frames	2
Physical	Move bits across media, Physical topology	EIA/TIA 232 serial, V.35 modem, Cat5, RJ45	Cable Connectors, Hubs, repeaters	Bits	1

(Table 30: Source: https://itdaddy.files.wordpress.com/2008/07/osimodel.png)

Here is a table (#31) that is helpful in memorizing what each layer does.

OSI MODEL		
7		**Application Layer** Type of communication: E-mail, file transfer, client/server.
6		**Presentation Layer** Encryption, data conversion: ASCII to EBCDIC, BCD to binary, etc.
5		**Session Layer** Starts, stops session. Maintains order.
4		**Transport Layer** Ensures delivery of entire file or message.
3		**Network Layer** Routes data to different LANs and WANs based on network address.
2		**Data Link (MAC) Layer** Transmits packets from node to node based on station address.
1		**Physical Layer** Electrical signals and cabling.

Layers 4-7 are **UPPER LAYERS**. Layers 1-3 are **LOWER LAYERS**.

(Table 31: Helpful table to explain what is done at each layer.)

Welcome to IPv6 Headers. Ok, so both IPv4 and IPv6 both have the IP header information as well as the payload but we are going to focus on IPv6 header here. The IPv6 data packet which is 320 bits (40bytes) in total is broken into 2 parts: the header and payload.

My table 32 below lists the header parts only in a more easy to understand view
(Note: I show the payload as well but this is not covered here).

Version (4bits)	Packet Priority Traffic Class (8 bits)	Flow Label / QoS mgmt (20bits)	
Payload Length (16bits)		Next Header (8bits)	Hop Limit / TTL (8bits)
Source Address (128bits)			
Destination Address (128bits)			
<Payload here> *<size=524280 bits/65535 bytes>* *<will be discussed later>*			

(Table 32: Inside look at the IPv6 header)

Note:
In this section; I'll refer to the IPv6 address mainly in Bytes with a small mixture of the use of bits. You can easily convert Bytes to bits by multiplying Bytes by 8 to get bits. Likewise, you can convert bits to Bytes by dividing by 8.

The first 40 Bytes (320bits) contain the header, source and destination addresses. The source and destination addresses are 32Bytes long (128 bits each x 2 = 256bits (32bytes)) This leaves 8 Bytes (64bits) for the header (aka: management of data) as noted above in the diagram.

Using the chart above lets talk about each of the fields:

1) Version (4 bits): This field explains whether the data packet will be in either IPv4 or IPv6 protocol. The size of this version field is the same size at 4 bits.

2) Packet Priority / Traffic Class (8 bits): This field defines the packet priority. For example if a company has a business class internet connection they can pay for business class internet levels which basically means the priority or their data is higher than that of residential. This also means that the datagrams with higher priority will be delivered before those of lower priority. The source is the device that sets the priority for the destination to read and communicate at the higher priority.

3) Flow Label / Qos Mgmt (20 bits): These 20 bits are used by the source (sender) to label a set of packets that belong to the same flow of data. In esscense making sure the data is sent as smoothly as possible. This is important when it comes to VoIP transmissions and remote locations that do not use a wired connection to their ISP. QoS is critical to ensure that voice communication is crisp and clear. If you have bad or broken voice transmissions then look at the QoS for your network. IPv6 has a Flow Label field incase the packet needs to be resent or resequenced.

4) Payload Length (16bits): The Payload length field puts a ceiling limit on the maximum packet payload size of 64 Kbytes. This is what's common for transmission between devices. However, when a higher packet payload is required (aka: Jumbo payload) a jumbo payload extension header is provided in the IPv6 protocol as indicated by the value of zero in the Payload Length field. Jumbo grams are frequently used to transmit heavy data payload. Total length (IPv4) == Payload Length (IPv6)

5) Next Header (8bits): Indicates the transport layer protocol that the payload will use. There are many however the two most common are TCP (6) and UDP (17). Protocol (IPv4) == Next Header (IPv6) Defines whether using TCP vs UDP protocols for the Data Packet.
    Same as "Next Header" in IPv6 but also defines what type of data is in the packet.

6) Hop Limit / TTL (8bits): This Time-to-Live (TTL) field is 8 bits long which give a binary version of 256. That means that there can be 256-2 = 254 hopes in the IPv6 address. A hop is when your connection crosses over a router. Then that router will decrement this hop count by one and pass it to the next router until it reaches zero. IPv4 is very similar to this however it only allows 30 hops per IPv4 connection.

7) Source Address (128bits): This is the source address of the originator. IPv4 = 32 bits and IPv6 = 128 bits (source and destination are both 4x longer in IPv6)

8) Destination Address (128bits): This is the destination address of the recipient device for the packet. IPv4 = 32 bits and IPv6 = 128 bits (source and destination are both 4x longer in IPv6)

Other items in IPv4 verses IPv6:

1) IPv4 (Header Checksum) == error detection during transmission.
    IPv6 = eliminated as it's addressed in other layers of the OSI model.
2) IPv4 there was no way to truly authenticate the source.. we had to believe what it told us (allowed for spoofing).
3) Encryuption of payload for while payload is in transit
4) There are no options and padding in IPv6 as there was before in IPv4. This would be handled in the Next Header field if needed
5) IPv6 Stateless auto-configuration means a new host can auto assign its own host address which is new and this eliminates the need for DHCP. This is done by the new host using its own mac address + servers host address to assign its own new IPv6 address.
6) IPv6 supports new IP security protocols (Authentication of source and payload encryption)
7) IPv4 and IPv6 both default to maximum 64KB payload size; however they both support jumbo frames but IPv6 now supports jumbo frames up to 4GB and these are called "jumbo datagrams". Note that if jumbo frames are used then all devices between the 2 sources must also 100% completely support and be 100% correctly configured for jumbo frames. Otherwise network degradation can occur resulting in slower performance than if you had never configured jumbo frames at all.

Internet of Things
(Explanation: connect all things to the internet)

What is this Internet of things? Maybe you've heard of it and maybe you have not. Let's take a step back and think about the internet when it first came about and ask yourself why did the internet come about? Ok if you said the Internet was originally the ARPA project for the Department of Defense then yes you are correct. In that case the internet started in 1958 when President Eisenhower requested funds for the project. It however didn't officially start until December 1966. Over a four month period of time spanning from September 1969 to December 1969; the ARPA project was able to establish 4 nodes. One node at each of the following sites: UCLA, Stanford, UC Santa Barbara and University of Utah. The next year there were more nodes that were established such as Cambridge Massachusetts in March 1970 and University of Hawaii in July 1970. This continued as time went on; however again we have to ask ourselves why are we connecting computers? Quite simply it was a way of connecting people and data. You see the military and government is very smart (I know this is a part where you may laugh at me for saying that but seriously the government has some pretty good ideas at times). Anyhow, this ARPA thing was a great idea and it is what spawned the internet many years later (now). So why did they create the ARPA net? As I was saying, they were facing some hard times with the possibility of war and incase a military base was wiped off the face of the earth they needed to be able to re-route data and communication quickly. Likewise they needed redundancy so there was not a gaping hole for the enemy to attack through. So that was one of the main reasons... to connect data and people. As time has gone on and the public has become more main stream this ARPA net project has evolved into the internet that we know today. So we can call this 'internet version 1.0' which can also be called the 'internet of people' or the connecting of people.

Now that we understand the beginning purposes of the internet and how to connect people we can see based on the previous IPv4 sections that there is a limit to the number of people and things that can be on the internet, remember 16 Million devices which are all used up. Hence comes the next version of the internet which we can call 'internet version 2.0' or better yet, 'Internet of Things' (IoT). The IoT has how many IPv6 addresses available? If you are thinking $2^{128} =$ 340,282,366,920,938,463,436,374,607,431,768,211,456 devices or addresses. Then you are still on the right track. That's enough IP addresses for way more devices than currently exist on the earth and then probably even more.

This means that with 2^{128} devices that not only can people have IPv6 addresses but so can things. Such as your refrigerator, TV, thermostat, car, smartphone, clothing, security systems (including cameras), street lights and intersection cameras. Now I'm not trying to set off the paranoid flag here but some may start raising it now and think that big brother is watching; I'm not trying to go down that path.. it was already travelled way to much back in the 1960's, 1970's and 1980's. (Trust me in today's world, it's not a big brother mindset you need to worry about, but instead you have to also think of little brother which is your family and friends taking pictures and posting them on the web.. but that's another story for a different book I may write some day). Instead let's look at this with our engineering minds at work here and think how great this IPv6 can be. First of all to have a camera at an intersection with its own IP address. To think how effective this will be for helping first responders determine what and who is needed onsite of an accident. When there is an accident the city personnel can log into the camera and see what has happened and auto-dispatch emergency personnel to that location and have a better understanding of the situation up to and including even saving lives.

Ok, I know there can be some negative ideas that we all need to address regarding IoT and yes they do exist however I'm going to be optimistic here and focus on the many wonderful things that can happen with the IoT and I'm looking forward to them. What positive thoughts can you come up with regarding the new IoT?

1. _____
   _____
   _____

2. _____
   _____
   _____

3. _____
   _____
   _____

4. _____
   _____
   _____

5. _____
   _____
   _____

6. Learning Check (IPv6):

1. What is IPv6 address?

2. What is an IPv6 address?

3. How many devices can an IPv6 address support compared to IPv4 address scheme:

4. Does IPv6 use subnet mask?

5. Does IPv6 use a gateway address?

6. What is a link-local address?

7. What is an Any-cast address?

8. What is a multi-cast address and why is it important:

9. How many Bytes is an IPv4 address compared to an IPv6 address?

10. Give an example of a link-local address in Hexadecimal notation:

11. Briefly explain what the IoT is and its importance:

12. Tools to troubleshoot the network and internet

1. What can I expect from this chapter? (dos>ping, traceroute, arp, netstat)

1. In this chapter I will discuss the tools we use to troubleshoot a network. There are many different programs for the computer as well as apps for the smart phones which can be downloaded for free or for a small fee. However keep in mind that there are also all-in-wonder programs that do have a heavy cost to them and they promise to make your life easier as a network admin. I'm not saying that one is better than the other or vice-versa. Instead I'm going to talk more about the basic tools we use to troubleshoot a network.

The basic tools are command line tools and are available in the Microsoft operating system. These tools are:

ipconfig
arp
ping
netstat
traceroute

You can access any of these above tools by simply typing them into a command prompt window. If you have any questions add the forward slash and question mark (/?) behind the command for more details.

Let's go through these command line (Dos) commands.

IPCONFIG:

Starting off with ipconfig this command identifies the computers overall network interface card IP configuration. This includes IP address, subnet mask, gateway, machine address code (MAC), DHCP information as well as DNS information. The ipconfig output looks like:

Example: C:\Users\testuser>ipconfig
Windows IP Configuration

Wireless LAN adapter Local Area Connection:
Media State . . . . : Media disconnected
Connection-specific DNS Suffix . :

Ethernet adapter Local Area Connection:
Connection-specific DNS Suffix . :
IPv4 Address. . . . . : 192.168.1.19

Subnet Mask . . . . : 255.255.255.0
Default Gateway . . . . : 192.168.1.1

However if you add a switch to this command such as /all then you get more information which includes all the interfaces and MAC, DHCP and DNS information. I've provided a copy of this as well here:

C:\Users\testuser>ipconfig /all

Windows IP Configuration
   Host Name . . . . : testuser-PC
   Primary Dns Suffix . . . . :
   Node Type . . . . : Hybrid
   IP Routing Enabled. . . . . . . : No
   WINS Proxy Enabled. . . . . . . : No

Wireless LAN adapter Local Area Connection:
   Media State . . . . : Media disconnected
   Connection-specific DNS Suffix . :
   Description . . . . : Microsoft Wi-Fi Direct Virtual Adapter
   Physical Address. . . . . : ##-##-##-L#-L#-#L
   DHCP Enabled. . . . . : Yes
   Autoconfiguration Enabled . . . . : Yes

Ethernet adapter Local Area Connection:
   Connection-specific DNS Suffix . :
   Description . . . . : Intel(R) 82579V Gigabit Network Connection
   Physical Address. . . . . : ##-##-##-L#-L#-#L
   DHCP Enabled. . . . . : Yes
   Autoconfiguration Enabled . . . . : Yes
   Link-local IPv6 Address . . . . . : fe80::L###:##L#:L##L:L###%4(Preferred)
   IPv4 Address. . . . . : 192.168.1.19(Preferred)
   Subnet Mask . . . . : 255.255.255.0
   Lease Obtained. . . . . : Thursday, October 13, 2016 3:36:01 AM
   Lease Expires . . . . : Friday, October 14, 2016 3:35:57 AM
   Default Gateway . . . . : 192.168.1.1
   DHCP Server . . . . : 192.168.1.1
   DHCPv6 IAID . . . . : 241447248
   DHCPv6 Client DUID. . . . : ##-##-##-##-#L-##-#L-##-##-##-##-L#L#-#L
   DNS Servers . . . . : 192.168.1.1
   NetBIOS over Tcpip. . . . . . . : Enabled

NOTE: The # and L above in addresses have been used to protect private information. However in order to keep integrity to the field I've replaced either the number with the # sign or the hexadecimal letter with an L.

To display the information on ipconfig, I've typed the command with the /? To display the help information on the command. I've done this below for your reference:

C:\Users\testuser>ipconfig /?

USAGE:
   ipconfig [/allcompartments] [/? | /all |

```
/renew [adapter] | /release [adapter] |
/renew6 [adapter] | /release6 [adapter] |
/flushdns | /displaydns | /registerdns |
/showclassid adapter |
/setclassid adapter [classid] |
/showclassid6 adapter |
/setclassid6 adapter [classid] ]
```

where
  adapter   Connection name
                 (wildcard characters * and ? allowed, see examples)

Options:
  /?   Display this help message
  /all   Display full configuration information.
  /release   Release the IPv4 address for the specified adapter.
  /release6   Release the IPv6 address for the specified adapter.
  /renew   Renew the IPv4 address for the specified adapter.
  /renew6   Renew the IPv6 address for the specified adapter.
  /flushdns   Purges the DNS Resolver cache.
  /registerdns   Refreshes all DHCP leases and re-registers DNS names
  /displaydns   Display the contents of the DNS Resolver Cache.
  /showclassid   Displays all the dhcp class IDs allowed for adapter.
  /setclassid   Modifies the dhcp class id.
  /showclassid6 Displays all the IPv6 DHCP class IDs allowed for adapter.
  /setclassid6   Modifies the IPv6 DHCP class id.

The default is to display only the IP address, subnet mask and
default gateway for each adapter bound to TCP/IP.

For Release and Renew, if no adapter name is specified, then the IP address
leases for all adapters bound to TCP/IP will be released or renewed.

For Setclassid and Setclassid6, if no ClassId is specified, then the ClassId is removed.

Examples:
  > ipconfig   ... Show information
  > ipconfig /all   ... Show detailed information
  > ipconfig /renew   ... renew all adapters
  > ipconfig /renew EL*   ... renew any connection that has its
                            name starting with EL
  > ipconfig /release *Con* ... release all matching connections,
                            eg. "Wired Ethernet Connection 1" or
                                "Wired Ethernet Connection 2"
  > ipconfig /allcompartments   ... Show information about all
                            compartments
  > ipconfig /allcompartments /all ... Show detailed information about all
                            Compartments

Exercise (ipconfig):

Open a command prompt and issue the same command as I've done above
so you experience how to look at these commands. Note any differences
between your system and the information that I'm providing in this book.

Now add in the options such as /all, /release, /renew and see how your output changes.

1. What is your IP address listed from the ipconfig command:
   _____
   _____

2. What is your subnet mask listed from the ipconfig command:
   _____
   _____

3. What is your gateway address from the ipconfig command:
   _____
   _____

4. What happened when you issued: "ipconfig /release"?:
   _____
   _____
   _____
   _____

5. What happened when you issued: "ipconfig /renew"?:
   _____
   _____
   _____
   _____

ARP:

Next item you will read about is ARP (Address resolution protocol). The dos command help file says that arp displays and modifies the IP-to-Physical address translation tables used by address resolution protocol (ARP). Ok what does that mean? Quite simply, arp is a command that you can issue which will tell the computer to send out an arp request to the network and announce that it's on the network. In simple terms it's like yelling into a dark room to announce that your there. Only the people in the room that hear you will respond. Arp works the same way.

To display the information on arp, type the command without any options. I've done this below for your reference:

C:\Users\testuser> arp <enter>
Displays and modifies the IP-to-Physical address translation tables used by
address resolution protocol (ARP).

ARP -s inet_addr eth_addr [if_addr]
ARP -d inet_addr [if_addr]
ARP -a [inet_addr] [-N if_addr] [-v]

  -a   Displays current ARP entries by interrogating the current
           protocol data. If inet_addr is specified, the IP and Physical
           addresses for only the specified computer are displayed. If
           more than one network interface uses ARP, entries for each ARP
           table are displayed.
  -g   Same as -a.
  -v   Displays current ARP entries in verbose mode. All invalid
           entries and entries on the loop-back interface will be shown.
inet_addr   Specifies an internet address.
-N if_addr   Displays the ARP entries for the network interface specified
           by if_addr.
  -d   Deletes the host specified by inet_addr. inet_addr may be
           wildcarded with * to delete all hosts.
  -s   Adds the host and associates the Internet address inet_addr
           with the Physical address eth_addr. The Physical address is
           given as 6 hexadecimal bytes separated by hyphens. The entry
           is permanent.
eth_addr   Specifies a physical address.
if_addr   If present, this specifies the Internet address of the
           interface whose address translation table should be modified.
           If not present, the first applicable interface will be used.
Example:
  > arp -s 157.55.85.212 00-aa-00-62-c6-09 .... Adds a static entry.
  > arp -a   .... Displays the arp table.

Exercise (arp):

Open a command prompt and issue the same command as I've done above so you experience how to look at these commands. Note any differences between your system and the information that I'm providing in this book. Now add in the options such as –a and see how your output changes.

1. What is your MAC address (list and explain why it is what it is):

   _____
   _____
   _____
   _____
   _____

2. What else did you notice in your ARP output:

   _____
   _____
   _____
   _____
   _____
   _____
   _____
   _____
   _____

PING

Ping is the next command line tool that we'll use in our troubleshooting. The ping command is issued from the computer that you're on (called pc1) and we'll use it to ping another computer called pc2 via an IP address. Ping will send over icmp packets to pc2 and if pc2 is turned on and present on the same network as we are on then it will reply with a successful ping. However if no connection can be successfully made then the router or switch will reply that destination is not reachable and this will be a fail.

The command prompt help file states:
C:\Users\testuser>ping /?

Usage: ping [-t] [-a] [-n count] [-l size] [-f] [-i TTL] [-v TOS]
            [-r count] [-s count] [[-j host-list] | [-k host-list]]
            [-w timeout] [-R] [-S srcaddr] [-c compartment] [-p]
            [-4] [-6] target_name

Options:
      -t   Ping the specified host until stopped.
                      To see statistics and continue - type Control-Break;
                      To stop - type Control-C.
      -a   Resolve addresses to hostnames.
      -n count   Number of echo requests to send.
      -l size   Send buffer size.
      -f   Set Don't Fragment flag in packet (IPv4-only).
      -i TTL   Time To Live.
      -v TOS   Type Of Service (IPv4-only. This setting has been
                      Deprecated and has no effect on the type of service
                      field in the IP Header).
      -r count   Record route for count hops (IPv4-only).
      -s count   Timestamp for count hops (IPv4-only).
      -j host-list   Loose source route along host-list (IPv4-only).
      -k host-list   Strict source route along host-list (IPv4-only).
      -w timeout   Timeout in milliseconds to wait for each reply.
      -R   Use routing header to test reverse route also (IPv6-only).
                      Per RFC 5095 the use of this routing header has been
                      deprecated. Some systems may drop echo requests if
                      this header is used.
      -S srcaddr   Source address to use.
      -c compartment Routing compartment identifier.
      -p   Ping a Hyper-V Network Virtualization provider address.
      -4   Force using IPv4.
      -6   Force using IPv6.

Example (ping):

Per my above ipconfig information; my computer IP address is 192.168.1.19 and my gateway is 192.168.1.1.

Therefore for this example I'll ping my gateway IP address to see if I have connectivity. If so then I will get 4 successful ping replies. However if not then a failure will be listed.

```
C:\Users\testuser>ping 192.168.1.1
Pinging 192.168.1.1 with 32 bytes of data:
Reply from 192.168.1.1: bytes=32 time<1ms TTL=64
Reply from 192.168.1.1: bytes=32 time<1ms TTL=64
Reply from 192.168.1.1: bytes=32 time<1ms TTL=64
Reply from 192.168.1.1: bytes=32 time<1ms TTL=64

Ping statistics for 192.168.1.1:
    Packets: Sent = 4, Received = 4, Lost = 0 (0% loss),
Approximate round trip times in milli-seconds:
    Minimum = 0ms, Maximum = 0ms, Average = 0ms
```

As you can see in the above results that the ping is successful and I have sent and received 4 packets with 0% loss. This is good and what we want to happen when troubleshooting. However as the word troubleshooting often means we are trying to find a problem and if packets are lost then that would be indicative of a connectivity problem somewhere between source and destination.

Let's play with this ping command one more time. You see ping will also work with websites as well. This time I'll try to ping google' website via its public address (URL) but your welcome to try any of your favorite URL's.

```
C:\Users\testuser>ping www.google.com
Pinging www.google.com [216.58.195.68] with 32 bytes of data:
Reply from 216.58.195.68: bytes=32 time=12ms TTL=53
Reply from 216.58.195.68: bytes=32 time=12ms TTL=53
Reply from 216.58.195.68: bytes=32 time=12ms TTL=53
Reply from 216.58.195.68: bytes=32 time=12ms TTL=53

Ping statistics for 216.58.195.68:
    Packets: Sent = 4, Received = 4, Lost = 0 (0% loss),
Approximate round trip times in milli-seconds:
    Minimum = 12ms, Maximum = 12ms, Average = 12ms
```

Exercise (ping):

If not already open from the previous exercise; open a command prompt and issue the ping command on your own IP address (obtained from your previous ipconfig output). This way you will experience how to look at this command. Note any differences between your command output and the information that I'm providing in this book. Now add in the options such as –n and see how your output changes.

1) What result did you get from pinging your own IP address?:

_____

_____

_____

2) What result did you get from pinging your local gateway?

_____

_____

_____

_____

3) What result did you get from pinging your favorite website?

_____

_____

_____

4) What result did you get from pinging www.google.com?

_____

_____

_____

_____

NETSTAT

Netstat is a command that will display the network statistics for the computer. It listens for TCP and UDP traffic as well as port numbers.

The help file shows:
C:\Users\chris>netstat /?

Displays protocol statistics and current TCP/IP network connections.
NETSTAT [-a] [-b] [-e] [-f] [-n] [-o] [-p proto] [-r] [-s] [-x] [-t] [interval]

-a	Displays all connections and listening ports.
-b	Displays the executable involved in creating each connection Or listening port. In some cases well-known executables host multiple independent components, and in these cases the sequence of components involved in creating the connection or listening port is displayed. In this case the executable name is in [] at the bottom, on top is the component it called, and so forth until TCP/IP was reached. Note that this option can be time-consuming and will fail unless you have sufficient permissions.
-e	Displays Ethernet statistics. This may be combined with the –s option.
-f	Displays Fully Qualified Domain Names (FQDN) for foreign addresses.
-n	Displays addresses and port numbers in numerical form.
-o	Displays the owning process ID associated with each connection.
-p proto	Shows connections for the protocol specified by proto; proto may be any of: TCP, UDP, TCPv6, or UDPv6. If used with the –s option to display per-protocol statistics, proto may be any of: IP, IPv6, ICMP, ICMPv6, TCP, TCPv6, UDP, or UDPv6.
-q	Displays all connections, listening ports, and bound nonlistening TCP ports. Bound nonlistening ports may or may not be associated with an active connection.
-r	Displays the routing table.
-s	Displays per-protocol statistics. By default, statistics are shown for IP, IPv6, ICMP, ICMPv6, TCP, TCPv6, UDP, and UDPv6; the -p option may be used to specify a subset of the default.
-t	Displays the current connection offload state.
-x	Displays NetworkDirect connections, listeners, and shared endpoints.
-y	Displays the TCP connection template for all connections. Cannot be combined with the other options.
interval	Redisplays selected statistics, pausing interval seconds between each display. Press CTRL+C to stop redisplaying statistics. If omitted, netstat will print the current configuration information once.

Example:
C:\Users\chris>netstat -a

Active Connections

Proto	Local Address	Foreign Address	State
TCP	0.0.0.0:80	PC1:0	LISTENING
TCP	0.0.0.0:135	PC1:0	LISTENING
TCP	0.0.0.0:445	PC1:0	LISTENING
TCP	0.0.0.0:1801	PC1:0	LISTENING
TCP	0.0.0.0:2103	PC1:0	LISTENING
TCP	0.0.0.0:2105	PC1:0	LISTENING
TCP	0.0.0.0:2107	PC1:0	LISTENING

...
...
...

TCP	127.0.0.1:49704	PC1:0	LISTENING
TCP	127.0.0.1:49705	PC1:49706	ESTABLISHED
TCP	127.0.0.1:49706	PC1:49705	ESTABLISHED
TCP	127.0.0.1:49707	PC1:0	LISTENING
TCP	127.0.0.1:49723	PC1:49725	ESTABLISHED
TCP	127.0.0.1:49724	PC1:49726	ESTABLISHED

Exercise (netstat):
If not open from previous exercise, open a command prompt and issue the same command as I've done above so you experience how to look at this command. Take a few moments to look over your output and note any differences between your system and the information that I'm providing in this book. Now add in the options such as –a, -f, -n and see how your output changes.

1) What do you notice regarding your netstat output?

_____

_____

_____

_____

2) do you see your own IP address and the ports that are open as well as their listening verses established states?

_____

_____

_____

_____

3) What are the most common ports listed in your output?

_____

_____

4) Do you see any ports that refer to port 80 or 443? Y or N? What does this mean for your computer?

_____

_____

_____

_____

TRACEROUTE (tracert)

Traceroute is a command that will allow you to see the full path a packets takes from source computer (pc1) to destination computer (pc2 or website). This is a way of providing validity to the connectivity between 2 locations.

I like to think of traceroute as a roadmap checker. If you were to drive across country wouldn't you like to have checkpoints you would go to such as national parks, museums, events, cities, etc. If you're like most people the answer is yes. Ok in my example of driving across country think of each park or city as a destination. In the networking world we call this a router. A router as we previously discussed does what? It connects networks together. So you could think of this router as a cross-road between networks much the same way as a city is a cross road to multiple paths across a country side. Ok, stick with me here. Every time we cross over a router we call it a 'HOP'. We have hopped from network A to network B and this is counted in the header as we previously discussed. Ok so when you look at a tracert output in the example below you'll see the HOP count and in IPv4 we can have a multiple of 30 HOPs to reach the destination. If however we reach 31 HOPs then the destination is pre-determined to be unreachable and dead. So you will never reach the 31 HOP. The good news is I've been able to reach every single valid webpage I've truly tried to connect to within 30 hops as I'm sure you will and have done as well.

NOTE: The actual command is 'tracert' in the command prompt.

The help file shows:
C:\Users\chris>tracert

Usage: tracert [-d] [-h maximum_hops] [-j host-list] [-w timeout]
       [-R] [-S srcaddr] [-4] [-6] target_name

Options:
-d	Do not resolve addresses to hostnames.
-h maximum hops	Maximum number of hops to search for target.
-j host-list	Loose source route along host-list (IPv4-only).
-w timeout	Wait timeout milliseconds for each reply.
-R	Trace round-trip path (IPv6-only).
-S srcaddr	Source address to use (IPv6-only).
-4	Force using IPv4.
-6	Force using IPv6.

Example (tracert):
C:\Users\testuser>tracert www.google.com

Tracing route to www.google.com [216.58.195.68]
over a maximum of 30 hops:

```
 1   <1 ms   <1 ms   <1 ms   READYSHARE [192.168.1.1]
 2    8 ms    8 ms    8 ms   96.120.14.191
 3    8 ms    8 ms    8 ms   xe-7-3-2-sur02.sacramento.ca.ccal.comcast.net [68.87.213.181]
 4    8 ms   13 ms    9 ms   te-9-1-ur01.visalia.ca.ccal.comcast.net [68.87.200.53]
 5    8 ms    9 ms    8 ms   ae-2-ar01.sacramento.ca.ccal.comcast.net [162.151.18.133]
 6   12 ms   11 ms   12 ms   be-33667-cr01.sunnyvale.ca.ibone.comcast.net [68.86.93.25]
 7   12 ms   12 ms   11 ms   hu-0-11-0-0-pe02.529bryant.ca.ibone.comcast.net [68.86.86.70]
 8   12 ms   13 ms   12 ms   66.208.228.70
 9   13 ms   13 ms   11 ms   108.170.242.81
10   12 ms   12 ms   12 ms   108.170.235.237
11   12 ms   12 ms   15 ms   sfo07s16-in-f4.1e100.net [216.58.195.68]
```

Trace complete.

Notice that traceroute only counts the router hops and not anything like my computers IP address.

Exercise (tracert): If not already open from previous exercise, open a command prompt and issue the same command (tracert) as I've done above so you experience how to look at these commands. Note any differences between your system and the information that I'm providing in this book. Now add in the options such as –d, -h, -4, -6 and see how your output changes.

1) What does tracert show you?

_____

_____

_____

2) How many hops did you count for your instance of the command being run?

_____

_____

3) Try issuing the tracert command on your favorite website and count the hops: _____

_____

Learning Check (Troubleshooting Tools):

1. Q: What command will display your hardware (MAC) address and list the correct syntax in how you would use it: _____

_____

_____

_____

2. Q: What will Ping allow you to do?

_____

_____

_____

_____

_____

3. Q: What does netstat allow you to see/check?

_____

_____

_____

_____

_____

4. Q: To check a path a packet is taking what command will I issue?

_____

_____

_____

_____

13. Summary Check: Networking

1. Q: What numbers are used in binary?

2. Q: What is the msb and lsb of an octet?

3. _____

4. Q: How many bits are in an octet?

5. Q: How many octets are in an IPv4 address?

6. Q: What is the maximum number for an octet if all bits are enabled?

7. Q: What is an IPv4 address:?

8. Q: What is an IPv4 subnet and why is it important?

9. Q: What are the different classes of IPv4 Addresses (List all classes, number of networks and number of hosts)?

10. Q: What are the different sizes of a IPv4 network? (Not classes)

11. Q: Which is best class of IPv4 addresses for home or small office use and why?

_____

_____

_____

_____

12. Q: Is there a difference between a Wi-Fi-Lan (aka: WAN) and a wide area lan (aka: WAN)? If so explain:

_____

_____

_____

_____

13. Q: Convert the following IPv4 address (192.168.29.57) to binary:

_____

_____

_____

_____

14. Q: Using your above answer; Apply the correct subnet mask to the above IP address answer (you provided) to net out the correct IP address when the subnet mask is active.

_____

_____

_____

15. Q: Convert the following binary address to decimal:
11000000.10101000.01100011.01101001

_____

_____

16. What is an IPv6 address?

_____

_____

_____

_____

_____

17. How many devices can an IPv6 address support compared to IPv4 address scheme:

_____

_____

_____

_____

18. Does IPv6 use subnet mask?

_____

_____

19. Does IPv6 use a gateway address?

_____

_____

_____

20. What is a link-local address? _____

_____

_____

_____

21. What is an Any-cast address?

_____

_____

_____

_____

22. What is a multi-cast address and why is it important:

_____

_____

_____

_____

23. How many Bytes is an IPv4 address compared to an IPv6 address?

_____

_____

_____

_____

_____

24. Give an example of a link-local address in Hexadecimal notation:

_____

25. Briefly explain what the IoT is and its importance:

_____

_____

_____

_____

_____

26. Q: What command will display your hardware (MAC) address:

_____

_____

27. Q: What will Ping allow you to do?

_____

_____

_____

_____

28. Q: What does netstat allow you to see/check?

_____

_____

_____

_____

29. Q: To check a path a packet is taking what command will I issue?

_____

_____

_____

5. File and Disk Management:

1. What can I expect from this chapter?

Welcome to File and Disk Management chapter. This is a fun chapter that really should be read by everyone on the earth. The reason I feel this way is that we all have data that needs to be backed up. For example think of all the pictures you have on your computer as well as special documents such as resumes, bank statements, and homework if you're in college, etc. This is why I feel and say that anyone who is using a computer and doing anything with documents or email or whatever should really think about date backups. Ok now that I've pushed that thought let's talk about what you learn in this chapter. In this chapter you will learn the following:
2. Why every hard drive will fail... The question is when it does will you survive?
3. What is a Backup and are they important?
4. How to manage files in Microsoft Windows?
5. How to clean up Unwanted files?

1.   Why every hard drive will fail... The question is when it does will you survive?

What can I expect from this chapter? In this chapter I'll cover why I say every hard drive is going to fail. Well let's just dive right into this and explain what I'm talking about. You see every hard drive that is mechanical will eventually wear out due to it being mechanical. This means that it may be an internal motor that fails resulting in the platters not being able to spin. It could be a circuit board error causing data not to be retrieved. In either case the hard drive is generically referred to as failed. That is why I say every hard drive will fail. The question you want to ask yourself is, "when it fails am I ok? Will I be able to survive my data loss?" You see you also have to keep in mind that a hard drive can fail right now as you're reading this or in 5 mins or in 5 years? This is the infamous question so many people ask, 'when will it fail?' and there is truly no way to specifically answer it. The hard drive companies are working on ways to predict when a hard drive will fail and provide you a heads up before hard drive failure occurs. Remember, your hard drive could have failed while you are reading this chapter. So the question that you really should be asking yourself is if every hard drive is going to fail what should I do to prevent from losing my data? The simple answer is to do backups. I'll cover this more in the next section.

1. Backups, Are they important?

1.   What is a backup? A backup is nothing more than a copy of the original file or directory structure. That's it in a simple nutshell. Think back to the time before computers and we had to use the 3 piece copy paper where each piece was a different copy (i.e.: the top copy was white, middle copy was ping and the bottom copy was yellow). For those who don't know what I'm talking about I've added image 80 below for your reference:

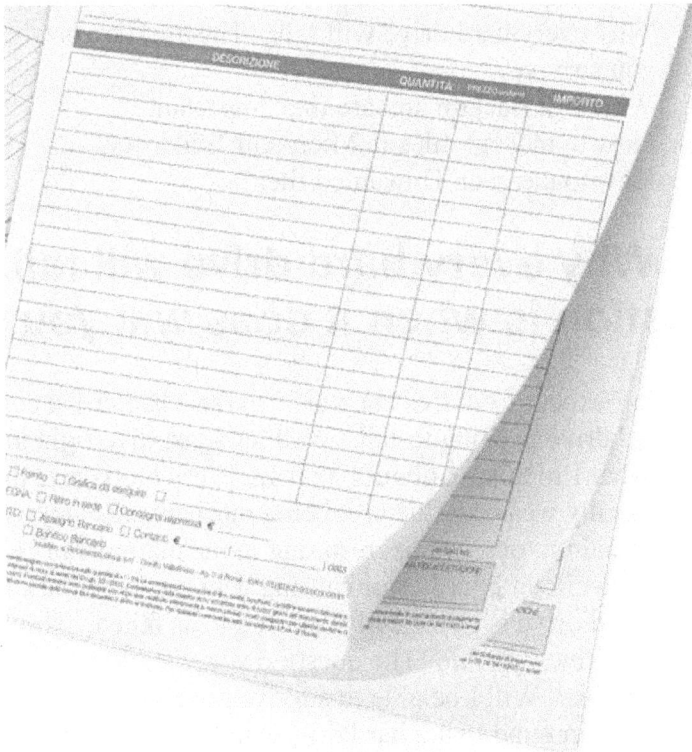

(Image 80: Example of Carbon copy paper Source: http://workflow-upload.s3.eu-central-1.amazonaws.com/files/010-va1mzmt6i-blocchi-e-fascicoli-copiativi-large.jpg?env=prd&v=1ZjxXL)

So how does this triple carbon copy work? You would have to use a pen to press down hard and then write. This would press the carbon from the bottom side of the paper onto the next sheet below it. The following graphic (image 81) helps demonstrate this better.

186

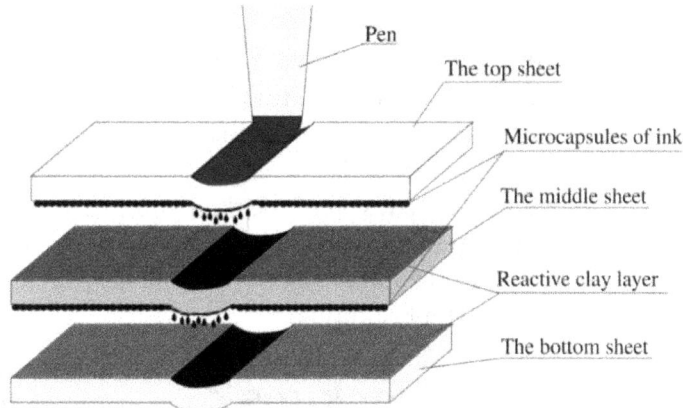

(Image 81: Example of how copy paper works when presure from pen is applied to the top sheet. Note how all 3 layers get the same information copied to each copy. Source: https://upload.wikimedia.org/wikipedia/commons/thumb/c/c1/Carbonless_copy_paper-en.svg/1066px-Carbonless_copy_paper-en.svg.png)

Ok so why did I bring up such an old concept? For demonstration purposes. You see if one of the copies (White, pink or yellow) were lost then you would have other copies of the same document to work from. In essence this was an early form of a backup or back in the days they called it 'duplicates'.

Lets take that same mental concept of duplicates and apply the concept to our data files and directory. If we want a duplicate we can click on the file and then copy that file and paste it into the same directory or anywhere we would like it within the computer file system. When we copy and paste that makes a duplicate and a duplicate is another word for backup. So when some some asks you if you have a backup of your data they are essentially saying did you make a secondary copy of the data.

Lets look at this another way just to make sure you really understand what I'm trying to convey here. Think about all your pictures or important data on your computer and in what folder does it reside in? Most likely it's in your Documents folder or MyPictures folder. Ok both of these directories reside on your local internal hard drive which again I said early will eventually fail. So if and when your internal hard drive fails what will happen to all of your pictures and documents... Kapoof! They will be lost in an instant and now you have a problem... However if you made a backup of your documents folder or pictures folder what does that mean?

187

You got it.. You made a secondary or chirchary (3rd) copy of the data on another hard drive. This secondary or chirchary hard drive can be internal to the computer or it could be an external USB drive or possibly a external network drive such as NAS (Network Attached Storage), SAN (Storage Area Network) or possibly on the cloud such as icloud, google drive or OneDrive.

In anycase since you made a backup of the data you can simply fix the damaged data structure up to and possibly replacing the drive. Once that's done you can simply copy the data back over to the new drive. Now you know and understand what a backup is.

2. **Do I need to do backups?** Yes everyone should do backups *(make a secondary copy of their data)* including you on the data that is important to you. I have been asked by my students over the years, "How do I know if my data is important or not?" My response is quite simply this; "If you can life without the data then it wasn't that important" and another way that I like to respond is, "If you can sleep soundly at night knowing what data you have could be 100% gone in the morning... Then you're probably ok due to the data is backed up". If you can look at both of these answers to the question and apply them successfully to your situation then you are probably ok.

3. There are so many different backup companies; which should I use? If you have ever asked yourself this question or had this thought you're not alone. Again what is a backup? If you're saying a secondary copy of your data then you're thinking correctly. So the next part to this mental equation for backups is do you want to manage the backups or have a third party company manage the backups.   There are many good external third party backup companies that will provide a service for you to backup your data to their company's server for a monthly fee for X amount of storage. The benefit to doing this is you don't have to worry about doing the backups, having the hardware equipment which could be as simple as an External USB drive or if you're thinking bigger it would be a server, raid array, etc.. So if you choose to use a third party backup service; you simply download their software, install it on your operating system and follow their setup instructions and you're backing up your data.

Now if you choose to do what's called in-house backups that means that you will be doing all the backups by yourself. The benefit to this is there is usually only a 1 time charge for initial purchase of equipment and you're good to go. What does this equipment mean? As I preluded to in the previous paragraph that an in-house backup depends on how elaborate you want to get. Again all we are doing is making a secondary copy of our data in case the original data is corrupted, lost or damaged. So I'll give a few examples of backups on the next page in Table 33.

Table 33: Types of Backups and their details:

Type	Knowledge	cost	Type	Location	Problem/Safety
File/Dir. Copy.	Simple	cheap	Directory 1 (hd#1) to directory 2 (hd#1) (local)	copy dir. To another dir. (same drive)	If HD#1 fails all data lost.
File/Dir. Copy.	Simple	cheap	Directory1 on Hd#1 to directory2 on h/d #2. (local)	copy dir. To another dir. (different drive)	Safer than above method.
USB backup	Simple	Cheap	Directory1 on Hd#1 to directory2 on USB drive. (local)	copy dir. To another dir. (different drive)	Safer than above method however can be slower due to USB speeds slower than SATA.
NAS (Network Attached Storage)	Intermediate	Medium	Directory1 on Hd#1 to directory2 on NAS drive. (local)	copy dir. To another dir. (different drive)	Similar to USB Backup only it's across your network. If a busy network it could be slow backup or cause latency for users.
Cloud (Network Attached Storage)	Intermediate (requires username & pw.)	Medium	Directory1 on Hd#1 to directory2 on Cloud drive. (requires username & pw.) (non-local)	copy dir. To another dir. (different drive)	Similar to NAS Backup only it's across your network and internet connection. If a busy network it could be slow backup or cause latency for users.

Ok so now that I've talked about whether a backup is local or non-local (remote) I think it's only pertinent that we also talk about the methods of doing the backups. There are different versions of backup strategies such as full, incremental and differential. Let's talk more about each of these:

1. Full Backup – A full backup is exactly what it sounds like. This method starts at the beginning of the file system (i.e.: c:\) and copies everything in full to the backup location. The benefit of a full backup is just as the name says, it's a full backup of everything. However the drawback to a full backup is it takes a lot of room on the backup medium such as the tape backup, usb backup drive or secondary hard drive which the full backup process is copying to. Again this can take some time to perform in both the backup and recovery process.

2. Incremental Backup – Incremental Backup is the process of doing a full backup but instead of doing it daily it's usually done 1 day a week such as Sunday (for example). Then you can run an incremental backup on Monday but it only backups data that has changed since Sunday as the files that were modified on Monday would not have an backed up flag set on them and that's how it would know to back them up. Now regarding the next day of the week (Tuesday), it would also need to have its daily incremental backup which would only backup the data between Mondays incremental backup completion and Tuesdays incremental backup start. This allows for the daily backups (Called dailies) to be smaller and occur quicker than doing a full backup each and every day.

The drawback to incremental is if you need to do a full system recovery you have to load the Sunday Full back up and let it process. When done then you need to load the Monday backup and let it recover the data to the file system. Then when the Monday recovery is done then you would have to load the Tuesday backup to get that tape to load and recover that data. As you can see this can take some time in order to recover certain data and/or a full backup to a specific day in-between the full backups.

3. Differential Backup – A differential backup is a process where a full backup is done (example: On Sunday) and then the differential backup backs up only the data that has been changed since that full backup was done.

If you need to recover the data you still need to load your weekly full backup (i.e.: Sunday full backup) however if it's currently Friday and you need to recover the data from Thursday; then you only need to load the Thursday differential backup media and you will have successfully backed up all of your data. This method is quicker and faster for recovering data unlike the incremental method which can be time consuming to recover the data.

4. What type of back-up should I do? This depends on how you want to do backups as well as how much you can afford. Most home users usually use an external USB Backup drive which you can pick up at most computer stores relatively cheap. Once you have this USB backup drive you can plug it into your computer via USB cable and then establish the method you want to use such as a full, incremental or differential. This process is the same for NAS devices as well.

5. What about backing up to the cloud; is this safe? There has been lots of different views of this over the years but essentially backing up data to the cloud is the same as backing up to a network attached storage (NAS) on your own home network. The only difference is instead of the NAS being in your home it's out on the internet at a given companies server such as Google, Dropbox, iCloud or OneDrive. There are many different companies that are all getting on board with this online storage.

So let me talk a bit more about this.. Is it safe? Well is anything really safe? The hard truth is no it's not.. If a criminal wants something bad enough and is willing to go through the hurdles to get to it.. eventually they will get to it. With that thought in mind what we do to make it safe or give us the illusion that it's safe is to put obstacles in between the bad people and our pot of gold. In this metaphor the pot of gold is your data. Bringing this metaphor back to the world of online data storage being safe. The companies that provide data backup and any online company that provides you a location for you to store data, pictures or backups want your business so they are going to take every opportunity to ensure your connection to their company website as well as your cubby hole on their website is as safe and secure as possible.

Why would they do this? It's about the money and don't forget that. Even if they are giving you a free online email and cloud storage of a few gigabytes. If you sign up with them and store your data on their server then you are using their services. Keep this in mind and multiply it by 100,000+

people from across the world. Now this online company can go to other companies and sell the point to other companies; that they have 100,000+ active users (people) on their website. This way it's a way of business to business marketing and there is a ton of money in this realm for advertisements.

Can you imagine what would happen if this online company didn't take your data security as high as they do and there was a data breach. You would instantly pull all your data from their website as fast as you could.. Again multiply that times by tens of thousands of people in only a few hours and that company could be in ruins as known by the world in only a matter of a few hours due to the speed of communication of social media today. So it's in every online company's best interest to provide the highest level of security for your data.

How do they provide the security to the public? Well when you go to their main website you access their public domain name site. This may or may not use ssl (secure socket layer) security. However as soon as you click on login then you will notice the address bar will change from
http://<www.companynamehere>.com to
https://<www.companynamehere>.com
Notice the letter 's' has been added to the http which means you are using a secure connection on port 443 instead of a common web port of port 80. I'm not going to go into the TCP ports much here but I want you to be aware that there are approx. 65000 ports that can be used to access the internet. Port 443 is a secure connection port for data traffic. If you want to learn more about this; please do a public internet search via your favorite search engine for tcp ports. There are other methods that are used for securing your data but for this terms of this book I will only call them out in general such as strong passwords or phrases as well as Kerberos which is a security method for authenticating your connection.

So yes in my opinion; online storage can be a great way to store data and to perform it on a 3rd party hosting site is probably a safe way to do it for the average home user.

Learning Check (Hard drives):

1. Will your hard drive fail? When?

_____
_____
_____
_____

2. Explain what a backup is and why it's important? _____

_____
_____
_____
_____
_____

3. Where is the average home users personal data kept in MS Windows
   Operating system? _____

_____
_____
_____

4. Who needs to do backups? _____

_____

5. List and explain the 3 method (types) for backups:

_____
_____
_____
_____
_____
_____
_____
_____

6. Can a backup device be internal or external to your pc/laptop and
   explain? _____

_____
_____
_____
_____
_____

How to manage files in Microsoft Windows?

What can I expect from this chapter? In this chapter, you'll learn how files are managed and where they are kept inside of Microsoft Windows.

It's no secret that Microsoft has been around of a long time. If you do a public internet search you can find the details of when it was incorporated but for simple terms and from my internet search, I'll say that it started in 1975 but wasn't until 1980 when it partnered with IBM and began its journey. Ok so between then and now Microsoft has had some time to pay attention to its users and how they use a computer as well as where they put their files. Despite what some computer folks say about Microsoft; they have actually done a lot of thing right. I'm going to focus on directory structures and how they are a benefit to the average home user.

As I said above, Microsoft has paid attention to the people who use the Microsoft Windows operating system for a very long time. What they found was that most people store their personal data into common directors with similar names even though they had different file extensions. Mainly these files are as follows:

Type of file:	Location	File extension
Documents	C:\users\<username>\documents	.txt, .doc, .wp
Pictures	C:\users\<username>\pictures	.jpg, .tiff, .gif
Music	C:\users\<username>\Music	.mp3, .wav
Desktop	C:\users\<username>\Desktop	Various
Videos	C:\users\<username>\Videos	.avi
Downloads	C:\users\<username>\Downloads	various

(Table 34: Directory pathing of common folders in Windows)

As time has gone on Microsoft has continued to pay attention to where data is being placed however I think that they got a lot of this right initially. So if you use Microsoft Windows OS then you can use the above chart to see where your data is being kept.

Now with the above said, that information is mainly for the average home or small business user knowledge. Yes I know there are more files and directories but I'm not going to cover them here as they are more for system/server administration purposes and I want to keep this somewhat beginner friendly.

Let's talk about Microsoft OS libraries. Microsoft has also incorporated this thing called a library. What is a library? A library is a tool that can refer to multiple different directories all at the same time and search for a given file format. If you are looking for pictures and you incorporate the libraries tool it basically conglomerates all your pictures from different directories into the pictures library providing you a single place to look for pictures. In other words, the picture library references any picture format with a listed directory path structure. You can add to this directory path list or remove your directory path from the pictures library by simply right clicking on the pictures library listing and click edit or properties. Follow the popup window for details on further actions.

Just like the pictures library; Microsoft has also done the same thing for Documents, music and videos as well. You can even add in external storage such as USB drives or cloud storage to your libraries.

6. Learning Check (Windows Managing Files):

1. Where does Microsoft keep your picture files inside of the operating system:

   _____
   _____ _____

2. Where does Microsoft keep your music files inside of the operating system:

   _____
   _____

3. Where does Microsoft keep your document files inside of the operating system: _____

   _____

4. What is a library and why is it important? _____

   _____ _____
   _____
   _____

14. How to clean up Unwanted files?

1. What can I expect from this chapter? I like to keep a clean environment and that includes my computer. How can I keep a clean and ordered file system? If you are thinking this or asking this question then you'll really enjoy this chapter.

In this chapter you will be able to determine where unwanted files could reside and could be taking up unneeded space on your storage system.

I'd say it's no secret that we all either on purpose or in-advert inly accumulate stuff on our computers. Unfortunately, this can lead to and cause unusual wear and tear on the system which holds, scans, backups, and make available all our stuff. If we accumulate to much miscellaneous stuff on our computer it can fill the hard drive above thresholds and cause Windows to slow down. You may have witnessed this some time or another when trying to surf the web or send or receive email or write a college term paper and your computer was just extremely slow due to the file system is to full. This can also lead to pre-mature hard drive failure if serious excessive use occurs.

With that said, its best practice for all of us to occasionally take some time to find unneeded items on our computers and delete them. These can be found in the most common places such as desktop, downloads, temp folders, etc...

Here is a good process to follow to find unwanted items and delete them occasionally. Look for unused, old, broken files in the following areas and delete them:

1. Temporary folders (C:\temp, All installed Web-browsers)
2. All users Desktops
3. All users Downloads
4. All users Documents
5. All users Music
6. All users Pictures
7. All users Videos
8. All users Personal Network Drives (i.e.: K:\, T:\, etc..)
9. When you find unwanted files; simply drag the items to the Recycle Bin on your Desktop or right click on them and select delete. When done with searching items 1-7 above you can empty your recycle bin.
10. To empty the recycle bin; right-click your Recycle Bin icon and select "Empty Recycle Bin". Keep in mind that after you empty the recycle bin that data is deleted from the system and unable to

be recovered. Well as far as the standard windows user is concerned with. (Note: There are data recovery experts that can recover some of the data if needed but they usually charge for this service).

11. You will also want to check your control panel > programs for any unwanted applications that are installed in your computer.
12. At the end of your pc usage; it's a good idea to restart Windows. This ensures that if there are any updates that need to process they do it before your next day starts. (again, this is best practice.. why wait for an update to complete when it can do it overnight when you're not there).

Note: It's not a good idea to mix your personal information with that of your work information. Computers as well as storage at work cost money and it's not typically best practice to store your own personal information, files, data on work computers. Therefore If you have personal stuff on your 'work' computer, you really should delete it or transfer it to a personal storage device and take it home.

2. Learning Check (File & Disk management):

1. In this section what folders are best for checking for unneeded files in a computer? _____

_____

_____

_____

_____

_____

_____

2. How do I delete a file or directory I no longer want?

_____

_____

_____

_____

_____

_____

3. If I empty the recycle bin what happens to the contents?

_____

_____

_____

_____

_____

4. What is the best practice method for keeping a clean computer operational?

_____

_____

_____

_____

_____

_____

_____

_____

15. Summary Check: File and Disk Management

1. Will your hard drive fail? When? _____

   _____
   _____
   _____
   _____
   _____

2. Explain what a backup is and why it's important?

   _____
   _____
   _____
   _____
   _____
   _____
   _____

3. Where is the average home users personal data kept in MS Windows Operating system?

   _____
   _____
   _____
   _____
   _____

4. Who needs to do backups?

   _____
   _____
   _____

5. List and explain the 3 method (types) for backups:

   _____
   _____
   _____
   _____
   _____
   _____
   _____
   _____

6. Can a backup device be internal or external to your pc/laptop and explain?

_____

_____

_____

_____

_____

_____

7. Where does Microsoft keep your picture files inside of the operating system:

_____

_____

8. Where does Microsoft keep your music files inside of the operating system:

_____

9. Where does Microsoft keep your document files inside of the operating system:

_____

10. What is a library and why is it important?

_____

_____

_____

_____

_____

11. In this section what folders are best for checking for unneeded files in a computer?

_____

_____

_____

_____

_____

_____

_____

12. How do I delete a file or directory I no longer want? _____

_____

_____

_____

_____

_____

_____

13. If I empty the recycle bin what happens to the contents?

_____

_____

_____

_____

_____

_____

14. What is the best practice method for keeping a clean computer operational?

_____

_____

_____

_____

_____

_____

_____

_____

6. Internet

1. What can I expect from this chapter?

In this chapter I'll cover a high level overview of the interview. This will be based on the fact that there are many many many different angles to the internet and to try and cover all the different usages is a crazy wild Pandora's box. So I'll cover some of the major common questions I get from my students in hopes that it will also help you. By the end of this chapter you should have a better understanding of the internet, how to search online, open your online email account as well as how to attach a document such as your resume.doc to your email to send to a future employer.

2. Explanation

Ok so I talked about the birth of the internet on page 109 and how important IPv4 is to the use of the internet. However what are some of the purposes of today's internet? Well that's a loaded question but many people use the internet for many things such as sending and receiving emails, paying bills online, chatting with friends and co-workers online using online chatting tools such as Facebook, Twitter, Google+ as well as listen to music by steaming online. Speaking of streaming online today's internet allows people from all around the world to stream music and movies 24 hours a day/ 7 days a week. With all that said there is probably even a stronger point to today internet and that is online shopping. You see the world of shopping has dramatically increased in the past 10 years with online shopping companies such as amazon.com, ebay.com and basically any of your regular stores are also now incorporating online shopping ability so you can shop from the convenience of your own home.

3. Example: How to navigate the internet

Navigating the internet can be a tricky process and in fact can lead you to websites that you never had any intension of visiting. I'm here to tell you, right now, that on average you are only 3 clicks away from being on a website that you don't want to visit at any given time and it's your responsibility to know where you are at all times. So you really need to pay attention to the address bar at the top of the web browser for the websites and URL's you are visiting. If it doesn't look right nor feel right then there may be a good chance you're not on the website you think you are.

Before I continue with this section of the book; I want to make sure that everyone is fully aware of how to read a web address. First off what is a web address? A web address is a way of using letters and numbers to identify a website for a remote organization or company. A web address would look something like www.google.com, www.microsoft.com, www.<companynamehere>.com. The name of the company is then translated by Domain Name Services (aka: DNS) into a specific IP Address and then routed to that remote companies public IP address. The companies information is then returned to your computer and displayed for your viewing.

So how do you read a webpage address? Quite simply you read it much like you do English. Starting from left with the http:// or www. and you read across to the right until you reach the first forward slash (/) after the domain name such as .com, .net, .edu, .gov, etc… For ease of this reading I'll use the .com/ and you can plug any of the above .net, .edu, .gov into its place.

Everything to the right of the first slash or anything after the first slash we can ignore for simplification. Now for my webserver techies I know you are totally cringing on this concept but again I have to say this for simplification. But for the record I'll say that anything to the right of the first forward slash after the .com/ is website specific for the web browser to properly navigate to the given data to be display for you. For us simple folks we don't need to worry about this extra information but instead be aware of it.

Ok so the next part is once you reach the .com/ of the website you then reverse and read backwards. That's right you now read from right to left starting with the .com which is the domain name and then the name of the company would be next (google) and then that would be followed by the www for the world wide web.

I think this may make since if you can see an example such as:
http://www.google.com/

reading from right to left it would be:
    a. .com
    b. Google
    c. www

Let's look at a couple other examples and you try to figure them out:
www.homedepot.com/
        a. _____
        b. _____
        c. _____

www.ashercollege.edu
        a. _____
        b. _____
        c. _____

placeronline.org
        a. _____
        b. _____
        c. _____

Great job on figuring that out.. It's not too hard. However the problem comes when you are redirected to another website which looks like the website you think you should be on but the URL is not correct. This may look something similar to:
http://www.google.badguysrus.com/happywebpage.html
www.homedepot.virusheaven.com/yourwrongwebpage.html

So what is different about the above 2 web addresses?: _____

_____
_____
_____
_____
_____
_____

If you said the above 2 websites had badguysrus and virusheaven in front of the .com then you are absolutely correct. Good detective work. Yes the simple answer here is the website directly to the left of the .com is the actual website you are truly visiting (i.e.: badguysrus and virusheaven.com) and if there is a another server on that bad website with a name of google or homedepot then that's a redirect within the badguysrus and virusheaven.com. So you see it's super easy for you to be redirected to websites that are not truly the websites you want to look at.

Ok I'm not trying to scare you but instead I'm trying to make you aware of what is and what should be. Remember you just need to pay attention to the URL address and you should be fine. Let's look at some good websites.

> http://www.server1.homedepot.com/webpage.html
> www.sacramentoserver.google.com/webpage.htm

Notice that both of these websites are valid. Why? _____

_____
_____
_____
_____
_____
_____

If you said, the word to the left of the .com was homedepot or google then you are correct. You now have the basics of how to read a web address URL.

4. Next I want to talk about how to go directly to a website. If you want to go to the website of Home Depot you would want to type in the address bar the following: www.homedepot.com which would then transfer to http://www.homedepot.com and this would take you to Home Depot website. The other way that many people would go to the Home Depot website would be to open a web browser and use their favorite search engine such as www.google.com, www.yahoo.com, www.bing.com, etc… and from within that search engine you could type 'home depot' and click on search. This would return a listing of from an open internet search with all the word Home Depot in the returned items (companies) websites. Your hopes in doing this would be that homedepot.com would be one of the results and you could click on their link URL to go to their website.

I would say that this is usually the case in a strong 95% of the internet searches for the major company's websites. However for the smaller company websites and the off the wall websites with non-common URL's there could be variances and there are the potential for website redirections to other websites. This is where you would need to know how to read a website URL as I covered above. Remember it's your responsibility to know where you are on the internet at all times. Did you catch that last sentence.. I'll say it again, "it's your responsibility to know where you are on the internet at all times."

If you don't know where you are on the internet and it doesn't feel right then you can always close your website and start over from the beginning. Sometimes it's the safer move to do that especially if you have been re-directed to a bad website.

Next I want to also say that everything you do on the internet has been logged by your computer, your internet service provider (aka: ISP) as well as all upstream routers. Now I'm not trying to make everyone paranoid to use the internet. I truly believe that the pros outweigh the con's here and in todays world the internet and sharing data is here to stay. So I want you to be smart about what you do on the internet and remember to use the litmus test in all of your internet activities. What do I mean by this? You can think of what I'm saying in this fashion. "if you could live your life tomorrow without shame or sorry with what you're doing on the internet right now then you are probably ok". Another way of thinking about this would be to think of your activities being broadcasted across a bulletin board in times square. How would you feel if that happened. If you wouldn't mind then you are probably doing everything right and in accordance with safe internet usage. However if not then you may want to re-think your internet activities.

5. Example: How to conduct a job search online.

In today's world of the internet doing a job search is almost as common as breathing and using technology is a must in order to find a great job. So how do you best do this? Well there are many ways of doing this but I'll provide you some of the ways that I did this when I was looking for jobs.

First off you will have to have a resume created for you and it would be a great idea for you to customize the resume for the given job you're searching for. Next you would want to use a job search engine for the field that you are using. For the tech industry I used www.dice.com, www.jobs.com, www.indeed.com, www.linkedin.com, www.facebook.com as well as state and local government websites.

You will want to create a username and password for each of these websites as well as remember each so you can regularly log in and check for posted jobs that match your job skills. The good news is that a lot of these websites have tutorials for helping you to navigate their setup processes so you can build your online profile. As you can see I chose not to provide screen shots of these websites here for many reasons. Mainly the webpages are changed as time goes on as does the long URL addresses however the main websites as listed above have been very static for many years.

6. Example: How to access your online email account (i.e.: Gmail acct).

Accessing your online email can seem like a very confusing task however it's really not that difficult if you understand how it works. First off you will need to have access to the internet. It does not matter how fast of a connection you have to the internet as long as you have a connection. With that said I would say that best practice is to have a good always on connection which could be via Wi-Fi, dsl or cable internet connection. However if you only have a modem to connect that will work to but keep in mind that you will need to have patience as the modem connection will be very slow.

Ok so provided your connection is now all established you will need to open a web browser of your choice and type in your online websites email address such as www.gmail.com, www.mail.yahooo.com, www.office365.com, etc... For simplification I'll use a test account that I have on gmail.com.

Google

Sign in to add another account

Enter your email

Next

Find my account

Create account

One Google Account for everything Google

G M ⚄ ▶ △ ⚗ ▶ ●

(Image 82: Google sign-in page)

Type in your email address and click next. You will then be prompted for your password and you can type that in and click next. After this you will be presented with your online email program.

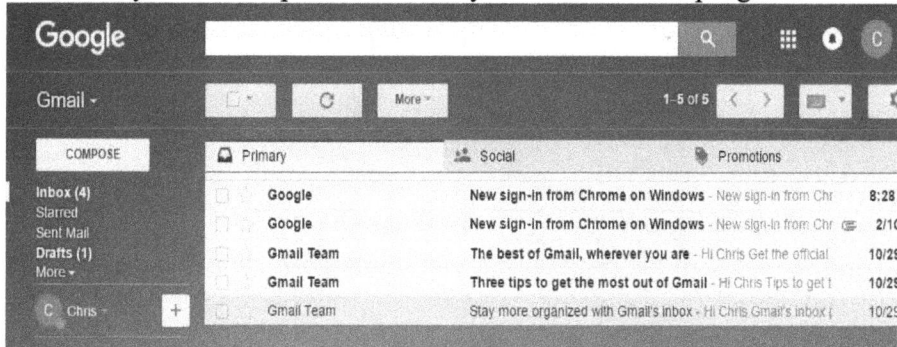

(Image: 83: Webmail format hosted by Gmail)

Now that you're into your online email account how do you send an email? If you are asking this question then I'm going to cover it now.

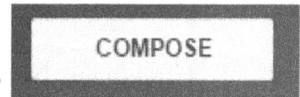

COMPOSE

You can simply click on the 'compose' button on the left hand side of the screen to open a new email for you to draft to someone. By this I mean you can write the email to send to another person. Notice that when you clicked on the compose button it should have opened a new window which looks something similar to:

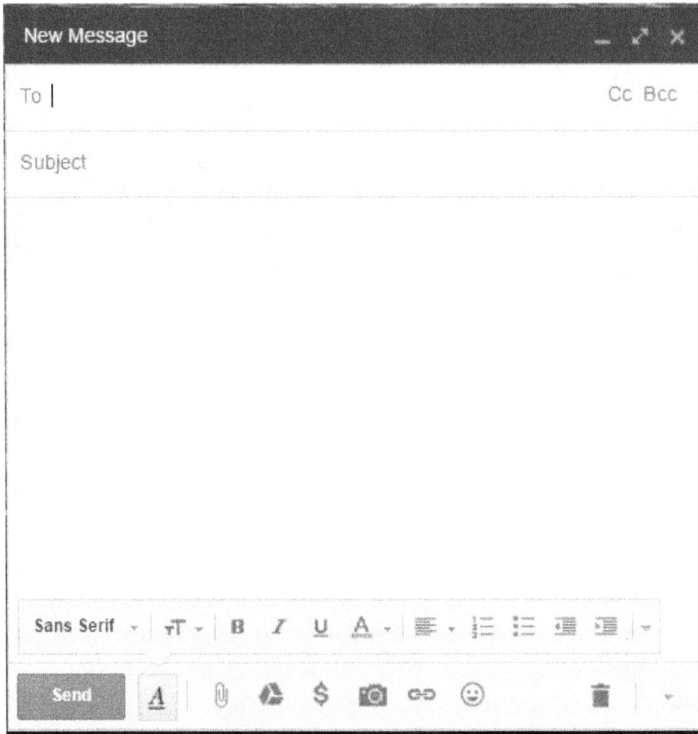

(Image 84: New Blank email window ready for you to compose email)

You can add a person's email address in the To: field as well as click on the CC: and Bcc fields to send this same email to multiple people on the same sending. The CC: stands for carbon copy and the Bcc stands for Blind Carbon Copy.

Notice at the bottom of the compose window is the formatting fields and you can choose how and what text to format with either larger or smaller text, the text color as well as whether it bold, italics, underlined, bulleted or location of the text. Also the paper clip is a univeral icon for adding attachments to your email. This is how you add your resume to your email and send to a potential employer for a job you found on a job website.

When you have the email completely done and formatted to your liking then you can click on send. It will then send the email to your recipent.

One very important item to remember is when you are using online email you always want to log out of the webpage when you're done. Never assume that you can click on the red X in the top right corner of the window (*left of the window for the Apple/Macintosh people*) and it will close your window so no one else can see your information. This is a false illusion. Instead always logout of the web session your currently in.

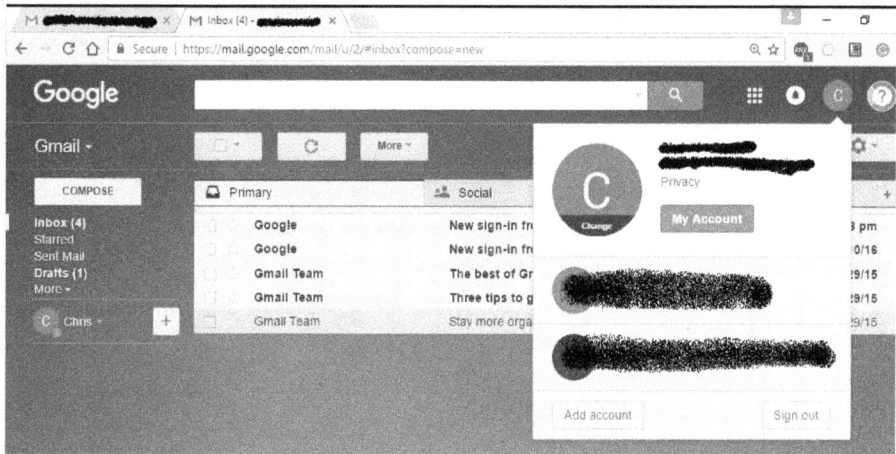

(Image85: email inbox with email you have received)

How to attach a document (resume.doc) to your online email account.

I was going to go into this much deeper but I think I've covered this in the previous paragraph. So with that said lets use this as a practice moment and please send yourself an email with the subject: test123.

Go ahead, follow the above items to draft an email and put your own email address in the To: field and if you are feeling advanced then please send an attachment to yourself as well. Try this now. Did it work? __Yes/NO?___
What is your findings/results? : _____

_____

_____

_____

_____

_____

7. Learning Check: Internet

1. List the reasons the internet is so successful in today world?

   _____

   _____

   _____

   _____

   _____

   _____

2. How do you read a webpage address?

   _____

   _____

   _____

   _____

   _____

   _____

3. Name some of the job search engines you can use to search for new jobs:

   _____

   _____

   _____

   _____

   _____

4. List some of the online email websites you can use for email:

   _____

   _____

   _____

   _____

   _____

5. Explain the process on how to log into your online email website?

   _____

   _____

   _____

   _____

   _____

   _____

6. How do you start an email?

_____

_____

_____

7. How do you send the email?

_____

_____

_____

8. In order to follow best practice; what should you always do when you are done with your online email session?

_____

_____

_____

9. Explain the process for your answer in step 8 above:

_____

_____

_____

_____

7. Troubleshooting

What can I expect from this chapter?
  9. In this chapter you will learn about:
      1. CompTIA 6 steps to troubleshooting
      2. Cpu-z (h/w info) and Prime95 (system stressor)
      3. Memtest86 (tests memory)
      4. TCP/IP = Wireshark and netperf

T his is a fun and interesting chapter which I hope helps you to better understand how to troubleshoot a computer. A lot of these examples if not all of them I have directly encountered and successfully fixed. But first I have to give props where props are due and I believe that the CompTIA 6 steps to troubleshooting process are an effective way to troubleshoot not only computer problems but also any problem you encounter. In fact I think I even use these same 6 steps in my daily life activities and in time as you get more and more comfortable with these steps; I think you may also find them helpful in your daily life activities.

After this I'll cover some troubleshooting tools such as cpu-z and prime95, Memtest86, and a brief overview of TCP/IP troubleshooting tool called Wireshark and Microsoft netperf.

Let's begin by talking about the 6 Steps to troubleshooting. This is something that every new technician that is working towards his or her CompTIA A+ certification will learn very well. I'll list these items out in a moment but first I want to say that if you are interested in learning more about the CompTIA A+ certification then please see your local education center for assistance in becoming ComptTIA A+ certified.

What are the 6 Steps to troubleshooting?
  1) Identify the problem
  2) Establish a Theory of Probable cause
  3) Test your Theory
  4) Establish a plan of action and implement the action (take action)
  5) Verify full system functionality after your action
  6) Document corrective action

Step1 (Identify the problem).

When you are identifying the problem it's best to never assume anything and always ask open ended questions such as:

- What happened to the computer?
- What was the last thing done on the computer before the error occurred?
- When did it happen?
- Is this the first time this error has occurred?
- Is this a repeat problem? (If so how often?)
- When was the last time it worked?
- Who was using it last? Can that person add any details?
- Where was it being used?
- What are your expectations of me to fix your computer?
- _____
- _____
- _____

(Reader; Can you think of a few open ended questions for the blank lines above?)

You really want to ask these types of question as it will help you to narrow down the true problem. If needed think of the game called "20 questions" and use that methodology to obtain the details needed to identify the problem. The more details (answers) you have from the above questions; the easier it will be to start your troubleshooting. If done properly, you should be able to determine if it's a hardware, software or networking problem.

After asking the above open ended questions you should be able to simply state the problem in 1 sentence or possibly 2 sentences. If you have to use a paragraph to state the problem then you don't have the problem identified tight enough and you need to ask more questions. Now I realize that identifying the problem may not be quick and easy but it's absolutely critical to you successfully fixing the problem. Keep with it until you have a 1 or 2 sentence statement of the problem.

After you have asked the open ended questions you've derived a problem at hand. This is probably the same problem your customer is referring to and if so then you're in the right area for troubleshooting. (Note: when I say customer I'm referring to anyone who is coming and asking you for help). If however the customer is referring to a problem which is not in line with your findings then you need to get clarity on the problem you have verses what the customer states and see if you can find some common areas where the 2 sceneries will overlap. If they don't then you have to treat them as individual problems and work them individually with these 6 steps.

Step2: Establish a theory of probable cause.

This next step (step2) can be easily done if you are able to ask the previous questions. You may even come up with multiple theories here such as theory a,b,c,d,e,f....etc. This is perfectly ok to do. Keep in mind that if you think it then it's a valid thought and it's ok to add it to your list of theories. So don't under estimate you're thinking when your troubleshooting and sometimes it's the "out of the box" thinking that provides the correct solution. Remember we have not done any actions yet… only thinking.

If you can't think of any probable cause then this is a great point in the troubleshooting process to ask your fellow teammate, technician, lead, supervisor or manager. Don't skip this step because you don't know what to ask. You will fail if this step is skipped. It's ok not to know something in this computer repair environment; but it's not ok to just stop at that point.. If you are going to become the successful computer repair technician that you are going to become, then you need to ask for help, phone a friend and if needed do your research online with your favorite search engine. Whatever you do is perfectly ok; just don't stop and don't skip this step… you need to eliminate all the possibilities.

Step3: Test each of your theories (in detail):

For each theory (a,b,c,d,e,f…etc) that you formulated above in step 2 you have to vet that theory to its fullness. This means that you have to run through each scenario in detail to see how it will play out. You need to determine if it is a true valid theory or does that theory fail when you really start thinking about the details. Any theory that fails then stop thinking about it and only focus on the theories that do seem to work. Continue to whittle down these theories and when you have them down to a few valid (correctly vetted) theories then proceed to step 4.

Important note: again we don't want to be vague here.. Vague-ness is also known as shot gunning the problem and that is not the best efficient way to troubleshoot a problem. Also do not rush the troubleshooting process. Sometimes this can take 5 minutes to diagnose and other times (depending on complexity of the situation) can take hours or even days or weeks to correctly diagnose problems. Especially if the problem is intermittent.

Back to being A+ certified and troubleshooting; we no longer want to do a broad shot gun approach to troubleshooting but instead we want to be as specific and narrow focused as possible. Think of this more as a sniper shot with a really powerful scope with laser assistance. When and where you put the laser on your target you know without a doubt that you're on your target/mark. Well you want to troubleshoot computer problems the same way. That's why I say you should get in the habit of identifying the problem in 1 or 2 sentences. Now will you be able to do that every time right from the beginning, the answer is no you won't. But with time this will happen or at least it will seem like it to you. Keeping in mind that not every computer problem is the same but you'll understand the concepts at hand and will be able to address them more efficiently. Lastly, most good technicians can still have difficulty in troubleshooting problems and they rely on using the 6 steps to troubleshooting so why don't you do the same.

Step4: Establish a plan of action and implement solution:
Of the valid vetted theories from step 3 above; you'll now go through these next steps and plan your course of action to correct the problem your working on. Some of the questions you'll have to determine are:
Will I:

    A) Do the easiest theory first?
    B) Do the most complex theory first
    C) Do the cheapest fix for this theory first?
    D) Do the most expensive fix for this theory first?
    E) _____
    F) _____
    G) _____

(Can you add any other questions above?)

Once you have a successful game plan thought and drawn out (physically or mentally) in its entirety; then it's time to take action.
For technicians who are new to troubleshooting this can be the most terrifying thing to do. You may be thinking that I'm crazy for mentioning this but let me tell you from my own experiences and from talking with fellow techs and admins that it can be really scary to power off a system or do maintenance on a live system while still in production. Usually the comments that comes about is, "What if I screw something up and make it worse?" Well there is no easy way to get over it other than to just do it.

Let's look at this a second way; Think about shutting down an enterprise server with hundreds or thousands of users connected to it right this very second and it's you that has to power off or do maintenance on this system. What are you thinking or feeling?

Now I have to also admit, that as a junior technician you will most like not be allowed to power off or restart an enterprise server without a more senior person's supervision or an approved work order from operations granting you to do a specific task. It wouldn't be fair to you nor the company. But when it's all done correctly and it still comes down to you issuing the shutdown or restart it can be somewhat scary but that's ok... rely on your supervisor and don't be afraid to ask questions. When you feel comfortable then make sure to take the action needed and implement your solution (fix).

ep5: Verify full system functionality after your corrective action

I think this is probably the most important of all the steps. You must fully verify the fix that you've just implemented before you leave the job site. I mean think about it... if your mechanic didn't do this but they said they fixed your car and you drive down the road and it breaks right after leaving the mechanic; wouldn't you be upset? The same goes for you fixing the computer problem you identified earlier. You must 100% verify the solution you were troubleshooting – again you're thinking like an A+ certified technician and therefore you must verify your fix.

Ask yourself did I fix the given problem? Is it now resolved? If not then you haven't correctly addressed the problem. Again being able to identify the problem correctly makes step 4 and 5 easier to do.

You can also test your fix by walking through the process the customer stated or even better yet have the customer use the system the way the customer is used to doing and see if the problem is still present. If the problem is gone then you have correctly addressed the problem and you can move on to step 6. If not then return to step 2 above and repeat the steps.

Step 6: Document your corrective action(s).

This is probably the step that is always talked about but for some reason is not always done by technicians. You need to document what the problem was, your steps to troubleshooting the problem and then the resolution and verification steps. In documenting the problem and solution you want to be very specific. Use the 1 or 2 sentence rule to correctly and specifically list the problem and solution.

This is also important for you if you ever have to come back and work on this same system again many years from now. It's also good to be as specific and detailed as possible in case you work with a team in shifts. You want the person on the shift before you to document in detail so you don't have to re-perform their tasks and likewise if you document in detail what you've done to troubleshoot the problem then the shift that starts after you will not have to wonder what you did. Nor will they have to duplicate any of the work you've already done. This saves time, effort and also money for you and the customer. Likewise your manager will really appreciate that you're not duplicating any un-needed work which correlates to wasting time.

Summary of 6 Steps:

If you adopt the 6 steps to troubleshooting then your success rate for troubleshooting problems will increase leading to more successful repair calls and your customer or manager will also look at you as an educated repairman/woman.

Computer Hardware Testing

There are multiple devices inside a computer as I've already covered above which includes CPU, memory, motherboard, I/O devices, etc... So how do we test these devices? This is a good question and I'll go through some simple free tools that are used in the industry. But first let me remind you that just using the computer on a regular basis is always a good way to test the equipment. Reason; if it works then it works and you usually know when it doesn't work the way that it used to.

Ok let's talk about some of the troubleshooting tools I've used over the years and found to be very helpful. First off, I think that it's important to understand what you're trying to get for a result before you start troubleshooting by testing. You need to first understand what you're testing for; what do you want as the result. What kind of problem are you testing for? If you don't know what you want then it's kind of hard to find it. Are you troubleshooting hardware, software, networking or something else (other)? Once you have identified what you want as the outcome and identified whether its hardware, software, networking or other then you can start using tools to help you whittle down the problem so you can find the true cause. Let's look at the troubleshooting tools in these 3 groupings (hardware, software and networking).

You must first know the environment that you're working on or in before you can understand the cause of a problem. When I refer to environment I'm not talking about the country side although you should always know the external environment you're in as it could also play into a problem with computers, networking and especially wireless. Narrowing in on environment I'm referring to the type of hardware you're working on, how old it is (less than 1 year old compared to 5 or 10 years old).

There's a good saying, "It's never a good idea to assume" and I'm going to agree with that statement here in troubleshooting computers as well. One thing I've learned over my years of troubleshooting is to never assume anything but instead verify. Listen to what is being said by the person who is reporting the problem. The reason is we need to listen for clues. Keep in mind that this person who is reporting the problem does not know computer-eze (the language of computers). Therefore this person will only report that it's broken. So you'll have to fall back to the 6 troubleshooting steps and ask open ended questions for the clues that lie between the lines (so to speak).

Before you start troubleshooting a computer problem it's best to understand what type of computer you're working on. I mean you really do need to know the situation in detail to properly troubleshoot a complex problem.

Some tools which I've found to be helpful in identifying the equipment (environment) that I'm working on are:
Information tools:
1. Piriform Speccy   (Provides overall system information)
2. Belarc Advisor   (Provides overall system information)

By using these above system information tools it can really help you to better understand what you're working on. Once I have a really good understanding of the environment, equipment, operating system and configurations then I can better determine what I need to do to fix a problem.

Now some will argue with my thought and just jump right into fixing the problem. I will say that if you have previous experience on the given situation as this is a duplicate or repeat call to the same office and situation then yes this is probably ok to do as you would understand the environment and hence what I said earlier still applies here. I have done this in the past and I think there is a point in a technician's experience where he/she does say yes I can do this; and just jumps straight to the fix part. Again, I want to highly caution the beginner and highly suggest you fall back to the CompTIA 6steps in troubleshooting process. However I'll leave that up to you to decide when and where that is in your journey. I'll also go as far as to say skipping the 6-step process is not best practice for a beginner to make and this type of cavalier decision of just jumping to a fix is not best practice. Once you understand the environment and/or equipment that you're troubleshooting you can proceed.

I'm going to say that electro-static discharge is always something that we need to be aware of and practice safe ESD processes. There are some that say it's not important but I'm here to tell you that ESD does cause problems in the computer world. ESD is the zap that can potentially bring down a computer. It's effects are not always immediate and the damage could be benign or fester up in 5 minutes to 5 days or even 5 years down the road. You see we don't know when ESD will cause the problem to rise however we have plenty of evidence of the aftermath of what ESD does to components.

What is ESD?

ESD is the immediate discharge or releasing of static electricity from one device into another device in a sudden burst and usually a tenth of a second. Think of this as when you were a child and you walked across the floor in socks and built up a charge and then touched your brother or sister and zap.. you got them. Ok, apply that same mental image to a computer and zap… you got it. ESD is measured in volts and for us humans to feel the zap it has to increase into the thousands of volts range. We refer to this as kilovolts. With approx. 20% humidity in the environment a person who walks across a typical nylon carpet can generate 2-4 Kilovolts (KV) of static electricity and vinyl floor can generate 10-12Kv. Remember that ESD is dangerous to a computer down in the hundreds which means this is well below what a human can feel. So even if a human cannot feel the ESD 'zap' occur doesn't mean it's not happening… it is and does! If a computer takes enough zaps then you start getting weird, rogue or intermittent errors occurring which can be hard to troubleshooting.

What does this look like? Well again you can do an internet search for 'esd damage images' and you'll see all kinds of images. I've placed a few here for your reference:

(Image 86: Images of ESD Damage)

When damaged components are put underneath a microscope looked at by x-ray or even frequency we can see what damage was done. As you can see ESD zap's can cause minor burns or deviations in the existing traces or computer chips which lead to failure.

How do we protect against ESD? Usually there will be a yellow image representing ESD safe procedures. It looks something like:

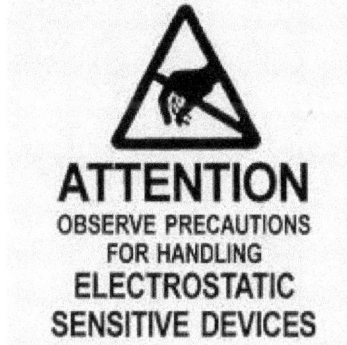

ATTENTION
OBSERVE PRECAUTIONS
FOR HANDLING
ELECTROSTATIC
SENSITIVE DEVICES

(Image 87: Example of Electronic Industry ESD protective sticker or label)

When you see an image like above then you can safely make the conclusion that ESD procedures are practiced.

What can you do personally to protect again ESD? It's quite simple really. When you work on computer equipment of any degree then you want to practice safe ESD procedures. This includes using ESD wrist strap, ESD Jacket and a grounding mat being connected to ground and the computer equipment. Again I've provided an image of these items below for your better understanding:

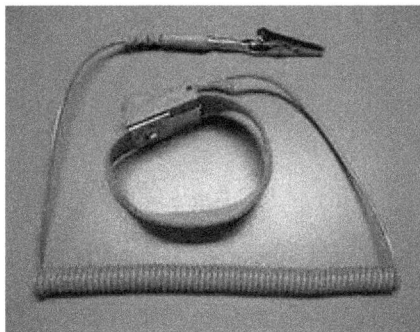

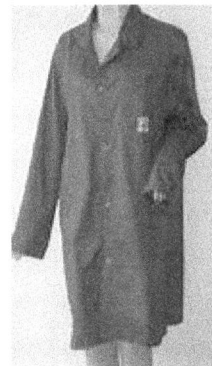

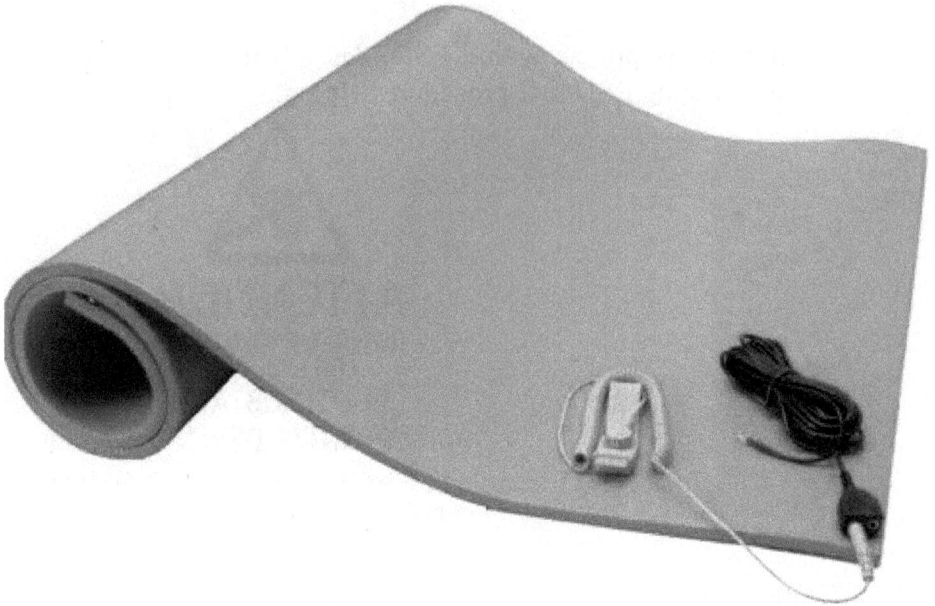

(Image 88: Esd Protective wear (ESD wrist strap, Jacket and Table mat)

With all that said it's always best practice to use proper ESD grounded mat, wrist-strap and ESD jacket to protect against ESD occuring.

Now that I've covered ESD; The first tool that I've used for physical testing is a power supply tester. These are relatively cheap and you can find them online. I suggest that every good technician have one of these in his/her set of tools. The main reason to have one of these power supply testers is to identify if your power rails are functioning correctly when troubleshooting a power problem. You have to identifiy whether the problem is power or motherboard. It's always best practice to start from the power source and then work inward toward the motherboard. Here is what a power supply tester looks like:

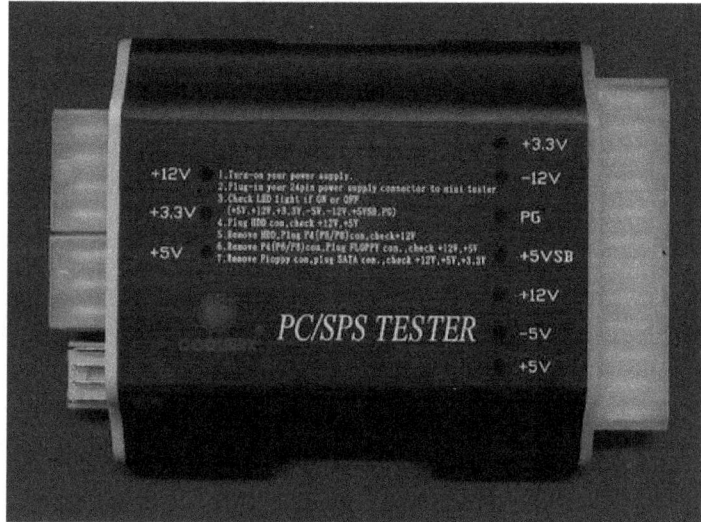

(Image 89: Power supply tester)

As you can see there are multiple connectors for you to connect your power supply connectors to. For exampleon the left side of the tester you will see the molex connector as well as floppy drive power connector. On the right side of the tester is where your P1 connector (which usually connects into the motherboard directly) would plug into. When you have your power cable connected to the tester you apply power to the power supply and then the power LED's will light up if the correct power is provided. As I recall a green led is good and a red is a fault. There are other power supply testers which you may have to press a 'test' button in order to enable testing.

Next, if there is a CPU or memory error that you've identified as a problem then I've used the following tools over the years to help me determine where the problem lies:

Hardware Diagnostic tools:

1. Cpu-z   (provides overall CPU and memory info.)
2. Memtest86   (tests and exercise cpu and memory)
3. Prime95   (stresses system for intermittent failures)
4. Power supply tester   (Tests p/s without motherboard)

CPU-z is a good program for providing information on your system. This program is created and distributed by www.cpuid.com. It includes the details of the CPU such as the revision, stepping, cache size as well as total memory installed in the pc and the memory configuration. It will also show the details of your video configuration as well. If you have a computer system and you need more detail specs this program is wonderful for the technician to use.

Another great tool that I've used to test a CPU or stress a CPU is prime95. You can do a simple internet search for prime95 and find it. Basically this program will load up a bunch of worker processes for each CPU core the OS can see and then run through a series of tests. When I did this on my computer I was able to capture the following screen images:

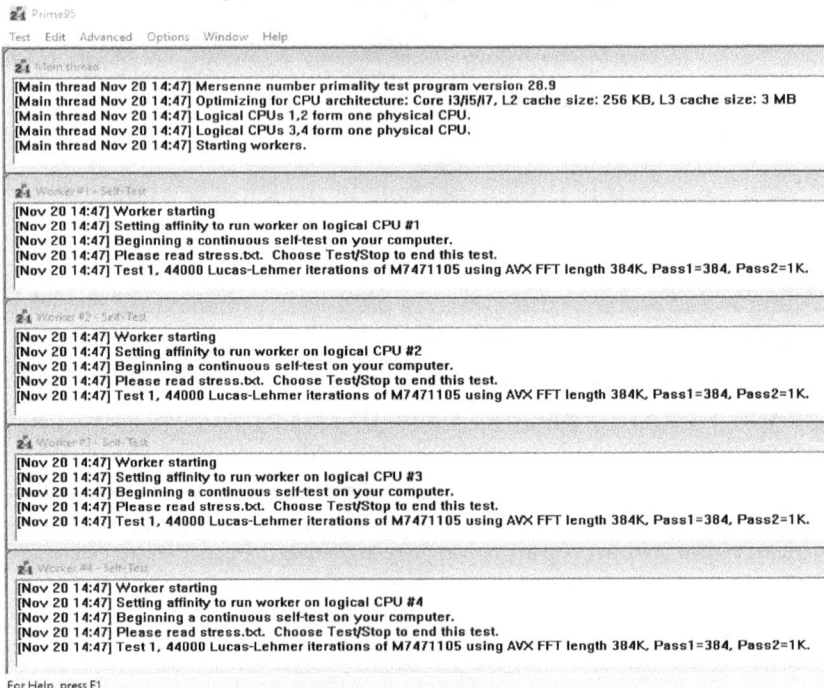

(Image 90: Prime 95 screen shot)

228

You can start and stop the exerciser by clicking on the Test menu item at the top. However you want to keep in mind that this will most likely max out your cpu performance and so if you are trying to do other tasks while this is running performance issues will probably be encountered. Lastly in regards to Prime95; since it does run your cpu at 100% this will generate more heat than what is typically encountered on normal operation. It's not advised to run this program and not monitor the computer and the internal temperature while testing.

If you believe you have a memory problem then Memtest86 is another great program that I've used over the years to exercise memory when I thought I had a memory problem. Keep in mind that it also stresses the CPU as well as it has to use the CPU to stress the memory. For example, Let's say you are troubleshooting a dimm problem. It wouldn't make since to replace all the dimms for a memory problem. That would be crazy and to expensive; plus your boss wouldn't appreciate the un-needed cost involved. Instead if you are able to identify which exact dimm is at fault then that's a much simpler and cheaper fix. So how do you identify the problem? Well there are multiple ways to do this but lets keep it simple as this is an introductory book. Let's take a simple pc with 2 dimm slots on the motherboard (slot 0 and slot 1) and both have a 512MB dimms installed for a total of 1 GB of memory installed in the system. For simplification I'll assign a letter to each of the dimm slots to help with my example. For the dimm in slot 0 I'll call that dimm A and for slot 1 will have dimm B installed in it. Again the A and B are only figurative for the point of this example.

Dimm slot	Physical Dimm
0	A
1	B

(Table 35: Dimm slot correlated to Dimms)

In troubleshooting this memory problem which I encountered on my mother-in-law's computer. I had to figure out where the problem truly was; was it a dimm or on the motherboard? The problem that I was told was the computer wouldn't boot and when I turned on the computer sure enough it would not boot at all.. it would error out in POST during the memory section of POST.

Here are my steps I used in troubleshooting:
1) Removed dimm B only (dimm A installed) = fail, no change.
2) Removed dimm A only (dimm A installed) = fail, no change
3) Replaced dimm A&B both   = fail, no change

Suspicion is it's a motherboard.

4) Moved dimm B into slot 0   = Booted to OS.
5) Moved dimm A into slot 1   = failed.
6) Replaced dimm A into slot 0   = Booted to OS.
    a. Ran memtest86 for 3 cycles   = no error reported.
7) Swapped dimm A and B in slot 0   = Booted to OS.
    a. Ran memtest86 for 3 cycles   = no error reported.

8) Conclusion: bad dimm slot 1 – system now only has ½ the capacity of ram it did before and there is no fixing this at this level of troubleshooting. I presented this information to my mother-in-law and she decided to buy a newer computer due to the age of this computer.

In regards to testing input and output devices (aka: I/O) there is a huge array of input and output devices and to list them here would take too long. I'm going to encapsulate the I/O troubleshooting tests into using the equipment is probably the best way to troubleshoot it. If you are having I/O problems make sure that the correct device drivers are installed and haven't been over written by an update or something that may have corrupted the drivers. Also in regards to troubleshooting an I/O error with regards to windows make sure to reboot the computer first. This usually fixes a lot of the I/O errors I've seen over the years.

Let's move on to software troubleshooting. I'm not going to cover anything in regards to programming as that's a whole different perspective on software and that's not the purpose of this book. There are many different ways of troubleshooting a software problem and there are many good ways to do it. I would say that since I'm primarily focusing this chapter on Microsoft Windows then I believe that Microsoft has done a great job on already creating the operating system. With that said I know I've hit a nerve for some people and they have their reasons for saying windows has its problems; Ok true and well nothing is perfect but come on lets give the people at Microsoft some credit too… They have constantly released multiple versions of Windows and yes they have had to also release updates (aka: patches) as well. Hence the term 'patch Tuesday' came into existence as that is when Microsoft would push out their patches or updates. So where am I going with this… I believe that it's best practice to have updates done on your computer. Either by automatically updating or by you reviewing the updates and then allowing them to install. I want to make it absolutely clear that doing no updates is not recommended. What are updates or patches? I think I've covered that earlier in the software section.

When you have software problems I've found it best practice to make sure the OS and applications updates are current such as:

1. Windows updates
2. Java updates
3. Web-browser updates
4. Flash updates
5. Specific applications updates (i.e.: office, antivirus, antimalware)

With that said here are a few other tools I've found to be helpful.

Software Diagnostic Tools:

1. Windows Update
2. Application/Program updates
3. Microsoft fix it tool.
4. Ccleaner.exe
5. Malwarebytes.exe
6. Secunia.exe
7. Driverpack

These are some of the common tools I've used over the years to resolve software problems. There are more than what I've listed above but by doing a simple internet search you can find these above tools as well as many more tools to help you troubleshoot your software problem.

Networking Troubleshooting Tools:

This is an interesting sections and I feel that in order to troubleshoot a networking problem you must cover the basics. By that I mean that I typically will use commands at the command such as:

      Cmd> ipconfig /all
      Cmd> ping *<website name here>*
      Cmd> netstat –a
      Cmd> tracert *<website name here>*

These simple commands that come in every instance of Windows as well as Linux and even apple can seriously help you to troubleshoot your network problems.

Let's take a look at these commands:

```
C:\Users\chris>ipconfig /all
Windows IP Configuration
   Host Name . . . . . . . . . . . . : This-PC
   Primary Dns Suffix  . . . . . . . :
   Node Type . . . . . . . . . . . . : Hybrid
   IP Routing Enabled. . . . . . . . : No
   WINS Proxy Enabled. . . . . . . . : No

Wireless LAN adapter Wireless Network Connection:
   Media State . . . . . . . . . . . : Media disconnected
   Connection-specific DNS Suffix  . :
   Description . . . . . . . . . . . : Intel(R) Centrino(R) Advanced-N 6205
   Physical Address. . . . . . . . . : NN-NN-NN-NN-NN-NN
   DHCP Enabled. . . . . . . . . . . : Yes
   Autoconfiguration Enabled . . . . : Yes
```

```
Wireless LAN adapter Local Area Connection* 2:
   Media State . . . . . . . . . . . : Media disconnected
   Connection-specific DNS Suffix  . :
   Description . . . . . . . . . . : Microsoft Wi-Fi Direct Virtual Adapter
   Physical Address. . . . . . . . : NN-NN-NN-NN-NN-NN
   DHCP Enabled. . . . . . . . . . : Yes
   Autoconfiguration Enabled . . . . : Yes

Ethernet adapter Local Area Connection:
   Connection-specific DNS Suffix  . :
   Description . . . . . . . . . . : Intel(R) 82579V Gigabit Network Connection
   Physical Address. . . . . . . . : NN-NN-NN-NN-NN-NN
   DHCP Enabled. . . . . . . . . . : Yes
   Autoconfiguration Enabled . . . . : Yes
   Link-local IPv6 Address . . . . . : fe80::NNNN:NNNN:NNNN:NNNN%4(Preferred)
   IPv4 Address. . . . . . . . . . : 192.168.1.19(Preferred)
   Subnet Mask . . . . . . . . . . : 255.255.255.0
   Lease Obtained. . . . . . . . . : Saturday, November 19, 2016 1:00:57 PM
   Lease Expires . . . . . . . . . : Monday, November 21, 2016 1:00:56 PM
   Default Gateway . . . . . . . . : 192.168.1.1
   DHCP Server . . . . . . . . . . : 192.168.1.1
   DHCPv6 IAID . . . . . . . . . . : 241447248
   DHCPv6 Client DUID. . . . . . . : 00-01-00-01-1C-78-2A-NN-NN-NN-NN-NN-NN-NN
   DNS Servers . . . . . . . . . . : 192.168.1.1
   NetBIOS over Tcpip. . . . . . . : Enabled
```

Another good tool is called ping and I've listed a simple ping command below:

```
C:\Users\chris>ping 192.168.1.19

Pinging 192.168.1.19 with 32 bytes of data:
Reply from 192.168.1.19: bytes=32 time<1ms TTL=128
Reply from 192.168.1.19: bytes=32 time<1ms TTL=128
Reply from 192.168.1.19: bytes=32 time<1ms TTL=128
Reply from 192.168.1.19: bytes=32 time<1ms TTL=128

Ping statistics for 192.168.1.19:
    Packets: Sent = 4, Received = 4, Lost = 0 (0% loss),
Approximate round trip times in milli-seconds:
    Minimum = 0ms, Maximum = 0ms, Average = 0ms
```

For example: by using the ipconfig /all command you can fully verify your current network configuration such as IPv4 and IPv6 addresses, masks and gateways. It can also show you if your DHCP connectivity is functioning correctly. If all looks correct then I would try to ping my local ip address (192.168.1.19) and if successful then I would ping the gateway (192.168.1.1) to see if I could ping my local network. After that I would proceed and ping a public website. I would then follow up with a traceroute to that same website to verify connectivity. You see by just using these basic command line tools you can easily troubleshoot a computer network connectivity. With that said there are 3rd party programs that do the same thing but they wrap the commands into their customized application to make it easier; but don't let these all in wonder programs fool you.. they are just using the basic commands as I've listed above.

Ok there are internet bandwidth testers such as www.speedtest.net which can test your internet connectivity speed and efficiency. This website has been around for a long time and is a safe website for testing with. You can also use www.pingtest.net which tests the quality of service (QoS), jitter and ping success rate on your internet line. I have to also say that there are other websites which also help in this area and you're welcome to use the one you are most familiar with.

Lastly if you think that you are having a lot of internal network problems then you could use a tool called Wireshark. This program has been around for a very long time and is used by the professionals. This tool has a steep learning curve so I won't try to teach it to you here but I want you to be aware of this tool. It can sniff the network and log packets that are being sent across your network. It allows you to see how packets and frames are transmitted across your network. If you are experiencing network congestion then this is a great program to help analyze what is going on. I would also suggest using Cisco packet tracer as well as netperf or iperf to troubleshoot a network. Again you can do a simple internet search for the latest URL of the above programs to successfully download, install and use them in your troubleshooting.

It never fails but sometime during your computer career you will come across a failing hard drive. The question is always, how to troubleshoot a bad harddrive? Well the simple answer in todays harddrive computing is that you will most likely receive some type of message from within MS Windows operating system indicating a hard drive has encountered a smart error. What is a smart error? A smart error is an acronym which stands for "Self-Monitoring, Analysis and Reporting Technology". This is a self-monitoring software within the harddrive itself that monitors the status and health of the hard drive. This software can provide a user heads up information of an error before the hard drive has actually failed. Think of this software as a predictive failure tool.

What happens is if there is a hard drive failure that's starting to occur then the smart software within the hard drive will notice the foot prints of the occurrence and register a smart error code. Then the OS will poll this registry to see if there are any smart errors and if so then report them to the system log as well as inform the user of the possible error. Why is this important? For the simple reason that if the user knows the hard drive is compromised and starting to fail then that user can backup their data asap before total failure has occurred. It's a way of trying to help the user not lose their data.

There is a list of 255 smart error codes which are available in the industry but my findings have shown that not all hard drive manufacturers are consistent with their smart code errors. With that said, if you encounter a smart predictive failure on your given disk drive then my suggestion is to do an internet search for that specific drive model number and manufacturer and include the word 'smart' in the search. This will provide some results specifically for that hard drive and the software (firmware) that correlates to that disk. Based off the results and the information you obtain from your search you can derive a corrective action plan to fix the problem. I would further note that if you have a hard drive that is starting to throw smart errors then pay attention to the type of error and the frequency (how-often) it's occurring. You may want to start thinking of replacing the disk drive. If your data is critical then you should already have a backup of the data or at least a RAID1 or greater setup.

How should you test your hard drive to determine if smart errors exist? This is a good question and there are many 3rd party software programs that can read smart errors and give you a report. The one that I use is called Victoria and you can download that for free from the internet; it's self-explanatory.

I want to also say that you can pull this information from a command prompt as well. I've pasted a copy from my local Windows10 machine for example:

Microsoft Windows [Version 10.0.10586]
(c) 2015 Microsoft Corporation. All rights reserved.

C:\WINDOWS\system32>wmic
wmic:root\cli>diskdrive get status
Status
OK
OK

wmic:root\cli>

As you can see above the windows management interface console is able to read the disk status for any smart errors. If no errors are present then you'll see the same output as I've noted above.

Understanding & troubleshooting Wi-Fi!

This is always a good topic to cover and yes troubleshooting Wi-Fi is easy and yet difficult at the same time. In today's world of home internet and small office I think we all know what Wi-Fi___33 is or at least you've most likely used it but for those who don't know let me show you what I'm talking about here. Here are a few images of wireless access points (aka: wap) that I've used over the years:

Linksys wrt54g   Netgear WCPS606
(Image 91: Common WAP's)

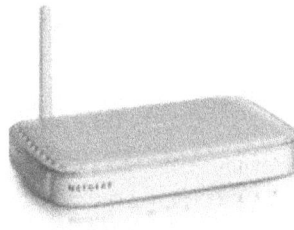

Both of the above router/switch combo's with wireless access were good in their days and for this example of troubleshooting I will use them for my references. However you may have a different wireless access point at your home or office and that's ok. The point that I'm covering here will be universal and the concept you'll be able to apply to your wap as well.

First off, I think it's best to refresh our thoughts on how Wi-Fi works and in regards to Wi-Fi connections. What I want you to think about in regards to Wi-Fi is to think of the Wi-Fi signal between the wap and your Wi-Fi device as a flash light. Imagine laying a flash light on top of your wap and pointing it at your Wi-Fi device. If your Wi-Fi device is close to the wap then the light is brighter on the Wi-Fi device just the same way the signal is stronger when you're close to it. You can try this by actually using your own flash light and pointing the beam close to a wall. Then slowly pull the light away from the wall and notice the beam of light. What happens?

Results:_____

_____

_____

_____

_____

_____.

Based on your own findings above, now image what would happen to the beam of the light if you did the same thing with your Wi-Fi device and walked away from the wap with the flash light on top of it?

Explain:_____

_____

_____

_____

_____

_____.

What you should have noted here is that the beam of light would enlarge the further you walk away from the wap as well as the beam may become diffused; this would represent the signal becoming weaker the further you walked away from the wap.

Next, Lets talk about Wi-Fi interferences. If you turn on a flash light (again representing the Wi-Fi signal between your wap and your Wi-Fi device) and hold it near the ceiling where there are not to many distractions then the beam of light is un-interrupted and is delivered to the other side of the room. However if you take that same situation and put the flash light near the floor does it make it to the other side of the room without disruption in the beam? The answer is typically no and the reason is there are more obstacles closer to the floor than there are near the ceiling. In a given living room for example you may have couches, chairs, tables, people, animals, etc... So you have to remember that everything in-between flash light and the opposing wall is a barrier or better yet a light blocker and this is just the same way for Wi-Fi connections. Anything in-between the wap and Wi-Fi device is a Wi-Fi signal blocker. If you get to many object in-between the flash light (i.e.: wap) and the opposing wall (i.e.: Wi-Fi device) then there is no light (i.e.: signal) delivered to the wall.

Now I have to take this one step further for my wireless folks out there who know about Omni directional antennas. Most wireless access points (wap) are omni-directional which means that the signal does flow out of the wireless access point in a 360 degree horizontal signal. I have an analogy to use to help better understand this concept. Think back to when you were at a lake and you threw a rock high into the air over the water and when it finally came down and entered the water; what happened?

_____

_____

_____

_____

Yes, that's correct when the rock did a Ka-plunk it caused a ripple effect from the point of entry and that ripple went out in 360 degrees on top of the water.. Remember this?

(Image 92: Rings of water waves from a rock thrown into water)

Ok, so I'm going to use this mental image now for understanding Omni-directional signal coming from your wap.

When a wap broadcasts it's Wi-Fi signal it does this in a 360 degree horizontal plane just the exact same way as the rock, water and ripple thing. Now i want you to replace the word water surface (in my above example) with the word horizontal plane. Now you're ready to better understand how this works. You see the wap Omni-directional antenna in regards to your Wi-Fi area of coverage can be thought of the exact same way as the rock being the center of the Ka-plunk ripple effect. The closer to the center the more strength the Wi-Fi has and the further away the less strength. I've placed a few images here to also better understand this concept.

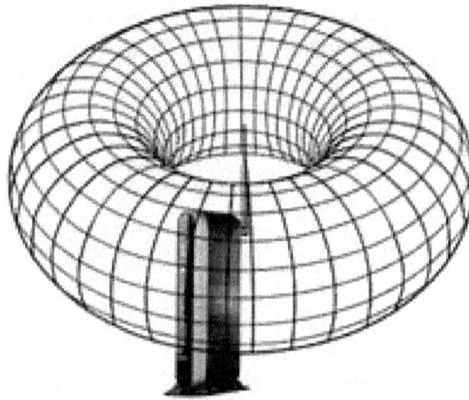

(Image 93: Radio signal radiates out in 360 degree horizontal plain from WAP (center point))

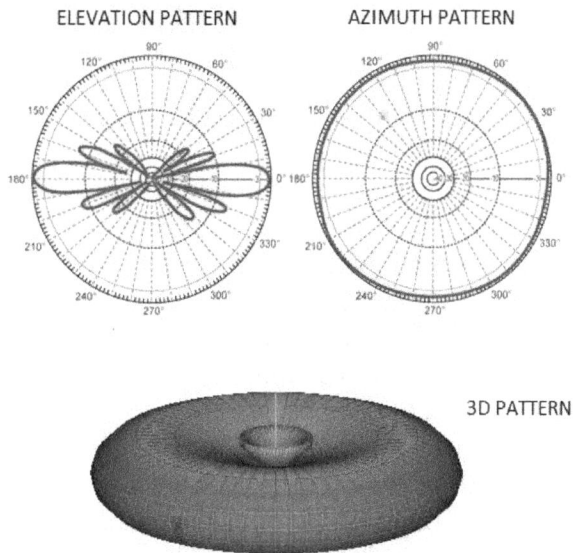

ELEVATION PATTERN

AZIMUTH PATTERN

3D PATTERN

(Image: 94: More examples of how the radio signal emits from the antenna (center point of origin)
source: http://www.mpantenna.com/wp-content/uploads/2015/02/FIGURE-2.png))

Azimuth and 3D pattern image shows how the signal radiates out 360 degree horizontal plain.

Regarding the Elevation pattern in the image above; I want you to think of this as a side view of your Wi-Fi environment. You see the horizontal plain is typically only at a 15 degree vertical angle which goes completely around in a full 360 degree horizontal circle from the antenna. This is what the elevation pattern is showing. See the next image for a better understanding of this.

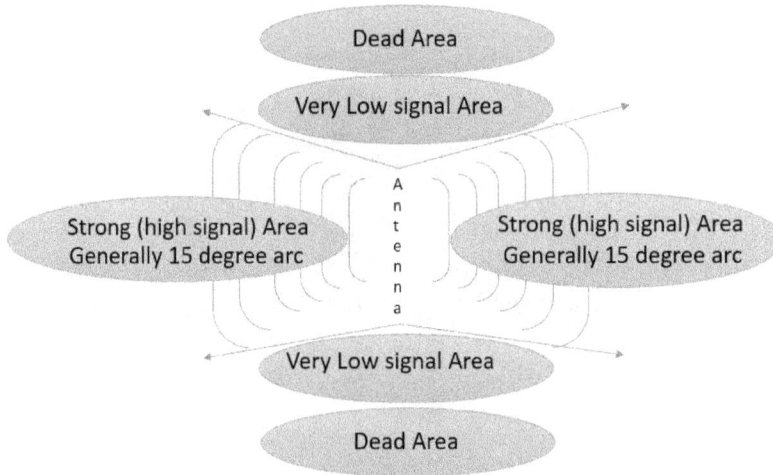

(Image 95: Example of how the Radio signal emits away from antenna)

Ok so now that we all are on the same page regarding Wi-Fi signal strength and how it radiates away from the center point of the Wi-Fi environment with less and less signal the further away from the CenterPoint. We can now look at troubleshooting Wi-Fi itself. Just by understanding the above examples you've already learned how to troubleshoot a vast majority of Wi-Fi problems. I think of all the home and small office Wi-Fi problems I've worked on; they have already been addressed in the above examples.

Remember to think of Wi-Fi signal as a line of sight technology. If you can see from point A to point B then the signal can also go between point A and point B. If you can't see between point A and B then that means there is an obstacle in-between and it can degradate your signal. For example a wall can drop a Wi-Fi signal up to 50% or more based on material and internal wall contents such as heavy wood or even cinder block or concrete. If you run into this problem then it's best to use a hard LAN cable and run around the obstacle to a repeater at the other side to continue your Wi-Fi environment.

Next lets talk about troubleshooting Wi-Fi security. There are multiple versions of Wi-Fi security that I've troubleshot over the years. For simplification of this book I'll generalize them in saying there will always be a need for security and I don't see it going away. Contrary to this I only see security becoming more and more complicated. Believe it or not; the reason is the industry is trying to protect you from the bad people of the world and not to frustrate you in your wireless connectivity problems. Ok with that said the newer securities will always be more complex and the older equipment which was made before the newer securities were created did not have the newer security protocols (rules). Therefore if you have an older Wi-Fi router, switch or WAP and you are trying to connect to a newer security protocol it may not work. Better yet, if you have an older Wi-Fi device and you're trying to connect it to a new WAP you just recently purchased at the store then your Wi-Fi device may not connect. The reason is your WAP has to high of a level of security (encryption) for the Wi-Fi device to connect to. Your solution is to log into the WAP and lower the encryption level so that Wi-Fi device can connect.

I ran into this exact situation when I purchased a new Netgear N600 switch and WAP combo unit. I setup my Wi-Fi to use WPA2 encryption and I set my SSID to broadcast. All of my Wi-Fi devises connected without problem when I provided the login credentials however the Nintendo Wii did not. It could see the SSID broadcast but it could not correctly mount it when I entered my credentials (password). The problem was the Nintendo Wii was created prior to the WPA2 even being created. So there is no way for the Wii to correctly map to the WAP. So my solution was to lower my encryption level on the WAP to an older version of encryption (WEP) and sure enough the Wii connected without error. This worked for my environment as there were no other surrounding neighbors that I had to contend with. Also the Wii was used for about a year and then removed from service and given to my grandson. At this point my security did increase on the WAP back up to WPA2. Example: WAP connecting to a Nintendo Wii.

An important note is to never not have encryption on your Wi-Fi environment. I believe that it's best practice to have some type of protection on your Wi-Fi environment. Something is better than nothing.

Let's next talk about a common problem where a browser is unable to connect to internet/Facebook. Usually if a person is unable to get to a website such as facebook.com, youtube.com (Note: it really doesn't matter what the website is).
Usually, it means that the web browser (Internet Explorer, Chrome, Opera, and Safari) cannot access the internet.

Here is a list of items I go through to troubleshoot when a web browser does not display the page I'm looking for:

1. Refresh the web browser
2. Try a different website or a website you don't go to often.
3. Try a different web-browser.
4. Try to access a different search engine.
5. Open command prompt and run ipconfig /all to see if you have a valid IP address on this computer.
6. In the command prompt window; ping the local IP address of the computer, it's router, it's DNS, and ping www.google.com to see if there is connectivity.
7. If items 1-5 fail then reboot the computer you're on and retest. This usually fixes most problems I've seen on windows client machines (which are what most versions of windows are for home users.).

7. **Learning Check: Troubleshooting**

1. What are the CompTIA 6 steps to troubleshooting (explain in detail):
    1. _____
    2. _____
    3. _____
    4. _____
    5. _____
    6. _____

2. What is the purpose of Cpu-z? _____
   _____
   _____

3. What is the name of a system stressor/tester program?
   _____

4. What is the name of the memory tester program?
   _____

5. What program helps network technician break down TCP/IP traffic?
   _____

6. What does ESD stand for?
   _____
   _____
   _____

7. Why is ESD so dangerous to computers? _____
   _____
   _____
   _____
   _____
   _____
   _____
   _____
   _____

8. At what voltage do humans feel ESD compared to what voltage can damage occur to electronics?

_____

_____

_____

_____

_____

9. What items can be used to combat ESD?
   1. _____
   2. _____
   3. _____

10. To test a power supply for functionality without using a motherboard; what is the best way to do so? (Explain)

_____

_____

_____

_____

_____

_____

_____

_____

_____

11. When troubleshooting an operating system what do you want to make sure is updated?

_____

_____

_____

12. List a few updates that you can do to verify the best performance for a computer?

_____

_____

_____

_____

_____

13. List 4 command prompt commands that come with MS Windows to troubleshoot its network connectivity? (Explain each in detail)

   1. _____
     _____
     _____
     _____

   2. _____
     _____
     _____
     _____

   3. _____
     _____
     _____
     _____

   4. _____
     _____
     _____
     _____

14. What output does ipconfig /all show you?

15. What 2 websites can test your internet connectivity and quality of service for your internet connection?

16. In regards to Wi-Fi; explain what a WAP is and does?

17. Explain how a WAP broadcasts its signal? _____

_____

_____

_____

_____

_____

_____

18. What can cause a blockage in a Wi-Fi environment?

_____

_____

_____

_____

_____

19. Are all Wi-Fi encryption levels the same?

_____

_____

20. Is one encryption level better than another? (if so, why and if not, why)

_____

_____

_____

_____

_____

21. List some steps you can do to test connectivity on a web-browser that does not show you a website of your choice?

_____

_____

_____

_____

_____

_____

8. Applications

What can I expect from this chapter?

In this chapter you will learn about the different applications (programs) that are installed in a computer.

Explanation:There are many different applications that can run on Microsoft Windows operating system. Many are written from Microsoft itself such as Microsoft office which includes Word, Excel, PowerPoint, Outlook and Access. This is the office program which is used in many small, medium and large office environments.

Microsoft also has the following plus more programs than I've listed here:

Basic	programming language
Cobol	programming language
Fortran	programming language
Dos	Disk operating system
Internet Explorer	web browser
Money	financial program
Project	project management software

(Table 36: Programming languages)

There are also many 3rd party apps that are written to work in MS Windows environments and provided the software programmers did their jobs correctly (which they usually do but sometimes there are programs that are not and these errors are called bugs in the software) the 3rd party software should work correctly and not cause errors.

These programs can be written in a variety of software languages such as C, C++, Java, J++, Perl, etc... The programming languages and the programmers who are using them are taking the programming field to all time high's in regard to performance. I really find it interesting to see what new things people are coming up with in regards to programming. If this is something that interests you then please find a local club to join regarding your flavor of programming and go have fun.

Web-Browsers:

Ok, now let's talk about Web-browsers. Specifically I'm going to talk about Internet Explorer as it's probably the most common browser for most of the new folks. However there are a list of browsers available in todays environment such as Internet Explorer, Chrome, Firefox, Safari and you can find the download website for each of these browsers by doing an internet search. Keep in mind there are over 10 different types of web-browsers currently on the market and to say 1 is better than the other I don't feel is fair to do. In all my years of using heave web browser usage I never said one is the best over all others. That's like saying 1 screw driver is better than all the other screw drivers in the tool box. That saying would only be true if every screw you had to tighten or loosen were all the exact same size... (did you catch the point where I said "every" screw you came across would have to be the exact same size). The reality is you will come across many different size screws and you'll need different size screw drivers to correctly tighten or loosen them.

Ok well the web-browser in my opinion is the same as my screw example. In fact I believe that I currently have 4 different web-browsers on my laptop. They are Edge (Windows 10), Internet Explorer (IE), Chrome and Safari. Most often I dance between IE and Chrome but sometimes when a website doesn't operate like it's supposed to then I'll try either Edge or Safari. You see that's the reason in my opinion that you need more than one web-browser. Websites are written by webmasters to operate best under certain web-browsers and therefore that's why it's good to have multiple browsers. In fact back around 2010 time frame the websites usually had a logo near the bottom of the main page that would say something like, "best viewed at 1024x768 resolution using Internet Explorer". This would tell the user what browser to view the webpage in as well as the resolution for best readability.

What I'm going to cover next is configuration of web-browser(s). I'll refer to internet explorer here but every web browser will be similar to what I'm talking about. Ok so lets begin, once you have IE open you will notice a

gear shape ⚙ device in the top right corner of the window. In Chrome this will be 3 horizontal or 3 vertical dots ⋮ . The point I'm making here is this is how you will go into setting for the web-browser. Click on the setting icon and then click on setting. Once you click on it you will see a new dialog box open up which will look similar to below:

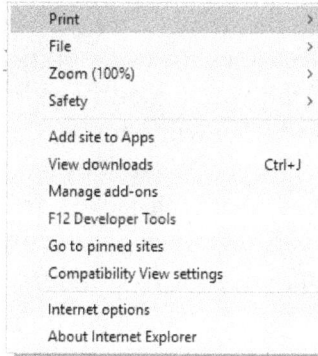

(Image 96: Web Browser options drop down menu)

Click on 'internet options' or 'settings' in chrome to get to the next options window.

(Image 97: Internet options)

From this window you can look at the main tabs across the top of the screen to identify the major subjects within that tab. The major tabs are general, security, privacy, content, connections, programs, advanced. I invite you to play around in these tabs so you learn what each does and the importance of each on. Don't worry about screwing something up bacause you can always click 'cancel' to exit without saving your changes.

Lets look at some of the key fields I've used inside of internet options. The first and main field I've modified is 'home page'. I usually set this to my favorite search engine and as I noted above in the picture it's:
https://www.google.com

One important thing to remember here is if you install 3rd party software it will ask if you would like to change or modify your webpage home page. This is the field it's asking you to modify and if you click 'yes' then the 3rd party software install program will remove https://www.google.com and replace it with it's home page. What does this mean? Quite simply this means your webpage has been high-jacked and you are now going to another website when you first open your IE. This is common with the following 3rd party programs such as Conduit, V9, Trovi, Search Protect, etc... Now these programs are not illegal programs and they are not doing anything legally wrong due to they ask you for permission to change your home page and if installed then it's means you granted them permission to change your home page. So keep in mind that if this happens and your webpage is going to a new/different webpage than what you're use to, then your homepage has probably been over written and you need to go in here to the home page screen and make the correction to the web address.

Next field I use is 'browsing history'.

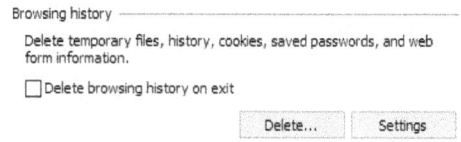

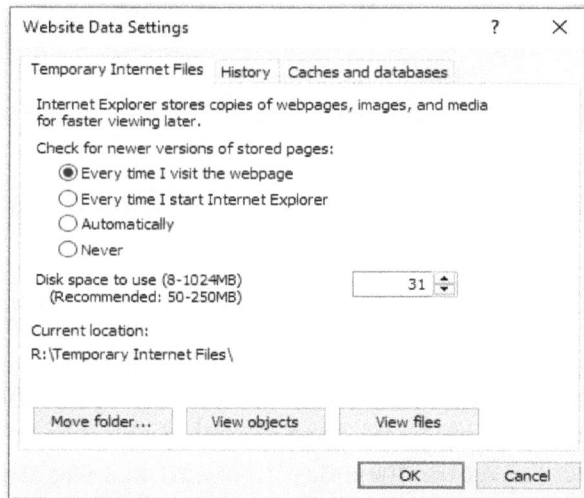

(Image 98: How to clear browsing history)

Probably once a month or there of, I go in and delete my browsing history. I've even been known to click 'delete browsing history on exit' and there are many different reasons why. However I think the more important thing to talk about here is the browsing history settings tab. I make sure to change Temp files to 'every time I visit the webpage'. This keeps the webpage from trying to update pages in the background and consuming your internet connection. It also provides a bit more control over the websites you're accessing. Maybe it's me but I like to know what I'm doing on the internet at all times as well as where my computer is going to do certain tasks.

The next tab I feel is of importance is security.

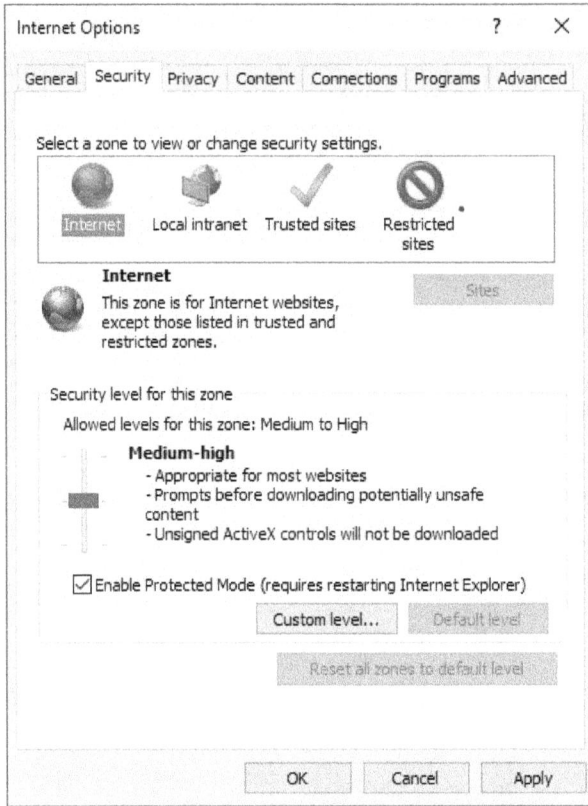

(Image 99: Internet options: security settings)

In all my years of using web-browsers and I feel really comfortable in saying what I'm saying here. Most of society and mean probably a strong 95% of society never use the internet browser in a way it's not designed to work. Therefore regarding web-browser security I usually click the button at the bottom which states, 'reset all zones to default level'. This has worked for me and even when doing level 3 engineering tasks I still used the default security configuration and didn't have much problems. If this setting worked for me then I'm going to say it will probably also work for you. Some apps and website may want to change this and that may cause you problems with other apps or websites. However, when in doubt, default it back to basic setting.

Privacy is the next tab and for that IE has a pop-up blocker that I find is helpful. Notice I didn't say it's fool-proof. It's easy to turn on/off and configure the settings under the Privacy tab as shown below:

(Image 100: how to enable/disable pop-up blocker)

The rest of the settings I'll let you play around with and become familiar with for your desired level of use.

Let's backup for a moment in case you are asking the simple question, 'what is a web-browser?' This is a good question. It is a program/application (aka: tool) which is installed into the operating system (i.e.: MS Windows) the same way as other programs such as Microsoft Word or the game solitaire. I want to make it clear that a web-browser is not Microsoft Windows as Microsoft Windows is the operating system which the browser will reside within.

Once installed the web browser program (example: Chrome) can read pre-made code which usually resides on a public website and you get to it by downloading the code using your internet connection. I've provided some screen shots I took from my local machine to help demonstrate what I'm talking about.

.(Image 101: Chrome browser looking at www.google.com)

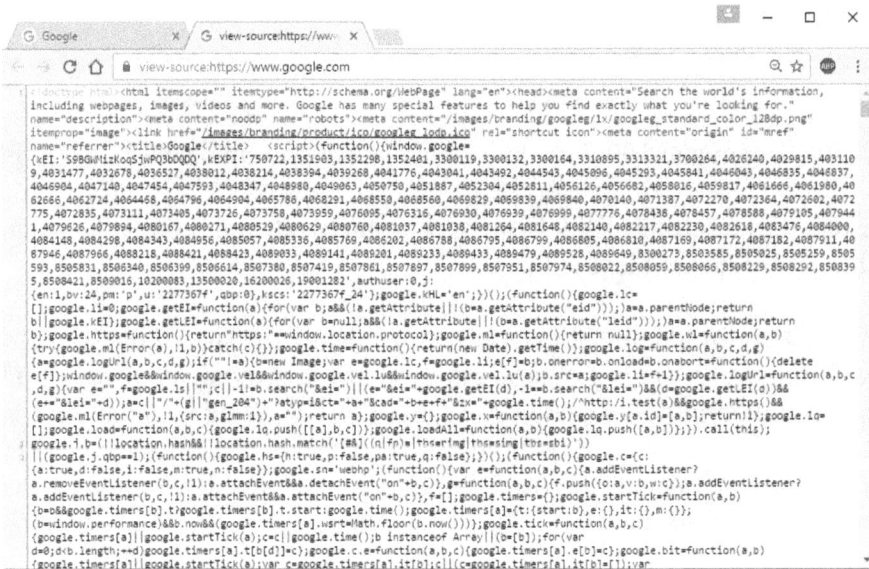

.(Image 102: Chrome browser looking at source code (*HTML*) for www.google.com)

Keep in mind there are other things a web-browser can do such as read local network (intranet) webpages and file systems; I'll cover that lightly in a bit. Once a web-browser successfully points to and connects to a remote web-server; it downloads that webpage information; it then deciphers (decodes) that code and converts it into a readable format for viewing.

> *Note:*
>
> *When I say external (in the above paragraph) I'm referring to external from the machine you're currently using the web-browser system on. If this is your laptop then your local system is your laptop and the external remote website might be* www.google.com*.*

We call this pre-made code Hyper Text Markup Language (also known as HTML). This HTML code is more configurable than just basic text. You can make the text different sizes, fonts, colors, shapes, shadows, etc…You can think of this in a similar fashion as to how an office product such as word, write, google docs manages text. You can do the same with webpages with a little bit of knowledge. A good way to better understand this is to open your web browser, go to your favorite webpage and then right click on the webpage and select properties. This will show you the HTML or XML code for that webpage. You can study it and almost teach yourself the basics. Just remember that when you're writing HTML code for every item you open, you must close it.

Example: <title>www.google.com </title>

254

Notice that I opened the title with <title> and closed the title with the same thing only I added a forward slash (/). I'll leave this with you to investigate more with your favorite webpage should you choose to proceed more in this direction.

There are 3 common question I've received over the years from new folks who are learning web browsers and they are:
1. What kind of web-browsers are there?
2. Which is best?
3. Which one should I use?

These are common questions most new folks using a computer and browsers ask..
Let me first start off by saying web browsing has been around for a long time.. in fact I can remember web browsing using Netscape back in 1994 using a bulletin board system; but that's another story. Let's come back to now; there are more than just a few browsers available especially in 2016. In fact based on an internet search I was able to find Some of the most common are Internet Explorer, Edge, Chrome, Firefox, Opera, Safari, Konqueror and Yandex and the list goes on. Remember these are browsers and not websites. You may know these programs by their symbols listed below:

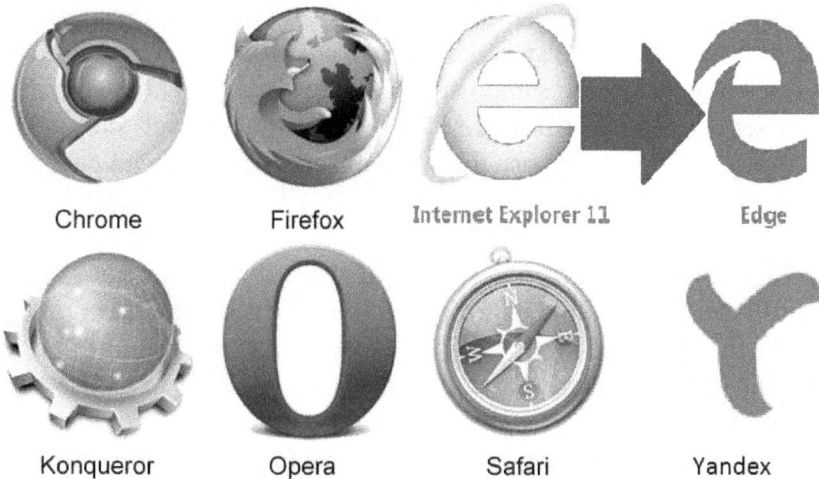

| Chrome | Firefox | Internet Explorer 11 | Edge |

| Konqueror | Opera | Safari | Yandex |

(Image 103: Logo's for some common internet browsers)

However I want to make it perfectly clear that there are more browsers than what I have listed here and you can find many different ones by doing a simple internet search.

Which is best and which should a new person use? Well that depends on the person. Think of this the same way as the car you drive. Why do you drive the type of car you do? There are many reasons; much the same way I want you to think of web-browsers. There are people that say a given browser is better than another and yes there are reasons for each to be used. That's why I have on average 4 different browsers that I commonly use which are Internet Explorer, Edge, Chrome and Firefox. However I do not have anything against the other browsers as I've used them over the years and it depends on my needs and what operating system I'm using as to which browser I use. For example if I'm using Linux then it will probably be Konqueror and Firefox (Mozilla). If I'm using Apple then it may be Safari or Opera. So you see it really depends on what OS you're using and where you are wanting to go. My suggestion to you is to use a few and understand how they work. When you understand one then compare it to another and another and another. Lastly, don't be afraid to have more than 1 browser loaded in your OS. Think of it similarly as screwdrivers in a toolbox; do you only need 1?

I mentioned that I would cover how to use a web-browser to read local networks (intranet) and file systems. Yes this is true in that a web browser can do this but how? In the same way that I previously mentioned that a web browser can read HTML code on a remote/external web site such as www.google.com. You can use the same exact process to read a website that resides on your own local network. Again the web browser is reading the remote file whether it be HTML, XML, etc... Where that file resides (lives) really doesn't matter; just so long as the web browser can successfully get to it, read it and interpret it on the remote system (again remote just means remote to the machine you're currently using). So if you look at your place of business and provided your business has a server on your network that is a web server; meaning the web server provides a source for HTML files to reside. Then you can use your company computer web browser to access company web pages, documents, video and audio files across the local company network. A local company network is called an 'intranet' and the open public internet is called the 'extra-net' but more commonly it's referred to as the 'internet'.

Instead of typing in the top of the web browser the external public website or address of the website such as below:

G Google   ✕

← → C ⌂ 🔒 https://www.google.com

You would type in the local server address of your local company file system you want to go to on your companies intranet.

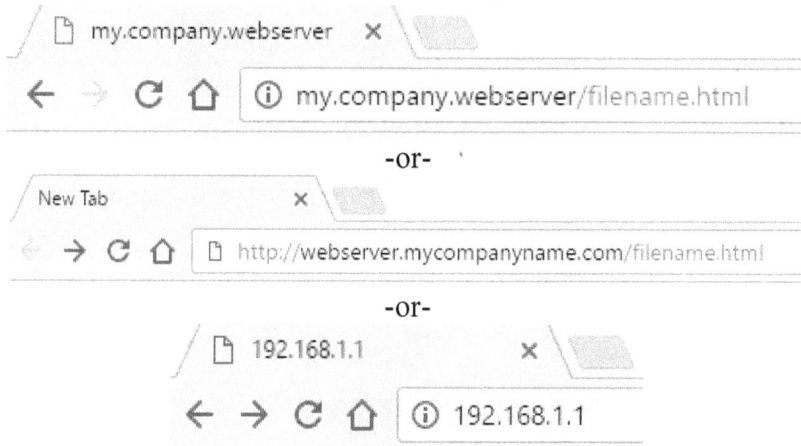

🗋 my.company.webserver   ✕

← → C ⌂ ⓘ my.company.webserver/filename.html

-or-

New Tab   ✕

← → C ⌂ 🗋 http://webserver.mycompanyname.com/filename.html

-or-

🗋 192.168.1.1   ✕

← → C ⌂ ⓘ 192.168.1.1

(Image 104: Examples of Web URL's and IP addresses)

Notice that this is directing the web browser to use your local network (intranet) web server and then after connecting successfully; it will read the filename. This only works if you have a company intranet, webserver and internal domain name service (dns) running or a host file configured on your local machine to resolve the names of the webservers to an internal IP address. If you don't have a local dns server running then you will be forced to use IP addresses to connect. Incase you don't know what I'm talking about here or are unsure you can always use the IP address of the remote machine such as your companies web or file server to get to the data. This is as far as I'm going to go with this topic for this page.

Next I want to discuss some of the codes that a person may get when using a web browser. This was more prevalent in early years of internet usage and intranet usage however in recent years I think the programming on webpages and browsers are doing a better job and possibly they are trying to hide a lot of these codes from the general public since the general public doesn't understand these codes and quite frankly it probably scares a lot of the public when they see these codes. None the less if you're reading this then you are proceeding above the basic user level and I'm sure you'll encounter these codes at some point in your life. With that... here is a list of codes that you may see either on your webpage or in the logs of looking at a webpage but keep in mind that there are many more and you can find all the codes by doing a simple internet search for 'html error codes'.

1xx	Informational.	(100=continue)
2xx	Success.	(200=OK, 202=Accept)
3xx	Redirection.	(300=site moved permanently)
4xx	Client Error.	(401=unauthorized (p/w typed wrong), 404=Webpage Not Found
5xx	Server Error.	(500=Internal server error, 502=bad connect to upstream server, 503=Service unavailable

(Table 37: List of common codes I've experienced in Web browsing).

Command Line Interface (AKA: CLI) Commands

There are 2 methods for entering information into an operating system. They are Graphical user interface (also known as GUI and pronounced 'Goo-Eee) and Command line interface (also known as CLI and pronounced C L I). So of course most everyone is familiar with the GUI version of Windows and using a mouse and keyboard to navigate and tell Windows what to do. However there is another way this can be done and as with any person who is familiar with system administration they would tell you that CLI is that other method.

CLI has been around since the beginning of the computer age and in fact CLI was the original method of computing prior to this application called Windows came along. For the folks who remember the days of 386 and 486 computers running MS-Dos operating system we would load hi-mem sys in the config.sys file of Dos plus modify the autoexec.bat file and then load this program called what? Ding Ding Ding... If you remembered the words "Windows 3.1" then you're as old as me and well we're dinosaurs in the computer world but so what.. We just have a lot of knowledge and we can enjoy reminiscing about the old days over a cup of coffee.

Ok so coming back to now. You see the Command line allows the user to enter commands at a black command prompt window such as:

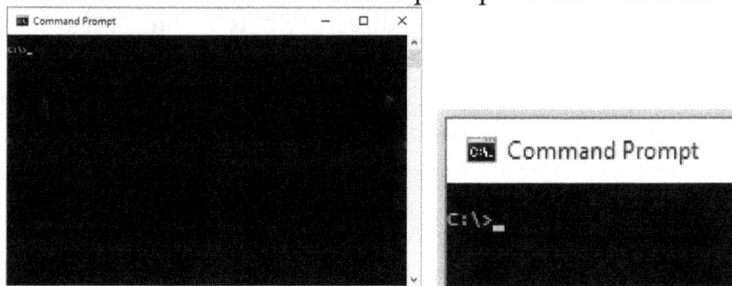

(Image 105: Zoom in on the C:\ prompt in command prompt)

How do you start a command prompt (CLI) window in Windows? This is quite simple and there are a few different methods you can do to do this (note: you only need to use one of these methods but they should all get you to the same point).

1. Start > All programs > Accessories > command prompt
2. Right click on start (menu/orb) > select command prompt
3. Press Windows key + R to open the run dialog box

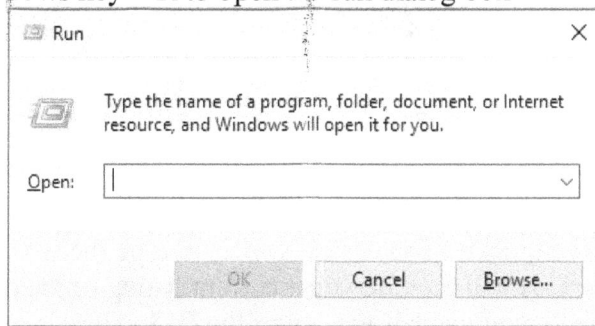

(Image 106: Run window)

4.   In the search box next to start menu or in file explorer you can type in 'cmd'

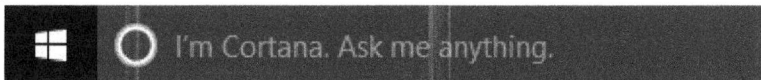

(Image 107: Cortana window in windows 10: type in 'cmd' in this box where being prompted.

It's imporant to note that there are 2 levels of command prompt to use. The first is the basic user level command prompt and the other is an elevated mode called Administrator.
To choose the elevated mode when you get to the point of selecting 'command prompt' to launch it. Instead of left clicking to launch it; do a

right click to list the options for the command prompt. When you do this you will see 'administrator'. It's also important to note that when you choose the administrator level your directory patch changes from the basic mode path of C:\users\<username> to the administrator mode path of C:\windows\system32. Make sure to make head of this directory path location. When in CLI mode you always need to know your current location.

Once you have used one of the 4 methods above to open a command prompt you will be looking at a blank screen such as:

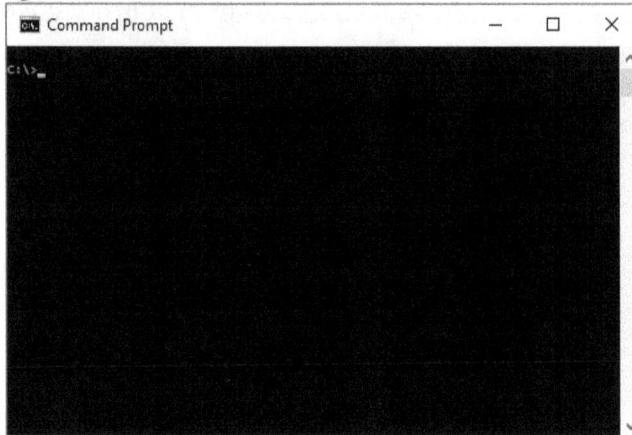

(Image 108: Basic Command prompt interface window)

From this entry window into the command line world where do you go from here? The quickest and easiest way is to type the word 'help' and press 'enter'. This will provide you a current listing of the commands that are available to you via that version of the CLI. Here is a listing I pulled from my Windows 10 machine:

```
C:\>help
For more information on a specific command, type HELP command-name
ASSOC       Displays or modifies file extension associations.
ATTRIB      Displays or changes file attributes.
BREAK       Sets or clears extended CTRL+C checking.
BCDEDIT     Sets properties in boot database to control boot loading.
CACLS       Displays or modifies access control lists (ACLs) of files.
CALL        Calls one batch program from another.
CD          Displays the name of or changes the current directory.
CHCP        Displays or sets the active code page number.
CHDIR       Displays the name of or changes the current directory.
CHKDSK      Checks a disk and displays a status report.
CHKNTFS     Displays or modifies the checking of disk at boot time.
CLS         Clears the screen.
CMD         Starts a new instance of the Windows command interpreter.
```

COLOR	Sets the default console foreground and background colors.
COMP	Compares the contents of two files or sets of files.
COMPACT	Displays or alters the compression of files on NTFS partitions.
CONVERT	Converts FAT volumes to NTFS. You cannot convert the current drive.
COPY	Copies one or more files to another location.
DATE	Displays or sets the date.
DEL	Deletes one or more files.
DIR	Displays a list of files and subdirectories in a directory.
DISKPART	Displays or configures Disk Partition properties.
DOSKEY	Edits command lines, recalls Windows commands, and creates macros.
DRIVERQUERY	Displays current device driver status and properties.
ECHO	Displays messages, or turns command echoing on or off.
ENDLOCAL	Ends localization of environment changes in a batch file.
ERASE	Deletes one or more files.
EXIT	Quits the CMD.EXE program (command interpreter).
FC	Compares two files or sets of files, and displays the differences between them.
FIND	Searches for a text string in a file or files.
FINDSTR	Searches for strings in files.
FOR	Runs a specified command for each file in a set of files.
FORMAT	Formats a disk for use with Windows.
FSUTIL	Displays or configures the file system properties.
FTYPE	Displays or modifies file types used in file extension associations.
GOTO	Directs the Windows command interpreter to a labeled line in a batch program.
GPRESULT	Displays Group Policy information for machine or user.
GRAFTABL	Enables Windows to display an extended character set in graphics mode.
HELP	Provides Help information for Windows commands.
ICACLS	Display, modify, backup, or restore ACLs for files and directories.
IF	Performs conditional processing in batch programs.
LABEL	Creates, changes, or deletes the volume label of a disk.
MD	Creates a directory.
MKDIR	Creates a directory.
MKLINK	Creates Symbolic Links and Hard Links
MODE	Configures a system device.
MORE	Displays output one screen at a time.
MOVE	Moves one or more files from one directory to another directory.
OPENFILES	Displays files opened by remote users for a file share.
PATH	Displays or sets a search path for executable files.
PAUSE	Suspends processing of a batch file and displays a message.
POPD	Restores the previous value of the current directory saved by PUSHD.
PRINT	Prints a text file.
PROMPT	Changes the Windows command prompt.
PUSHD	Saves the current directory then changes it.
RD	Removes a directory.
RECOVER	Recovers readable information from a bad or defective disk.
REM	Records comments (remarks) in batch files or CONFIG.SYS.
REN	Renames a file or files.
RENAME	Renames a file or files.
REPLACE	Replaces files.

RMDIR   Removes a directory.
ROBOCOPY Advanced utility to copy files and directory trees
SET   Displays, sets, or removes Windows environment variables.
SETLOCAL   Begins localization of environment changes in a batch file.
SC   Displays or configures services (background processes).
SCHTASKS Schedules commands and programs to run on a computer.
SHIFT   Shifts the position of replaceable parameters in batch files.
SHUTDOWN Allows proper local or remote shutdown of machine.
SORT   Sorts input.
START   Starts a separate window to run a specified program or command.
SUBST   Associates a path with a drive letter.
SYSTEMINFO   Displays machine specific properties and configuration.
TASKLIST   Displays all currently running tasks including services.
TASKKILL   Kill or stop a running process or application.
TIME   Displays or sets the system time.
TITLE   Sets the window title for a CMD.EXE session.
TREE   Graphically displays the directory structure of a drive or path.
TYPE   Displays the contents of a text file.
VER   Displays the Windows version.
VERIFY   Tells Windows whether to verify that your files are written correctly to a
disk.
VOL   Displays a disk volume label and serial number.
XCOPY   Copies files and directory trees.
WMIC   Displays WMI information inside interactive command shell.
For more information on tools see the command-line reference in the online help.
C:\>

(Note: I've bolded the above commands to show the most common commands I use)

Ok so now that you know how to open the command prompt as well as have a list of commands how do you get the details for each command. This is simple and you start off with the name of the command you want followed by a space and then '/?'.

Here is an example of getting the different flags (options) to use with the directory command. To save space I'm not going to do this for every CLI command but please keep in mind that you can do this same method for any of the CLI commands.

C:\>dir /?
Displays a list of files and subdirectories in a directory.

DIR [drive:][path][filename] [/A[[:]attributes]] [/B] [/C] [/D] [/L] [/N]
[/O[[:]sortorder]] [/P] [/Q] [/R] [/S] [/T[[:]timefield]] [/W] [/X] [/4]

[drive:][path][filename]
        Specifies drive, directory, and/or files to list.

/A   Displays files with specified attributes.
attributes D Directories   R Read-only files
            H Hidden files   A Files ready for archiving
            S System files   I Not content indexed files
            L Reparse Points   - Prefix meaning not
/B   Uses bare format (no heading information or summary).
/C   Display the thousand separator in file sizes. This is the
        default. Use /-C to disable display of separator.
/D   Same as wide but files are list sorted by column.
/L   Uses lowercase.
/N   New long list format where filenames are on the far right.
/O   List by files in sorted order.
sortorder N By name (alphabetic)   S By size (smallest first)
            E By extension (alphabetic) D By date/time (oldest first)
            G Group directories first   - Prefix to reverse order
/P   Pauses after each screenful of information.
/Q   Display the owner of the file.
/R   Display alternate data streams of the file.
/S   Displays files in specified directory and all subdirectories.
/T   Controls which time field displayed or used for sorting
timefield C Creation
            A Last Access
            W Last Written
/W   Uses wide list format.
/X   This displays the short names generated for non-8dot3 file
        names. The format is that of /N with the short name inserted
        before the long name. If no short name is present, blanks are
        displayed in its place.
/4   Displays four-digit years

Switches may be preset in the DIRCMD environment variable. Override
preset switches by prefixing any switch with - (hyphen)--for example, /-W.

C:\>

Ok if you're like me you are probably thinking it would be nice to see some examples. To base your knowledge on and my response is right in line with your thought. Sure I can provide this and I'll do some common CLI commands over the next few pages.

Student LAB:

As I'm showing the following examples; I highly recommend you open a command prompt window and duplicate what I'm showing. Do each step as you read over this section of the book.

NOTE: There will be directory and file differences between your computer and what I have listed here in these pages. The reason is that each computer and user will have different files saved and used. The point here is to understand what the commands are doing when issued on your computer.

CLI Example1: In this example I will show how to show my current location in the CLI environment as well as show the listings of the directory contents using the 'dir' command:

C:\>dir
 Volume in drive C is Windows
 Volume Serial Number is 8AAB-A8B6

 Directory of C:\

08/17/2015 12:42 PM   <DIR>   AdwCleaner
05/04/2016 07:18 AM   55,948 cc_20160504_081825.reg
05/04/2016 07:19 AM   10,858 cc_20160504_081914.reg
01/15/2016 07:27 AM   <DIR>   chris' directory
09/14/2014 04:05 PM   116,214 compete-header-long2.bmp
08/24/2015 05:43 AM   <DIR>   cygwin64
10/29/2014 05:41 AM   37 DevMgr.bat
02/19/2015 04:24 PM   <DIR>   Drivers
12/07/2015 08:33 AM   <DIR>   inetpub
12/07/2015 08:50 AM   <DIR>   Intel
09/11/2016 04:53 PM   <DIR>   iolo
03/22/2016 02:22 AM   <DIR>   LogFiles
02/19/2015 04:20 PM   231 model.bat
08/24/2015 03:19 AM   <DIR>   NPE
10/29/2015 11:24 PM   <DIR>   PerfLogs
11/18/2016 10:54 AM   <DIR>   Program Files
11/18/2016 10:57 AM   <DIR>   Program Files (x86)
09/24/2015 05:58 AM   <DIR>   SharedForVM's
10/25/2015 12:31 PM   <DIR>   Swsetup
08/27/2015 10:45 AM   <DIR>   System.sav
08/17/2015 10:09 AM   651 task.vbs
09/07/2015 10:23 PM   <DIR>   TEMP
02/23/2016 11:42 PM   <DIR>   TestDataFiles
08/17/2015 09:49 AM   45 user.js
12/07/2015 08:57 AM   <DIR>   Users
03/12/2014 04:11 AM   52,398 usm_icon.ico
05/07/2016 12:56 PM   <DIR>   VM Images
11/19/2016 01:12 PM   <DIR>   WINDOWS
              10 File(s)   250,176 bytes
              20 Dir(s) 13,586,210,816 bytes free

C:\>

Notice the above output shows a listing of directories and files along with each entry having its own date and timestamp and classification. This is helpful information to know what you're working on and what subdirectory I can change directory into.

CLI Example2: In this example I will make a test subdirectory under the root of C:\ Using the make directory (mkdir) command. I will then change into the newly created sub directory using the change directory (cd) command. Note: when making directories or subdirectories you will use the same process as I show here:

```
C:\>mkdir test_subdirectory <enter>
C:\>cd test_subdirectory     <enter>
C:\test_subdirectory>        <enter>
```

CLI Example3: In this example I will list the contents of the newly created (test subdirectory) again by using the directory (dir) command:

```
C:\test_subdirectory>dir
        Volume in drive C is Windows
        Volume Serial Number is 8AAB-A8B6

        Directory of C:\test_subdirectory

        12/06/2016  02:31 PM   <DIR>          .
        12/06/2016  02:31 PM   <DIR>          ..
                0 File(s)              0 bytes
                2 Dir(s)  15,280,726,016 bytes free

C:\test_subdirectory>
```

Important to note what is in the directory. When looking at an empty directory you will notice there are always 2 directories listed. This is dot (.) and dot dot (..). There is actually a lot of information behind these 2 directory entries but I'm going to simply refer to them as a single dot refers to the current working directory that you reside in and the dot dot (..) refers the parent directory above where you currently reside in.

I'm always believing that you should be able to prove what you say especially in the computer world. With that said lets try another example.

CLI Example3: change directory from (test subdirectory) into the dot (.) directory. Pay attention to where you are and where you end up.

    C:\test_subdirectory>cd . <enter>
    C:\test_subdirectory>

Notice that you did issue the change directory (cd) command and the destination you wanted to change directory to was dot (.). But when you look at your current location after you hit enter where are you at? The same location before you issued the command. Why would this be? The answer is quite simple. Sometimes you need to issue commands or reach files which resides in a sub directory below where you currently are. This might look something like: copy ./dir1/dir2/file1.txt ./dir1/file1.txt What this command does is copies the file1.txt from the subdirectory called dir2 and copies it up one level to dir1.

CLI Example4: In this example I will show you how to change directory from (test subdirectory) into parent directory (../) which again resides above the test_subdirectory. In this case there is no directory above the test_subdirectory so we will be changing location into the root of the main hard drive called C:\

    C:\test_subdirectory>cd .. <enter>
    C:\>

As you can see if you change directory into the directory called dot dot (..) then it will change locations into the parent directory location above where you currently reside.

CLI Example5: In this example we will be removing a directory. To remove a directory use the remove directory command called rmdir. Important note that you cannot remove a directory if you currently reside within that directory. That would be equivalent to using a wrecking ball to remove a building with you still being inside that building. This is never good practice and the command line world follows this same practice. So before you remove a directory you must not be in it. Likewise; the directory that you're removing needs to be empty before removal otherwise you'll get an error message stating the directory is not empty. How do you know if you're inside the directory or if there are files and subdirectories in that directory you're trying to remove? You should have already answered this by thinking the 'dir' command.

IMPORTANT:
Remember in the CLI environment it's always your responsibility to know where you are at all times. If you don't know then you're doing something wrong and you need to find out immediately.

```
C:\test_subdirectory>dir
        Volume in drive C is Windows
        Volume Serial Number is 8AAB-A8B6

        Directory of C:\test_subdirectory
        12/11/2016  08:12 AM   <DIR>          .
        12/11/2016  08:12 AM   <DIR>          ..
               0 File(s)          0 bytes
               2 Dir(s)  15,228,686,336 bytes free

C:\test_subdirectory>cd ..
C:\>rmdir test_subdirectory

C:\>dir test_subdirectory
 Volume in drive C is Windows
 Volume Serial Number is 8AAB-A8B6

 Directory of C:\
File Not Found
C:\>
```

Student LAB:

Now that I've covered the basic navigation of the command line interface (CLI) world with you it's time to see if you can do some practice. I want you to perform the following tasks:

1) List your current directory location and contents
2) Make a temporary directory called bananas
3) Change directory into bananas
4) Inside bananas directory, make 3 subdirectories called dir1, dir2, dir3
5) Inside bananas directory, make 3 files called file1.txt, file2.txt, file3.txt
   Note to create a file from CLI; type 'notepad <filename>'<enter>
   You will notice a pop-up window which will look similar to image 109 below.

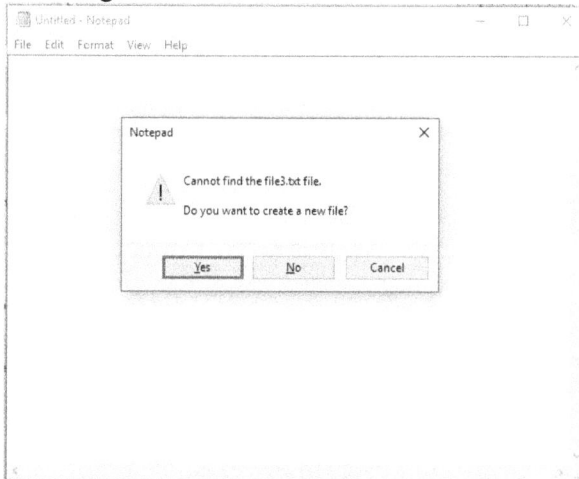

(Image 109: notepad window to create a new file)

6)   List directory contents of bananas

Answer: When done with step 6 your directory should look like this:
        C:\test_subdirectory>dir
            Volume in drive C is Windows
            Volume Serial Number is 8AAB-A8B6

        Directory of C:\bananas

        12/11/2016 07:54 AM   <DIR>   .
        12/11/2016 07:54 AM   <DIR>   ..
        12/11/2016 07:52 AM   <DIR>   dir1
        12/11/2016 07:52 AM   <DIR>   dir2
        12/11/2016 07:53 AM   <DIR>   dir3
        12/11/2016 07:53 AM   1 file1.txt
        12/11/2016 07:54 AM   0 file2.txt
        12/11/2016 07:54 AM   0 file3.txt

             3 File(s)   1 bytes
             5 Dir(s) 15,246,651,392 bytes free

Ok now that you have a basic familiarity with the basic CLI environment and moving around. I want to talk to you about the limitations. I want you to know that CLI has been around for a very long time and for many years; even before the MS Windows graphical user interface (GUI) and for those that remember that means that CLI has been around prior to the late 1970 and early 1980's. Back then the CLI environment was called disk operating system (aka: DOS) and it was limited to 8 characters for the file name plus 3 characters for the type of file (I covered this in the software section earlier in the book). Why do I bring this up again. Well it's due to the limitations of CLI. You see long filenames are not native to the CLI environment. When I say long filenames I'm referring to the 255 character filenames (including spaces). Let's take a look at the next example.

Example: cd c:\backyard patio\jobs

You see the space in between backyard and patio tells the CLI environment that there are additional options that are to be applied and they are following the space after c:\backyard. However, in my example above, the option 'patio' is not a valid CLI command nor valid option and so CLI errors.

Example: C:\>cd backyard
The system cannot find the path specified.

Notice you don't get into the directory you want to go into which is c:\backyard patio\jobs. To overcome this you need to use double quotes ("") around the long filename (which includes the spaces in-between the words) such as:

RULE: Must use quotes if path has spaces
Example: cd c:\"backyard patio"\jobs

If you type in the above example; then CLI will change directory correctly. Go ahead and try this on your machine now.

STUDENT LAB:

1.   Create a sub-directory called 'backyard patio' (This can be on your main C:\ drive)
2.   Change directory into that 'backyard patio' directory
3.   Make a new directory called jobs
4.   Change directory into jobs
5.   List the contents of the jobs directory.

Lab Results: (this is what you should see:)

1. C:\>mkdir "backyard patio"
   Volume in drive C is Windows
   Volume Serial Number is 8AAB-A8B6

   Directory of C:\backyard patio\jobs

   ```
   12/20/2016  10:27 AM   <DIR>         .
   12/20/2016  10:27 AM   <DIR>         ..
   12/20/2016  10:27 AM   <DIR>         backyard patio
                  0 File(s)          0 bytes
                  3 Dir(s)  9,537,540,096 bytes free
   ```

2. C:\backyard patio>dir
   Volume in drive C is Windows
   Volume Serial Number is 8AAB-A8B6

   Directory of C:\backyard patio

   ```
   12/20/2016  10:28 AM   <DIR>         .
   12/20/2016  10:28 AM   <DIR>         ..
                  0 File(s)          0 bytes
                  2 Dir(s)  9,537,183,744 bytes free
   ```

3. C:\backyard patio>mkdir jobs

   C:\backyard patio>dir
   Volume in drive C is Windows
   Volume Serial Number is 8AAB-A8B6

   Directory of C:\backyard patio

   ```
   12/20/2016  10:29 AM   <DIR>         .
   12/20/2016  10:29 AM   <DIR>         ..
   12/20/2016  10:29 AM   <DIR>         jobs
                  0 File(s)          0 bytes
                  3 Dir(s)  9,536,978,944 bytes free
   ```

4. C:\backyard patio>cd jobs

5. C:\backyard patio\jobs>dir
   Volume in drive C is Windows
   Volume Serial Number is 8AAB-A8B6

   Directory of C:\backyard patio\jobs

   ```
   12/20/2016  10:29 AM   <DIR>         .
   12/20/2016  10:29 AM   <DIR>         ..
                  0 File(s)          0 bytes
                  2 Dir(s)  9,536,954,368 bytes free
   ```

   C:\backyard patio\jobs>

Congratulations you are on your way to navigating the command line environment. Once you have these basic steps under your belt then the rest is easy… it's time and practice to really concrete this information into your head.

Let's continue our thoughts here on MS-DOS (aka:command line interfacing) and lets talk about trying to connect to a remote location such as a network drive. For this example I'll use the letter T: MS-DOS will allow you to change file systems by just typing in the drive letter you want to change to. For example your MS-DOS window currently shows C:\backyard patio\jobs and you insert a removable USB drive and it's mapped as F:\ How do you change from C:\backyard patio\jobs to F:\? You simply type at the prompt ">" the letter of the alphabet followed by a colon (C:\backyard patio> F: <press enter>).

Example: C:\backyard patio\jobs>f: <enter>

```
F:\>dir
 Volume in drive F is USBdrive
 Volume Serial Number is 57A8-8390

 Directory of F:\

08/17/2015 10:21 AM    <DIR>        dir1
09/28/2015 07:10 AM    <DIR>        dir2
09/28/2015 07:11 AM    <DIR>        dir3
11/28/2016 02:55 PM           13,189  File1.txt
09/28/2015 07:16 AM    <DIR>        dir4
12/13/2016 01:29 PM           39,936  File2.jpg
11/16/2015 10:55 AM    <DIR>        downloads
11/17/2015 09:15 AM    <DIR>        Pictures
02/13/2016 06:31 PM           49,728  3345847.pdf
02/18/2016 08:50 PM           62,202  harddrive.notebook
02/18/2016 08:50 PM          933,122  harddrive.pptx
07/18/2016 05:19 PM              966  batchfile1.bat
07/29/2016 05:13 PM    <DIR>        backups
              6 File(s)      9,944,049 bytes
              7 Dir(s)  17,118,724,096 bytes free
(Note: I've removed some listing to protect my example data)
F:\>
```

Ok now that we have that understood lets move to a networked drive. You see you cannot access universal naming convention (UNC) paths through MS-DOS. Dos came out before UNC's were common. Therefore DOS has no ways of understanding what a UNC is. You're probably wondering what a UNC is. UNC stands for Universal naming convention and it's a way that Microsoft machines are able to map to remote drive locations. If you are on machine#1 and you want to connect to a remote drive location on machine #2 then the easiest way is to map a drive from machine#1 to machine #2. To do this on machine#1 open My Computer and click on map network drive.

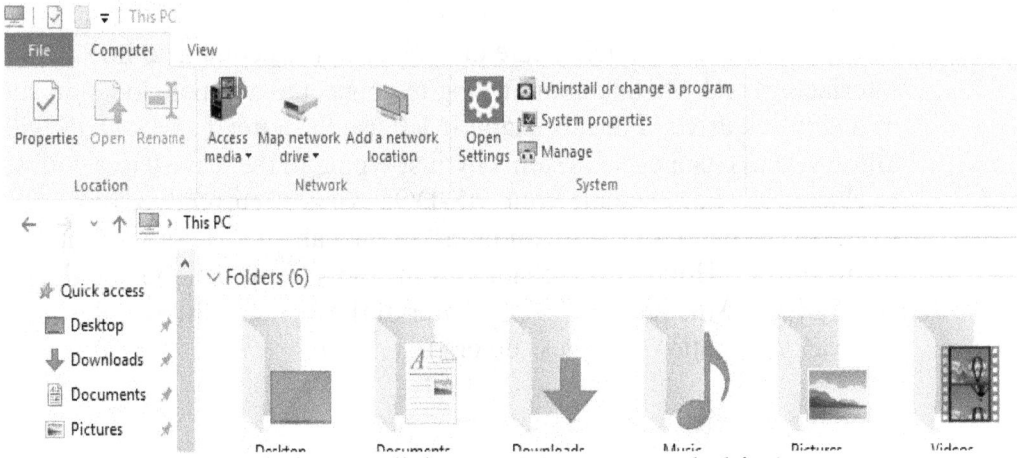

(Image 110: Window to click on to Map a network drive)

This will bring you through to the next window (Image 111) which is where you will associate a drive letter with the remote system. Remember, while you're on machine#1 you will pick a drive letter and then associate it with a UNC. The UNC format is
\\<remote server name or IP address>\remote share name.

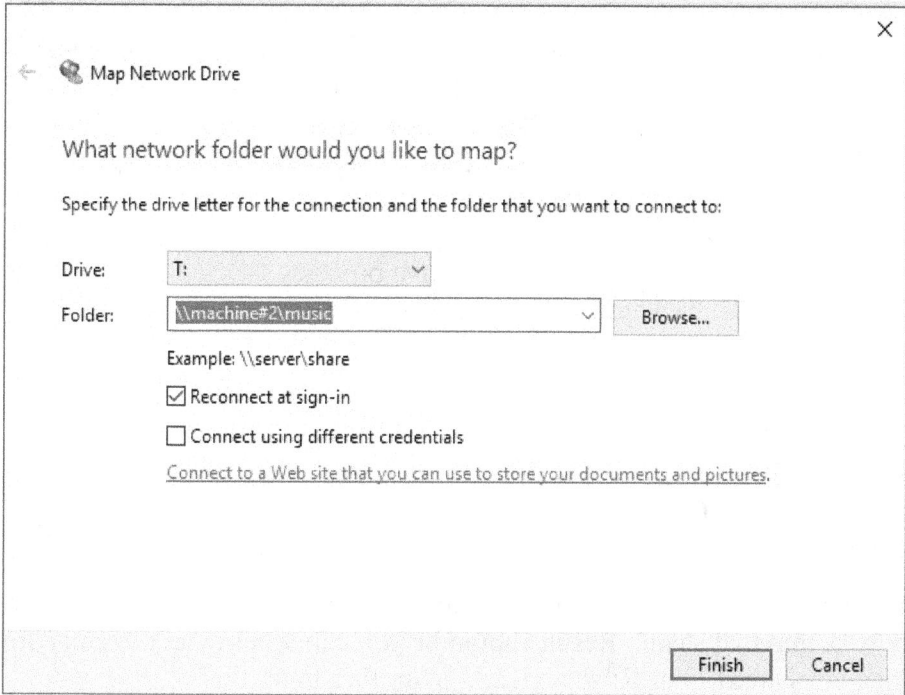

(Image 111: Map Window drive)

In my running example here I want to map the music folder on machine#2 to machine #1 at the T:\ drive. Now you try this on your machine to make sure you understand what I'm doing.

Once you click finish then Windows OS will have a drive mapping to the T:\ drive which will point to the remote shared folder called music on machine#2. Ok back to DOS; Please remember that Dos cannot access \\machine#2\music. If you try to type cd \\machine#2\music this will fail. Instead you have to use a 2 step process.

1. Map drive to T:\ (See above process)
2. C:\backyard patio\> T: <enter>

Ok I think I've beat this into the ground pretty good now.

STUDENT LAB:

NOTE: Most of you will only have 1 computer and so the sharing process is still the same. You do NOT need to have 2 computers to try this lab. Simply share a folder and then use map network drive to map across the network into that share. Result should be you can access that directory from either C:\shared123 or R:\shared123. Your turn to try this.
1. Create a shared folder on your computer called C:\shared123. (This can be on your main C:\ drive)
2. Follow the mapping process I described earlier and map the drive letter R: to the c:\shared123 directory you just created.
3. Make a new directory in R:\shared123 called happy. (result: R:\shared123\happy)
4. Change directory into happy and create subdirectory 'ness'
5. List the contents of the jobs directory.
6. Now change to C:\shared123 and list the directory contents. (Do you see shared123?)
7. Change directory to C:\shared123\happy\ness

If you have done your steps correctly then you should be seeing the exact same output on both C:\shared123 and the R:\shared123 directories. Why is this?

_____
_____
_____
_____
_____
_____

Lastly, as with any file system you need to know and remember that directories and files have what's called permissions. Permissions are the items that protect the file or directory from unwanted actions occurring. I believe I spoke about this earlier in the book. Well permissions are still present when we are dealing with DOS. You need to remember that you cannot access paths that you don't have permissions for. It's that simple. So just because you are in a DOS world you still need to remember about permissions. To find out what permissions are available on a given directory or file you can use the attrib command or directory command to inquire about the file or directory. If either of these commands do not provide you the information you're looking for then what else could you do?

_____

_____

_____

_____

_____

_____

If you said to use the help command then you are absolutely correct.

Ok I've mentioned this off and on but if you feel good about MS-DOS and the power it can provide for you then you'll also enjoy the CLI environment of another operating system called Linux/Unix. I covered this a bit earlier in the book but please keep in mind that Linux and Unix is nothing more than a CLI environment as well. Lastly, if you get really good a DOS and you need even more ability then I would encourage you to look into the world of PowerShell. A PowerShell is a windows based program which for the purposes of this book you can think of it as a powerful DOS program. In fact some of my students have refereed to PowerShell as DOS on steroids.

Learning Check: Command Line Questions:

1. How can you find a command you need to use in DOS if you forget the command?

   _____

   _____

   _____

   _____

2. In Dos, what does the . mean in a directory listing?_____

   _____

   _____

   _____

3. In Dos, what does the .. mean in a directory listing?

   _____

   _____

   _____

   _____

4. Using Dos; how do you change directory into a folder called, 'my backyard projects'?

   _____

   _____

   _____

   _____

   _____

5. In Dos (CLI) environment how would you map the U:\ drive letter to a remote computer shared folder called umbrella:

   _____

   _____

   _____

   _____

6. What other programs are command line interface based:

   _____

   _____

7. What is PowerShell:

   _____

   _____

MS Office Environment:

This section is designed to introduce you to basic office environment applications. The most common office application used by many people is Microsoft Office. Microsoft office has been around for a long time. Based on a simple internet search *(which anyone can do; and I like doing open basic internet searches for the research of this book due to it's the same thing that you can do at any time. I always encourage my students to get use to doing this as it's a tool that can be used to help you to learn).* Anyhow, based on a simple internet search; I was able to find that MS Office originated in 1990 with office version 1.0 however there were other typing programs prior to office such as starwriter 1.0 which appears to have originated back in 1985 and has evolved over the years into what is known today as either open office (www.openoffice.org) or star office (www.staroffice.org). Both of these programs are good programs and I've used both of them. They are both open source programs and are controlled by their respective groups. The nice thing about these programs are they are free for you to download (as of the writing of this book and it's believed they will continue to be free). If you are interested in more information about these websites then I would highly suggest that you go to their respective websites listed above for more detail.

For the purposes of this book I'll be concentrating on the Microsoft Office versions. Now if you have been using MS office for a long time then you are probably familiar with the old format of the MS Office environment which had the menu items across the top which were labeled from left to right as: 'File', 'Edit', 'View', etc. This is reflected in image 112 below which I took from my lab. Image 112 below is of the MS Word program but all of the other office 2000 applications such as Excel, PowerPoint, Outlook and Access all have the same similar command bar at the top. This is why these products have been referred to as the Office sister products. They are completely separate programs but they all have a similar feel based on the Menu bar at the top. This is why some refer to these as sister products. They are all within the MS Office Suite but do different tasks.

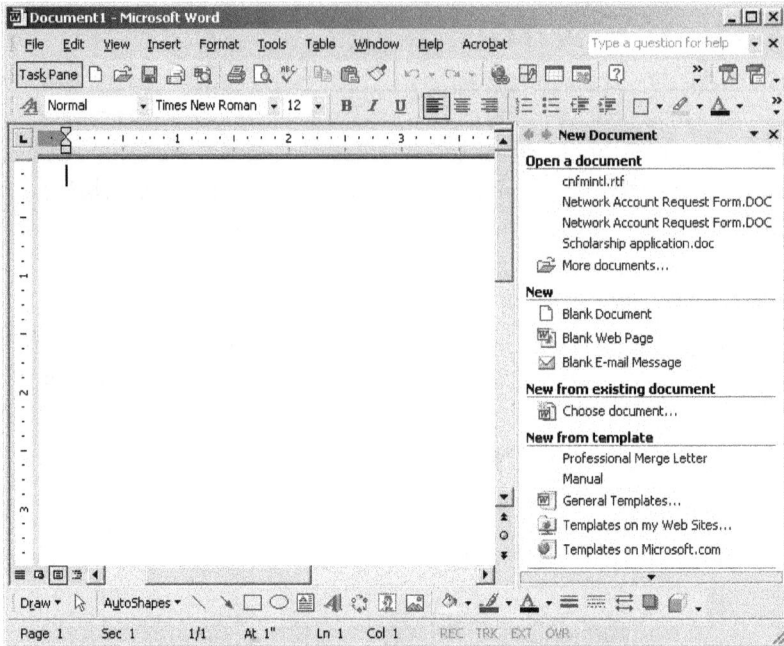

(Image 112: Microsoft Word:Office 2000
with File, Edit, View, etc.. Menu Items)

However with the release of MS Office 2007; Microsoft revamped the 'File', 'Edit', 'View' menu bar and came out with the new 'ribbon' across the top which is really quite nice. The 'ribbon' has also been continued in later versions of MS Office such as MS Office 2010, 2013 and 2016. Just like before the same goes for each version having a similar look and feel (making them sister products) however they have completely different purposes. This new ribbon view is reflected below:

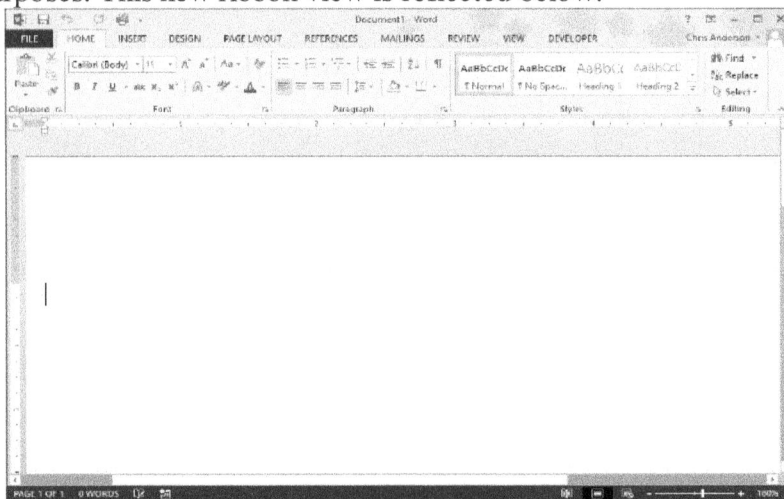

(Image 113: Microsoft Word:Office 2007 and Greater with new "RIBBON" Menu Item)

Why would Microsoft change up this format of the menu bar into the 'ribbon'? I've been told many reasons over the years by different resources but the one that makes the most since to me is that Microsoft was actually trying to help all of us to be able to easily navigate the tool bar inside of the office products. You see in the previous versions of MS Office there were many different drip down menu items and the command you were looking for might not be in the menu bar you thought it should be in. This led to a good amount of confusion for the end office user and un-needed frustration. So Microsoft listened and their engineers came up with an idea to use contextual menu's. In short what does this mean? Quite simply they will put the most common commands on the ribbon for the end user to have access to the most. However for the other commands that are not needed until they are needed they will be hidden from view until needed.

Side Note: You see if you tell an engineer to make something more simple even when that engineer knows you still need these options then that engineer will come up with a way of providing to to you when needed and not before. This is on of the concepts that were relayed to me from my research.

So with Microsoft Engineers working to make our lives easier and not more difficult they came up with the contextual menu and that is what is reflected in the ribbon. So lets look at what Wikipedia has to say on the Microsoft ribbon .

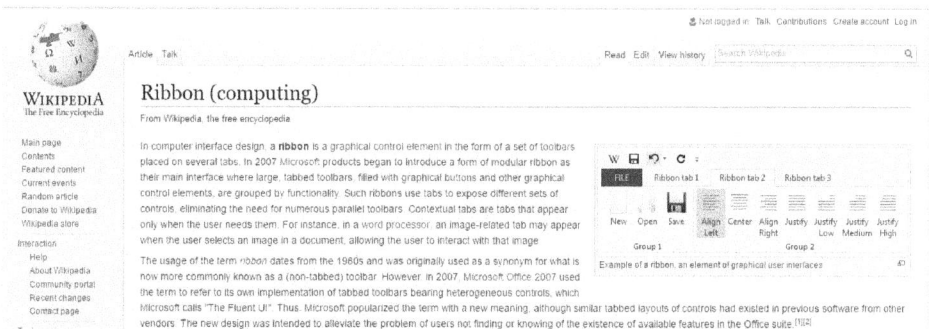

(Image 114: Source: https://en.wikipedia.org/wiki/Ribbon_(computing) Dec, 2016)

<ins>Here is what the Wikipedia image (Image 114) says:</ins>

*In computer interface design, a **ribbon** is a <u>graphical control element</u> in the form of a set of <u>toolbars</u> placed on several <u>tabs</u>. In 2007 <u>Microsoft</u> products began to introduce a form of modular ribbon as their main interface where large, tabbed toolbars, filled with graphical <u>buttons</u> and other graphical control elements, are grouped by functionality. Such ribbons use tabs to expose different sets of controls, eliminating the need for numerous parallel toolbars. Contextual tabs are tabs that appear only when the user needs them. For instance, in a <u>word processor</u>, an image-related tab may appear when the user selects an image in a document, allowing the user to interact with that image.*

The usage of the term ribbon dates from the 1980s and was originally used as a synonym for what is now more commonly known as a (non-tabbed) toolbar. However, in 2007, <u>Microsoft Office 2007</u> used the term to refer to its own implementation of tabbed toolbars bearing heterogeneous controls, which Microsoft calls "The Fluent UI". Thus, Microsoft popularized the term with a new meaning, although similar tabbed layouts of controls had existed in previous software from other vendors. The new design was intended to alleviate the problem of users not finding or knowing of the existence of available features in the Office suite.[1][2]

So what is an example of a contextual menu? Here is an example of a normal ribbon:

(Image 115: Ribbon with Contextual menu)

Notice that the major tabs across the top are listed as home, insert, design, page layout, references, mailings, review, view and developer (Note I had to enable developer under File, options, customize ribbon feature). The point of this ribbon image is this will be the main "common" ribbon most office users will see and use on a regular basis.

Now if I want to edit a picture there is no real option listed to edit the picture. So I have to insert a picture first and I can do that by clicking on the 'insert' major tab on top of the ribbon and then click in the illustrations group and then click on the 'pictures' icon to insert a picture.

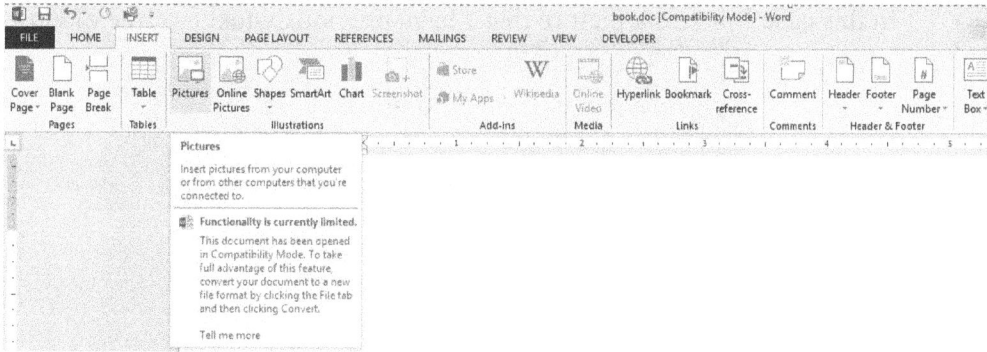

(Image 116: Ribbon without Image header, Click on Insert followed by Picture)

Once you click on the Pictures button then you will be presented with and insert picture window where you can navigate to your picture of choice.

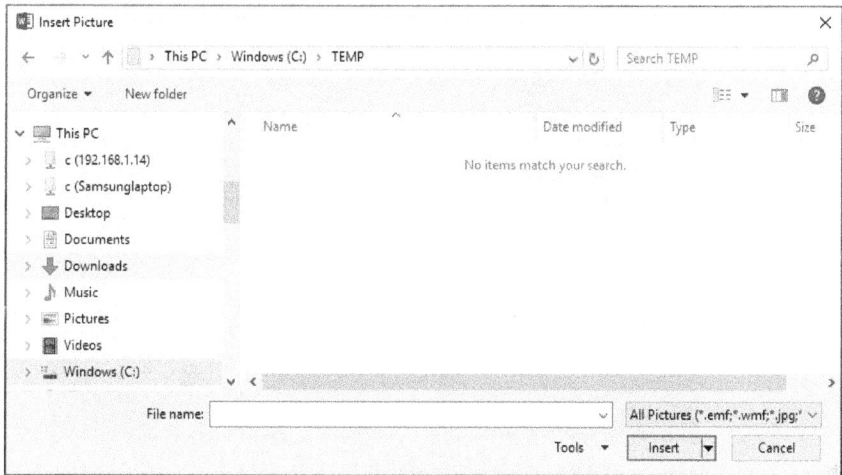

(Image 117: Insert picture pop-up window)

Once you have navigated to the directory (usually it's under your pictures directory) then click on the image and click on insert. This will insert your picture into your word document where your cursor resides. If this is not in the correct location then move your mouse to the location where you want to insert the picture and repeat the above process.

In this case I picked a picture that I have previously taken of the clouds.

(Image 118: Cloud Picture)

Now if I want to edit this picture all I have to do is use the mouse and click on the picture with the left (primary) mouse button to correctly select the picture for working on. This will surround the picture with a dotted line.

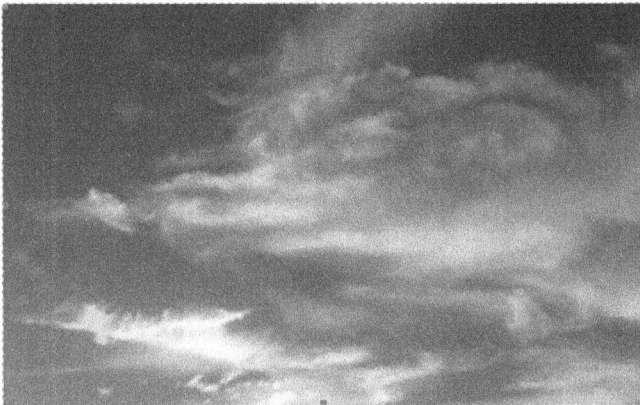

(Image 118a: Notice dotted line around cloud picture)

After clicking on the picture; you'll notice that back on top of word in the ribbon section; the ribbon now has a new major tab listed on the top right hand corner of the ribbon called 'picture tools'. It looks like:

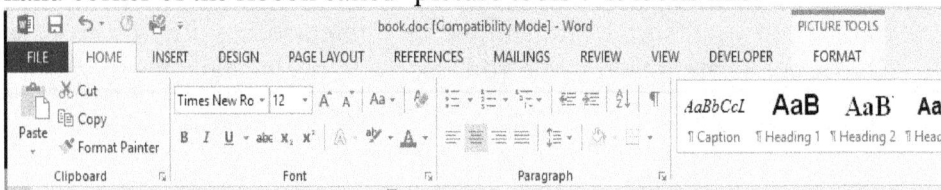

(Image 119: Ribbon with new "Picture Tools, Format" Menu bar added)

If you recall a few moments ago the 'pictures tools' major tab was not there (Look back to the previous page for review if needed). The reason for this is due to the "picture tools" tab is a contextual menu which again means it will not be displayed until you're ready to use it. This really helps simplify and make navigating the ribbon easier for the masses of people around the world. However I also have to say that this can be frustrating as well for newbies who want to do something but don't have word set in the correct position to display the contextual (hidden) menu. So keep this in mind that if you want to do something and you can't find the tab you want to use then it very well may mean that you don't have MS Word, Excel, PowerPoint, Outlook or Access in the proper mode to display the contextual menu.

<u>Student practice:</u> Now you try the above steps on your machine.

Ok you now know that the Microsoft office suite of products had a major revamp with the release of Office 2007 and the later versions continued this ribbon concept. This new ribbon is across all the office *aka: 'sister'* products such as Word, Excel, PowerPoint, Outlook and Access for each release of MS Office suite such as office 2007, 2010, 2013 and 2016. However what do each of these products do specifically and why would a person use them? Good question and I've made a simple chart below for your reference:

Product	Primary	Details	File Extensions 2007+ / Pre-2007
Word	Writing	Writes and edits documents, resumes, letters, etc.	.docx / .doc
Excel	Math	Creates, edits formulas for managing mathematical data.	.xlsx / .xls
PowerPoint	Presentations	Creates, edits presentations	.pptx / .ppt
Outlook	Email, Calendar	Manages Email, calendar, appointments, tasks, etc.	.pst / .ost
Access	Database	Creates, edit and manage small ended databases	.accdb/.mdb

(Table 38: What each MS Office program is primarily used for and the file extensions)

Keep in mind that a person can use the MS Office programs for many thing ranging from:
- Work/Office – performing work related functions and reports, creating/editing resumes, pay their personal bills and keep track of them in word or excel.
- Homework – Students can perform homework tasks such as writing papers, creating power point presentations, emails, etc.
- Personal letters – A person could write a letter to a family member or friend.

One very important thing to remember with the above products is they are all inter-twined with each other. By this I mean that if you want to insert an

Excel sheet (.xlsx) into a word document (.docx) or into a PowerPoint (.pptx) you can do this and work the excel sheet inside of the word or PowerPoint file.

Another important point to note is the difference in the extensions. Some of them have an 'x' and others do not. The reason for this is the 'x' refers to a newer version such as office 2007 and afterwards will have the same extension as files that were prior to the Office 2007 change over only these newer versions will add on an 'x' at the end to represent it's of the newer file format.

Some will ask if you have to have different versions of Office installed to read the different version and the answer is no. If you have a newer version of office such as Office 2013 and you try to open an older word document with a .doc extension then office 2013 is backwards compatible and will open it without error. However if you have an older version of office such as office 2000 and you try to open a document created in Office 2013 (.docx) then you will probably have to download an office compatibility pack from Microsoft in order to read it. If you are unable to do this then take the file to another computer with a newer version of office to read the file. The other option would be to try using MS Word 203 Reader (download from Microsoft for free) or use an alternative office program to read the document such as Libre office (URL: www.libreoffice.org), google docs (URL: https://docs.google.com/) or Microsoft OneDrive (URL: http://onedrive.live.com)

There are many reasons and tasks that can and are done on a regular basis in Word, Excel, Power Point, Outlook and Access. In fact there are more than I could list here in this book. So instead of trying to mention all the different things that can be done in the Office suite of tools I'll instead focus on a few common tasks.

Since 1990's some of the most common and basic formatting features in Microsoft Word have been:
1. how to open a new word documents
2. how to save a new word documents.
3. how to adjust the font size, font style, and margins.
4. how to insert bullet points

I'll now walk through how to do each of these common tasks that new folks are asking help with. Remember, when it comes to doing tasks in a computer and even office; I'm going to refer to what I've said before:

> *"On average; there are at least 3 different ways to do anything in a computer and I highly suggest you find the best way that works for you and stick with it; but keep in mind there may be other ways that are faster, easier and even more convenient than the method you know. So be open to these other ways as it will only help you in the long run". (Chris Anderson, self-2015)*

My above saying also proves true here as well for opening, saving and modifying a document.

1. How to open a new word documents

Method1: To open a new word document you can click on the MS Windows Start button followed by navigating the start menu to find the 'Microsoft Office 2013' listing, click on it and then select 'Word 2013'

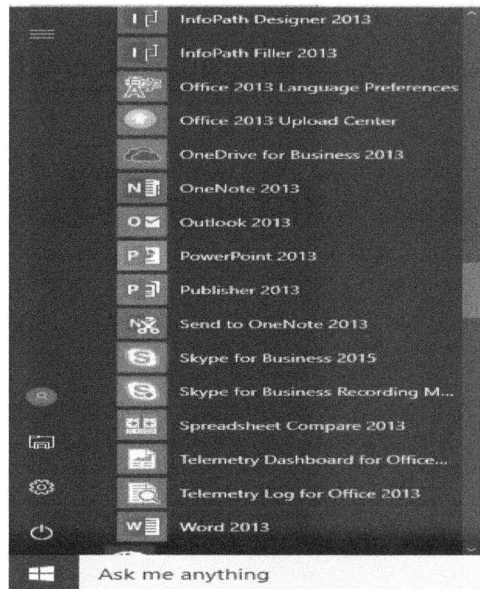

(Image 120: Windows 10 Start Menu to Start MS Word 2013)

This will open the Word Program and by default will bring you through to a new document listing page such as:

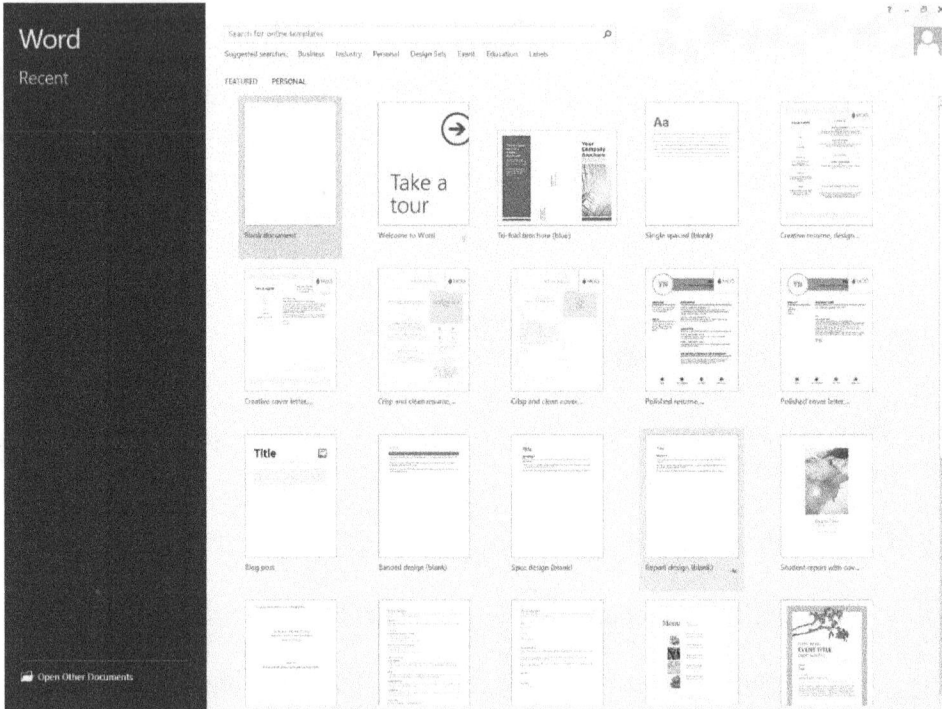

(Image 121: MS Word Start page to select the new document type you want to create)

From this page you can click on Blank Document to open the new document.

Method2: You can open file explorer and navigate to the directory you want to create the new document within and right click inside of the directory. From the options that are presented when you right click choose 'New' followed by different items you can create such as Text Document or Word. See below for an example:

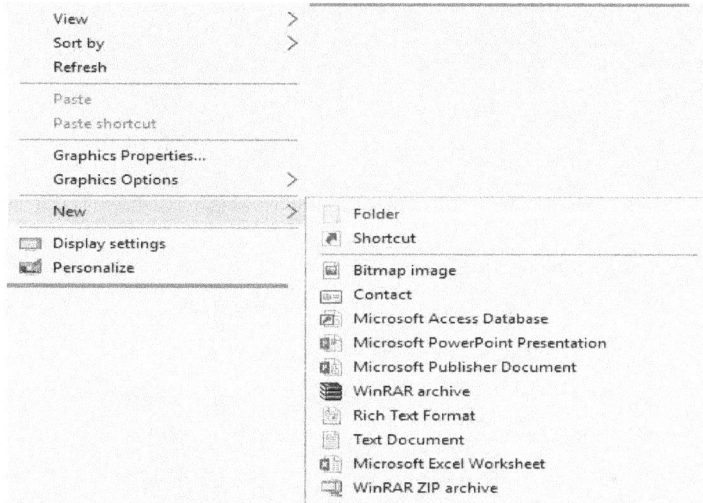

(Image 122: Images of how to create file using file explorer)

Method3: You can press the Windows Key [icon] on the keyboard followed by the 'r' key to launch the Run window. From there you can type in 'word' and press enter. This will also launch MS Word and from there you can press File followed by New and click the blank document.

Note: There are other methods as well so I'll let you do some exploring to see what works best for you.

2. How to save a new word documents.

When you are creating your first document it's very important that you save your work. Remember that the power can go off at any time and if you don't have your work saved then it may be gone. Note: Microsoft has created an auto recovery file that saves by default every 15 mins but you don't want to rely on this for saving your work… it's not best practice.

So how to do save your work? Here are 4 methods that work very well so choose what works best for you:

1. Method 1: Inside of MS Word program, click 'File' followed by 'Save'. If this is your first time saving the document it will launch the 'save as' window which will ask you how you want to save the document. It looks like:

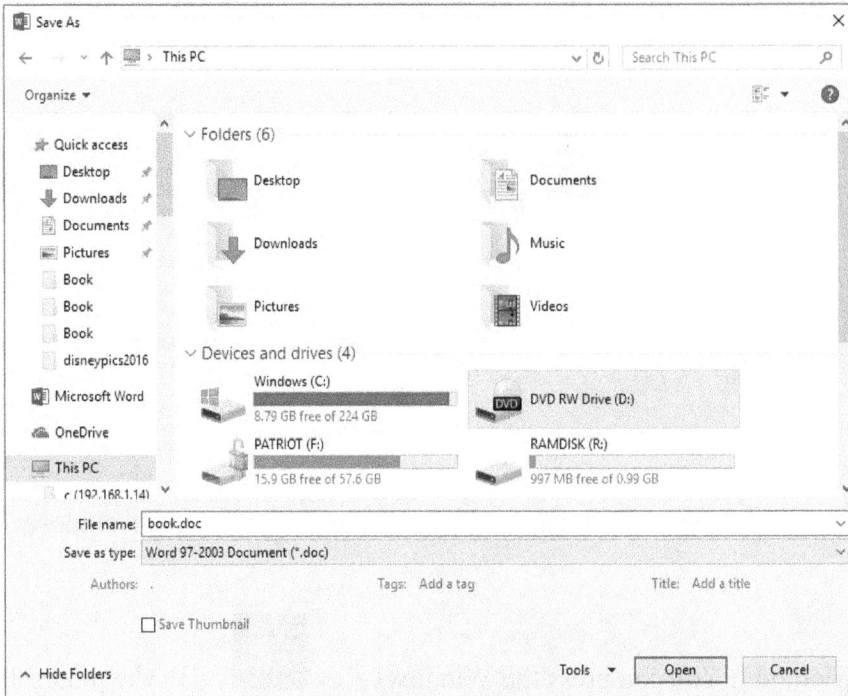

(Image 123: Save As screen)

From this window you can navigate the directory tree to the location you want to store your document. Name the document you want. Remember you have up to 255 characters to name the file with. I believe in newer versions of Office that may increase but still with 255 characters that is usually more than enough to properly name your file whatever you want.

Method 2: This method I've already explained above by clicking on 'File' followed by 'Save As' and choose your location. The main difference is sometimes you want to save the document into a different directory or possibly save it as a different file type such as .doc instead of .docx. Maybe you want to save it as a .pdf document and 'save as type' field will provide you with the list of options on how to save the document.

Method 3: This is a command line way to save the document and that is to press the following keys in this order: Alt+f+s. This will save the document provided there is already a filename in a directory which this document refers to. This is what most people who are proficient with word will use as it save so much time when saving a document.

Method 4: This is another command line way to save a document. Just like method 3 above you could also use the 'Ctrl+s' key sequence to save the document. Again there needs to be a name already created for the document otherwise it will prompt you with the Save-as window.

3. How to adjust the font size, font style, paragraphs and margins as well as inserting bullet points:

Most of my students who start with MS office products end up at some point wanting to adjust their font size, styles, paragraphs and margins. MS has done a wonderful job of providing these adjustments for you. All of these features can be done from the ribbon under the 'Home' tab.

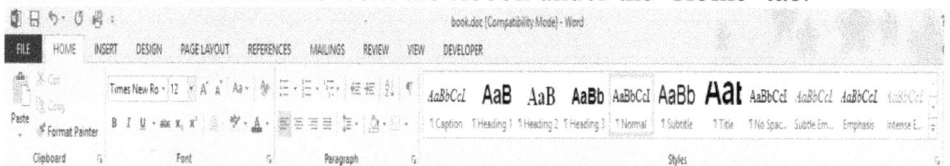

(Image 124: MS Word - Home menu)

Notice the font type, size, bold, italics, underline, font color, highlighter can all be addressed in the Font group. If however there is something that is not listed then you can click on the dialog box in the bottom right of the Font group (look for the diagonal arrow in bottom right of dialog box) to get more options. The same tode for paragraph alignment, double spacing, outlining a paragraph, etc.. If you want to insert bullets then you would click on the bullets button in the paragraphs group. Again if it's not listed on the main ribbon then always use the dialog box button to see more options available.

Learning Check: Applications:

Questions:
1. How can you find a command you need to use in DOS if you forget the command?

   _____

   _____

   _____

   _____

2. In Dos, what does the single dot (.) mean in a directory Listing?

   _____

   _____

   _____

   _____

   _____

   _____

3. In Dos, what does the double dots (..) mean in a directory listing?

   _____

   _____

   _____

   _____

   _____

   _____

4. Using Dos; how do you change directory into a folder called, 'my backyard projects'?

   _____

   _____

   _____

   _____

   _____

5. In Dos (CLI) environment how would you map the U:\ drive letter to a remote computer shared folder called umbrella:

   _____

   _____

   _____

   _____

6. What other programs are command line interface based:

_____

_____

_____

7. What is PowerShell:

_____

_____

_____

8. What are the different products which make up the MS Office suite?

_____

_____

_____

_____

_____

9. What is the term that we refer to these products as?

_____

10. List all the file extensions for:

    a. Word:

_____

    b. Excel:

_____

    c. PowerPoint:

_____

    d. Outlook:

_____

    e. Access:

_____

11. List 2 ways on how to open a new word document?

_____

_____

_____

12. List 4 ways on how to save a word document?

_____
_____
_____
_____
_____
_____
_____
_____
_____
_____

13. Can these 4 ways of saving a word document be used across other office products?

_____

14. In MS Word what is the dialog box and why would you use it?:

_____
_____
_____
_____
_____

9. Glossary / TERMS (aka: definitions)

Its common knowledge that computers use many, many, many acronyms and I would say that the computer industry is probably second to the military when it comes to using acronyms. That's why this section will be the Glossary of TERMs to help answer TERM questions such as:

"What does that mean?"

"Huh?"

Disclaimer:

So I don't leave other industries out; I do know there are many other industries that also use lots of acronyms as well such as the Medical and Automotive industries and I'm sure there are more that do as well; so for all the others I don't have listed here I apologize for not mentioning you here. I'm not trying to leave you out of this statement and therefore you're included as well.

I will attempt to answer question but please keep in mind that there are more than I will be able to answer in this book. Therefore if you don't find a term in this book then I suggest you type your acronym into your favorite search engine (i.e.: www.google.com) to look up its definition...

(Note, For simplicity I've placed these terms in Alphabetical order to help you)

Access point = This is a wireless connection device and its used to connect a wireless device such as laptops, smartphones and TV's to a wired (cabled) network.

Applications = Programs (examples: MS Word, Internet Explorer, Calculator, or a Game such as solitaire

Authentication = A validation process that is used to ensure a user's true logon information.

Authorization = A process that allows specific permissions (access levels) to be used for each username.

Back Up = duplicate copy of a file such as a program or data. The duplicate copy is called a backup. (Example: Think of making a photocopy/Xerox copy of a document (afterwards you have the original copy and a duplicate(backup) copy).

Bit = A single digit which is either a 0 or 1 but nothing else. (Notice this is referenced with a lowercase b. Example: 64Mb would be 64 Megabits. A bit is the smallest value used in computing.)

Byte = A quantity of 8 bits combined together to form a Byte. (Notice this is referenced with a capital B.   Example: 64MB would be 64 MegaBytes)

Cache (CPU) – On die internal memory on the cpu/processor. There are 2 or 3 layers of internal CPU cache which are referred to as L1, L2 or L3 cache. L1 cache is the fastest and most expensive as it is located closest to the CPU core(s). L2 is the next level away from CPU core(s) and it's a bit slower in performance and is cheaper. L3 cache is the furthest cache away from the CPU core(s) and again it's the cheapest of the cache as well as it's the slowest of the 3 levels of on die internal CPU cache.

Cache (Memory) = this is temporary computer memory used to store data files when you browse the Internet or use a program that needs to save volatile (non-permanent) information.

Client = A Client is simply any device (PC, laptop, smartphone, tv, etc..) connected via wire or wireless to a computer network which gets its affiliation from another computer (Server) on that same network. Typically this is done via TCP/IP network connection.

Central Processing Unit (CPU) = The central processing unit (CPU) is the primary hardware device that interprets and runs the commands you give to the computer. Many people think of the CPU as the main 'brain' of the computer. During production of the CPU it's usually cast at one time and the internal cores are referred to as on-die or built internal to the physical CPU device (aka: physical brick).
> Note: For us humans and to think in simplistic terms. I like to think of the CPU as the
> fastest speed reader or the fastest mathematician which can read or do repetitious math
> extremely fast. (granted computers only work in binary so there is no true reading occurring).

Computer = term used to describe all components of a computer as a single object. (Example: computer tower or laptop)

Communication Channel = transfer information between computers or peripheral devices. (Example: computer tower to external printers and external disk drives)

Compact disc (CD) = Typically a plastic storage device (approx. 4.7 inches in diameter and approx. 1 mm thick) which is used to store data in a digital format. Compact disc's usually store 700MB worth of data such as files, music, videos, etc.... The CD was replaced with newer technology called DVD's since early 2010.

Computer Privacy = A method to keep a person's data, such as personal data files, e-mail, and messages secured, so the information is not accessible by anyone without appropriate permissions.

Computer Security = the protection of a computer system and data from accidental or intentional loss and tampering.

Cookie = A small file which is placed on to your computer when you visit a Web site. Websites use cookies to identify a user who visits their site, and also track the preferences of the users. There are different levels of cookies and not all cookies are bad. Some cookies are performance cookies while others are tracking or history cookies. Some people believe in turning off cookies in their browsers; but this can lead to poor performance on some web activities and websites.

Copyright = protects the legal rights of an author or creator of creative work. (Example: text, music, painting, or computer program).

Cables (pwr, IDE, Sata) = wires that are assembled in an industry pre-determined manner to efficiently allow power or data to transfer between computer components in the best method possible. They come in different sizes and are typically color coded to refer to specific power voltages or to send data at different speeds.

CPU speed = The CPU speed is the rate at which the CPU can perform a task, such as moving data to and from the chipset, RAM or I/O devices. CPU speed is usually measured in Frequency and the higher the frequency the faster the processor however this also generates heat which is not good for a computer. Therefore more cores and hyper threading have been introduced which lowers the frequency and also lowers the heat to accomplish the same performance levels.

Chassis Frame (metal) = This is the metal structure inside the computer case which the motherboard is mounted to. It gives the structure for all hard drives, cd/dvd drives to be secured to for operation. It's usually covered by an external covering of metal which provides the secure environment inside from ESD and other foreign items.

Column = The vertical divisions in an Excel worksheet are called columns. Each column is identified by a letter. For example, the first column in a worksheet is column A and the next column to the right is column B and so on.

Data = Data is the plural for the Latin word datum, meaning an item of information.

Database = A database contains objects that help you to store, edit, and format information. A low level database is Microsoft Access which comes with Microsoft Office suite.

Decryption = Part of the security process to protect data; this process reconverts encrypted data into a usable form.

Desktop = This term can be used for many things in the office environment such as the work space on your desk that you use daily. However there is another meaning for this term in the computer world and that is the desktop is the on–screen work area that uses a combination of menus and icons and is usually the main screen available after a computer successfully boots and is ready for operation.

Desktop Computers = are made to site on top of a desk or next to a desk and are made up of individual components such as a computer case, monitor, keyboard, mouse, and a printer.

Digital camera = A camera that stores images digitally on a memory flash card and can connect to a computer via a USB cable to transfer pictures to the computer. This can be an input and output device with the newer digital cameras.

Digital versatile disc (DVD) = Much like the CD-ROM, this is a plastic storage device used to store data in a digital format. Typical sizes are the same as CD-ROM (4.7 inches in diameter); however the storage capacities are much greater ranging from ~4.7GB for single layer and ~8GB for dual layer.

Electronic mail (E-mail) = A method to communicate across the internet or within a network. Email allows for the exchange of letters, text messages and computer files over the network or Internet. Email is the electronic form of postal mail and is much faster and less expensive to relay information.

Encryption = The process of converting data into an unreadable and unusable form. This prevents unauthorized access to data.
Fan - device which uses 12Volts typically to remove heat from either the CPU, GPU, Chipset and/or chassis.

Faraday Cage = a completely grounded metal screen surrounding a piece of electronic equipment to protect from electrostatic and electromagnetic influences.

Firewall = This can be a hardware or software device that blocks unreliable information coming from the Internet before it reaches your computer or a private network. It provides protection against external remote threats such as hackers and viruses as well as it helps ensure computer privacy by restricting external users who do not have proper access.

Flash drive = A device that is used in the same manner as a hard drive or cd/dvd rom.
Usually they have a male USB connector on them so they can be inserted into a computer for file system access. They come in different physical styles and they come in a full range of storage capacities from 1GB, 2GB all the way up to 64GB and I've seen lately 128GB.

Folder (directory) = Just like a manila folder that is used in an office environment to file paperwork for storage. A folder (aka: directory) in the computer environment is a container which can hold data such as programs, files, pictures, music, videos, etc.

Gigabyte = One gigabyte (GB) is equal to 1,024 MB, which is approximately equal to one billion bytes.

Graphical User Interface (GUI) = A graphical user interface (GUI) is the most common methods today for interacting with a computer. It displays images and pictures that allows a computer user to interact with a computer easily as compared to command line.

Hacker = This is a person who uses their computer knowledge to gain unauthorized access to a computer, and then misuses or tampers the programs and data stored on the computer.

Handheld Computer = Handheld computers are smaller in size and provide fewer features compared to desktop computers or laptops. They are used for specific everyday tasks, such as managing personal data. These handheld computers can be used for many purposes such as inventory, medical, barcode scanning, etc.

Hard Drive = storage device to store data on. This can be internal or external to the computer chassis (case). They come in different physical sizes as well as different storage capacities and data can be accessed at different speeds. There are different types of hard drives such as Pata, Sata. The newest Sata connection drive is the SSD which is much faster that the older PATA technology drives although SSD is more expensive for the size of the storage compared to PATA at the printing of this book.

Hardware = This term refers to all the physical components of a computer (inside and outside)

Home office = This is usually a converted bedroom or spare area in a person's home that allows that person to work from home. Typically the home office needs to have a door to provide a quiet, safe and secure work environment to mimic the true work environment.

Icon = This is small picture or image which is displayed on the screen to represent a program, file or directory.

Input Devices = An input device is used to provide information into a computer. A keyboard and mouse are an example of an input device.

Internet = this is referred to as a super highway of information and it is a worldwide collection of networks that are linked to each other for information exchanges. It is not an

Intranet but instead an external network to corporations and people's homes. It was created originally by the department of defense (DOD) with the code name of Darpa-Net.

Internet Service Provider (ISP) = this is a company that provides Internet connectivity to individuals, businesses, and organizations for a monthly service fee. If you are connecting to the internet then you are using an ISP.

Intranet = this is a special type of network which is housed within a company or organization. It traverses the company or organization to provide network connectivity to allow communication and share information within that company or organization. Note this is not the internet.

IP address = this is a numeric address that specifies the exact location of a computer on the Web. It resides on the layer 3 level (protocol) of the OSI model and is 48 bits long. We usually refer to it using 4 sets of 8bit groupings called octets. This has the following format ###.###.###.### Each octet ranges between the decimal values of 0-255.

Keyboard = A device which looks like a type-writer and allows the user to press keys to send data into the computer. This is an Input device.

Kilobyte = One kilobyte (KB) is equal to 1,024 bytes.

Laptop Computers = Laptop computers are lightweight and portable personal computers. Laptop computers are also called notebook computers. They are becoming more light weight with the new laptops having SSD.

Local Area Network (LAN) = This is a topology style that connects devices (computers, smartphones, tv's, etc.) whether cabled or wireless together within a small limited area, such as a home or a small office.

Megabyte = One megabyte (MB) is equal to 1,024 KB.

Menu = this is a list of options a user can choose from to select a desired action, such as starting a program from the start menu, choosing a command or applying a particular format to part of a document. Most graphical user interface (GUI) based programs will use menus to provide the end user a method to operate that program. This is what makes the GUI environment attractive to new users. However it doesn't allow the user to use any other options which are not presented in the drop down menu. For this reason some power users prefer to use command line to issue commands so they can use all the other features and options available. This is a power user move and typically not done by newbies.

Menu bar = The menu bar displays a list of commands that are grouped into sections. Some of these commands have images next to them, so that you can quickly associate the command with the image. This image is also on the button that corresponds to that command.

Modem/NIC = This device is what allows the computer to talk to the outside world (internet) via a telephone core or a network cable. The modem can convert digital data into analog information to transmit across the telephone lines.

Motherboard = This is the main part of the computer hardware. It is the item to which all other internal computer parts plug into such as the cpu, ram, peripheral cards and it holds the I/O bulkhead which sticks out the rear of a computer tower.

Mouse = The mouse is an input device which a user places their hand on to control the mouse pointer within the computer screen. The Mouse typically has 2 buttons on it however it can have a single button (such as the Apple mouse) or it can have more than 2 buttons such as some of the gamers and power users mice have multiple buttons and scroll wheels.

Mouse pointer = The mouse pointer is an on–screen arrow or other (customizable) shape that moves when you move the mouse or other pointing device.

Network = A group of computers linked together across a Local Area Network to share resources and exchange information.

Network Drives = This is becoming a very common item in a computer environment as this is a disk drive that is shared with other computers on a network. It can be multiple disks that are RAID 'ed together for data protection and then presented as 1 single drive to the network. The benefit of network drives is that multiple users can access that drive at the same time across the network.

Nibble = 4 bits make a nibble and 2 nibbles makes a byte (see bit or byte for more info.).

Netstat = A DOS command to show you network information on a client/server machine.

Notification Area = This is the area in Windows operating system which is located on the bottom right side of the taskbar when the taskbar is located at the bottom of a screen. The notification area displays the time, a volume icon, and icons of some programs that are running on a computer. NOTE: Typically for best performance you do not want a lot of programs running in the notification area as they also take up memory resources.

Online = A computer is online when it's connected to the internet.

Operating System (OS) = The operating system controls the computer's hardware and provides services and access to the hardware to programs. It also manages the computer's operations and tasks, such as logging on, logging off, and shutting down. Common OS's of today are Microsoft Windows, Linux, Unix and Apple OS.

Output devices = An output device is used to send information outside of a computer. (Example: external devices, monitors, sound for speakers, printers are all examples of output devices.

Password = this is a protected unique string of characters which a user will customize by their choice to use at a later date to login into a computer or website. It is a security measure used to restrict access to computer systems and sensitive files.

Ping = A DOS command that will send icmp packets to a given remote destination (usually an IP address) to determine if it's network device is working correctly and responsive.

Platform = The hardware and the operating system together are referred to as a platform.

Plug-in = A web component that provides added functions by enabling the Web browser to access and execute files that are included in Web pages. Plug–ins are programs that help you view files, such as animations, audios, or videos, which are included in Web pages.

Portal (Web) = this offers information that is related to a specific topic in the form of a directory. A portal acts as a starting point to a number of resources on the Web.

Power supply = One of the most important items in a computer which goes un-noticed. This device converts AC power into DC power for the computer to use. The DC output is usually 3.3Vdc, 5.0Vdc, 12Vdc as the main power feeds however there are other voltages as well. The power supply has an octopus of cables with connectors at the end of each cable. This connectors connect to devices within the tower such as hard drives, motherboard and floppy drives.

Power surge = this is a sudden increase in A/C line voltage, which may lead to the damage of electronic devices, such as computers. This can occur in bad weather or if there is an accident down the street and the power poll was hit causing a sudden, rapid and/or severe increase in the A/C line voltage. This can come through and effect your computer and potentially damage your computer. The remedy for this is to be pro-active and purchase a surge protector (not a power strip which looks identical) and place between the A/C outlet and your equipment. Usually your equipment will plug into the surge protector. This goes for computers, TV's, anything electrical you want to keep safe from a power surge.

Presentation Programs (MS PowerPoint) = Presentation programs are used to present information in the form of slides. Microsoft PowerPoint is probably the most common program for doing this. It allows you create and edit presentations by adding graphics, texts, music and videos.

Programs = A pre-set sequence of instructions (code) that can be executed by a computer. A program is also known as software. When Apple Corporation released their iPhone, Apple coined the phrase, "There's an app for __<fill in the blank>__" to help sell all the different things that it could do.. These things called Apps are also known as programs.

Protocol = When you think of this word I want you to think of the word 'rules'. A protocol is a predetermined standardized communication method for transferring data between different devices or for computers it's across the network.

RAM = Random Access Memory. RAM is broken up into different sizes from 1k, 2k, 4k, 8k, 16k, 32k, 64k, 128k blocks depending on the Master Memory Controller decides what can be allocated where. Note; this is information changes and is not easily calculated so we won't cover that here. These blocks will be used in pages of memory. When a software application needs a page of memory then it would use a combination of these allocated block allotments. Then that page would be used by the software as a contiguous memory for the application even though the blocks may not be contiguous between the RAM itself and the page memory on the hard drive.

Reports = You can create reports in a database program, such as Microsoft Office Access, to organize, summarize, and perform calculations on data stored in a database.

Resolution = in regards to monitors; resolution refers to the clarity and sharpness of a picture.

Rows = The horizontal divisions in an Excel worksheet are called rows. Each row is identified by a number. For example, the first row in a worksheet is 1 and the next row down is row 2.

Search engine = A search engine is a program that helps you search and retrieve information over the Internet. Some of the most common search engineers are www.google.com, www.yahoo.com, www.bing.com. A search engine is not 'Internet Explorer', 'Chrome', 'Firefox', 'Safari', etc.

Server = the server is the main computer on a network that provides services to other computers on the network. A server decides which computers are allowed to access the hardware and software on the network. There are specific servers for specific tasks such as printing, user access control, web services, etc.

SSD (solid state drive) = This drive is the newest of the hard drive environment. There are no moving parts in the SSD as compared to the older style hard drives which required 12Vdc power to move the actuator motor and arm across the platters and to spin the platters. Therefore the SSD requires less power to operate than its predecessors. SSD typically have the SATA connector on them and transfer speeds at 6Gb/second. SSD come in various storage capacities up to 2 TB as of the writing of this book.

Software = this is very similar to the program definition listed above. It's a sequence of pre-written code (instructions) that a computer can execute to perform a given task. It is also referred to as programs.

Software Piracy = This is a real thing and yes you do not want to do this as it's a punishable offense. Basically it's the unauthorized copying (duplicating) of copyrighted software without obtaining the license or permission of its copyright owner is software piracy.

Sound = This is what we human hear however in a computer environment we are refereeing to the sound card. This is an output device which allows the computer to process data and then output the data to a sound jack (typically 1.5mm jack) for an external speaker system for our ears. This also includes headphones.

Spreadsheet Programs = The most common spreadsheet program today is Microsoft Excel. It's used to create budgets, manage accounts, perform mathematical calculations, and convert numerical data into charts and graphs.

Status bar = This bar displays information about a programs the current status.

Storage Devices = Storage devices are used to store data. (Examples: Floppy disk, hard disk drive, CD/DVD drive, USB/Flash Drive, MMC disk, network disk drives and cloud drives such as Icloud, Google, Onedrive are all example of a storage devices.

Tablet Computer = A tablet is a small, compact form of a computer. It can be carried very easily by most people and it allows you to write directly on the screen by using a tablet pen called a stylus.

Taskbar = this is used in Microsoft Windows and is usually located across the bottom of the screen. You can use the taskbar to keep track of your running programs. You can minimize a program when not in use by sending it to the taskbar and when you're ready to use that program you simply click on the minimized program within the taskbar.

Telecommuting = this is a feature that many home office people have to use in order to work from home. It's called telecommuting and it's an arrangement that allows people to work from home or from a remote office.

Terabyte = One terabyte is equal to 1,024 GB, approximately equal to trillion bytes.

Title bar = In most Microsoft windows, the title bar is the horizontal bar at the top of each window that contains the name of that window or the name of the program that's running in that window. Most title bars also contain buttons to close, minimize, and resize the window.

Toolbar = this is a tricky controversial item as some people love them and others do not. I have found in my personal usage that toolbars which are programs that reside within a web browser house many sub programs within them. This in turn consumes memory (RAM) which could be used for other items. Therefore I don't typically use them in my web browsers however to be fully neutral in my saying, I have heard there are some good ones. But what is it? The toolbar is a bar across the top of your web browser that houses multiple sub programs to try and make your internet usage easier. It contains a block of buttons or menus that you can use to quickly perform common tasks.

Traceroute = A DOS command that will show the number of hops (across external routers) from your current source location to a remote IP destination. For IPv4 the max number of hops is 30.

Trojan Horse = Just like in Greek mythology; it's a destructive computer program disguised as a game, utility, or software. When run, a Trojan horse does something harmful to the computer system while appearing to do something useful.

Usb ports = Ports on a computer for a USB cable to connect a remote external device to for use. USB ports speeds are USB 2.0 (max speed of 480Mb/sec) and 3.0 (max speed of 5Gb/sec). These allow for input and output to occur for the remote device.

Universal serial bus (USB) cable = A cable that helps you connect external digital devices to a computer without turning off the computer.

UNC = Universal Naming Convention = A method windows uses to connect to remote systems. It is not available in the DOS environment.

Username = the name by which a user is identified to a computer system or network. To access a computer protected by username and password, a user needs to enter the correct combination of username and password.

Video = This is referred to as an output device since the computer will send data out of the tower or laptop to a monitor for visual use.

Virus = A computer program that is designed to cause malfunctioning of a computer or damage the data stored on the computer. It's best to have an anti-virus on your computer however you only need one antivirus. I've found it to be good practice to also have an anti-malware and if needed a rootkit to resolve some problems.

Web (The Web) = Many folks refer to the Web but it's true name is the World Wide Web (WWW). The WWW is a giant collection of information which is housed on many different computers and servers (known as web servers) around the world and this housing is data is accessible on the Internet via this WWW.

Web address = Just like a house has a home address so do these web servers around the world. The address we use to access these remote web servers is called a web address. We humans like to refer to a word address such as www.google.com however the computers use a DNS to cross reference this address into a given IP address for a web server for google. Once connected to the web address then data (the webpage) is transferred between the 2 computers. A Web address is also known as the URL.

Web browser = A Web browser is a program that helps you view and interact with various resources on the Web. Typically a web browser will read HTML code or some form of Java, Perl, or other web programming language and convert that into a visual webpage for the end user to view. Some typical web browsers are Internet Explorer, Edge, Chrome, Firefox, Safari, etc.

Wide Area Network (WAN) = A WAN is a large global model for a topology plan for a given network that connects multiple smaller networks such as Metropolitan Area Network (MAN) and Local Area Networks (LANs) in geographically separated areas.

Window = In Microsoft Windows when the software opens a window it is rectangular area on the monitor that displays a given program. For every program that is opened or running it has its own process which means it has window.

Windows audio wave (WAV) = this is a type of digital file which is associated with audio music. It was developed by Microsoft.

Windows media audio (WMA) = this is a type of digital file which is associated with general media audio.

Word processors = this type of program assists a person to create documents which are text based. Microsoft Word is the most common word processor in today work environment. The format for word documents ends in .doc (prior to 2007) and .docx (2007 and later versions of MS Word)

Workbook = A workbook is a file created in Microsoft Excel. A workbook can contain one or more worksheets and related items.

Worksheet = A spreadsheet is called a worksheet in Microsoft Excel. There can be multiple worksheets in a workbook just as there can be multiple pages in a book.

Workstation = this is usually used in a work environment and it typically a bit stronger of a computer than the typical home pc. It usually has a stronger CPU and more memory than the normal home PC but we have to keep in mind it's still an end client machine for an employee to use on a company network.

10. Appendix A

(Various types of software, URL's and approx. costs)

Note: you will need to verify these applications and costs as this information may change over time.

a. Paragon Backup & Recovery (http://download.cnet.com/Paragon-Backup-Recovery-Free-64-bit/3000-2242_4-10972187.html
b. Acronis True Image 2015   (cost:~$49.99)
c. Retrospect   (cost: ~$119.00)
d. EaseUS Todo Backup   (cost: Free http://download.cnet.com/AOMEI-Backupper/3000-2242_4-75833997.html?part=dl-&subj=dl&tag=button
e. Acronis Software   (cost: ~$89.00 - $999.00)
f. NTI Backup Now EZ   (~$30.00)
g. Macrium Reflect Standard   (~$44.99)

NOTE: You can also get a lot of free trial software from doing a simple internet search for the program you're looking for by adding the word free to it. I've listed some common websites which many people use on a regular basis.
   i. www.download.com
   ii. www.filehippo.com
   iii. www.ninite.com

Appendix B (Answers)

Learning Check: Page 12 Items:

1. _Chassis Frame (metal)_____
2. _Power Supply_____
3. _Motherboard (Include Chipset)_
4. _CMOS (BIOS)_____
5. _CPU (Processor)_____
6. _RAM (Memory)_____
7. _Cables (Power, IDE, Sata)____
8. _Fans_____9
. _Input/Output Devices_____
10. _Mouse, Kybrd, USB, Modem,
Sound_____
11. _Hard drive, Disk Drives_____
12. _Operating Systems_____

a. Provide Structure to PC layout_
b. convert A/C power to D/C power
c. Main platform for connections___
d. Pre-OS Environ. to configure h/w e.
Main processor of data_____
f._Random Access Memory (RAM)
g. _Connects internal devices_____
h. _Remove hotter air from case____
i. _Gen. term for input/output items._
j. _i/o devices_____
k. _storage devices_____
l. _Windows, Linux, Apple_____

Learning Check: Page 20:

1. What does a chassis (frame) do for a computer?
   __(Provide structure to mount MB on)_____

2. What is the importance of the chassis?
   __(give structure for internal components)_____
   _(provide chassis ground for motherboard items)

3. What are the different Chassis styles?
   __(AT, ATX, BTX, MINI ITX)_____

Learning Check: Page 27:

2) What does a CPU do for a computer?
   ___It is the central processing unit and it processes data in a very fast method using binary computations and sends the data to the chipset for distribution throughout the computer__

3) How does the CPU interact with the different components within the computer itself?
   _The cpu interacts through the chipset to send and receive data across the front side bus__

4) What are the most recent CPU models for each of the CPU manufacturers?
   _____Intel = I7 6th Generation _____
   _____AMD = FX-9### Series _____

5) What are the 2 most commercial common cpu manufactures today?
   _____INTEL and AMD_____

6) What does RISC stand for and what OS primarily uses it?
   _____Reduced instruction Set Code. This type of processor is used primarily by
   UNIX environment.____

7) What does CISC stand for and what OS primarily uses it?
   _____Complex instruction set code. This type of processor Is used primarily for
   the Windows environment_____

8) What type of socket set does Intel use in the newer i3,i5,i7 processor family?
   _____Land Grid Array (LGA) sockets. There are different processor sets such as
   LGA-1150, LGA-1151, LGA-1155, LGA-1156, LGA-1366_____

9) What type of socket set does AMD use in the newer
   _____ There are different AMD sockets that match accordingly with each level of
   cpu such as: AM2, FM1, FM2, FM2+, FS1,etc.._____

Learning Check: (RAM) Page 28:

1. What does the acronym RAM stand for? _____Random Access Memory____

2. Explain how RAM interacts with the CPU and chipset?
   _____Ram interacts directly with the CPU at the same frequency across the
   front side bus and this is done via the chipset.._____

3. What is the FSB and why is it important? _____The Front Side Bus (referred to
   as the FSB) is the grouping of data lines (referred to as a bus) that lies between
   the CPU, chipset and the memory (RAM). The FSB must be the same width as
   that of the CPU, chipset and memory and operate at the same frequency as the
   devices on the FSB. For example the FSB is either a 32 bit bus or a 64 bit bus.
   In the future it's very conceivable that the FSB will consist of 128 or 256 bits in
   width. But this is well into the future.

4. Why is RAM so important?

_____ *RAM is the device that allows for the virtual operating system environment to be established in, as well as allow for software applications to operate from. Without RAM there would be no environment for the operating system nor applications to reside within during normal operations.*_____

5. What uses RAM?

_____*The operating system is the primary users of RAM however all additional software applications are also loaded into RAM and therefore it's easy to say that all software products are the users of RAM.*_____

What programs or applications use memory (a.k.a: RAM)?

_____As mentioned above *The operating system is the primary users of RAM however all additional software applications are also loaded into RAM and therefore it's easy to say that all software products are the users of RAM.*_____

6. Can contiguous memory be reused between operating system and applications; provided that the program was written correctly to release memory when done?

Yes/No: *Reason: Memory is designed to be contiguous if at all possible and this does lead to better software utilization of the memory pool.*

8. What is a memory leak?

_____*A memory leak is when software is not written correctly and during the usage of the software program the memory is consumed for normal operation how the program never releases the memory when done and instead it continues to consume more and more memory. In essence consuming all the available memory and leaving none left for any other applications nor operating system to use when needed. This will sometimes lead to either an application crash or operating system crash. This was common in earlier operating systems and or earlier versions of applications however in recent years the operating systems and application developers have become more aware of this and commonly write cleaner code resulting in less memory leaks.*

Page 61 learning check (Input/Output):

1. What does input and output mean in reference to the computer?

_____*Input and output refer to how communication occur travels into or out of the computer itself. If data is being sent from a mouse or keyboard that would be referred to as input. Whereas if data is being sent from a VGA card to an external monitor then that would be referred to as output. There are also other devices which are both input and output such as USB drives, Network cards_____*

2. Why so many devices are generically called input and output (I/O)
   _____*The reason so many devices are generically called input and output devices (also referred to as I/O) is because they are sending and receiving data into and out of the computer itself just as previously mentioned. Some of these devices are mouse, keyboard, hard drives, DVD-ROM and Blu-Ray, USB, Audio, networking, etc..._____*

3. Classify the device as either input or output and Explain the details of the following I/O items:
   a. *Mouse = (Input) - The mouse allows the end user to select items in the computer to perform given tasks.*

   b. *Keyboard = (Input) – The keyboard allows the end user to use various keys to type and input data into the computer.*

   c. *VGA =(Output) - The VGA adapter sends data out of the computer main compartment and to the external Monitor.*

   d. *USB = (Input and Output). The USB adapter is a bi-directional serial bus that allows data to flow from various devices at a high rate of speed.*

   e. *Hard drive = (Input and Output) A computers hard drive whether Pata or Sata connected are both bi-directional devices and allow data to flow at high rates of speed (Sata being even higher than Pata) and the data is stored in a non-volatile manor for safe keeping.*

   f. *SATA = (Input and Output) Sata stands for Serial ATA and it is the new faster bus for connecting hard drives.*

   g. *Video (PCI-e) = (Input and Output) There are multiple forms of PCI-e but for Video I'll refer to the x16 which is primarily used for high speed video data transfers and it comes directly off the cpu avoiding the chipset and the slower I/O bus.*

4. Why do we need I/O devices?

_____*We need I/O devices in order to effectively communicate with the computer in many fashions. We need to issue commands to direct the computer and we need to be able to get feedback from the computer via output devices._____*

Page 70 learning check (Printers):

1. What are the different types of printers that exist?

_____*Dot Matrix (Impact printers), Dot matrix and Laser_____*

2. What are the pros and cons for each printer type?

_____Dot Matrix was good in that you could easily feed reams of paper into it without reloading and you could easily use it for multiple layered paper due to its impact abilities. Cons was it was slower and the ink cartridge was either a single color (black) or possibly a 2 tone cartridge (black and red)

_____Ink Jet was the next version of printer to come out and it allowed for more colors to be printed but it lost the abilities that the impact printer provided.

_____Laser was the next printer to come out and it was faster to print material and it could be both black or in color. The primary drawback here was the cost of the laser printer and the ink. _____

3. Which printer will you choose and why? _____To be determined by reader. This is readers' choice._____

Page 71 summary check:

1. Write down all the hardware equipment in the left column and in the right column fill in what it does:

	9._Input/Output Devices_____
1._Chassis Frame (metal)_____	10._Mouse, Kybrd, USB, Modem, Sound_____
2._Power Supply_____	
3._Motherboard (Include Chipset)_	11._Hard drive, Disk Drives____
4._CMOS_(BIOS)_____	12._Operating Systems_____
5._CPU(Processor)_____	
6._RAM (Memory)_____	a.Provide Structure to PC layout__
7._Cables (Power, IDE, Sata)____	b.convert A/C power to D/C power
8._Fans_____	c.Main platform for connections__

d.Pre-OS Enviro. to config h/w____ i._Gen. term for input/output items.
e. Main processor of data_____ j._i/o devices_____
f._Random Access Memory (RAM)
g._Connects internal devices_____ k._storage devices
h._Remove hotter air from case___ l._Windows, Linux, Apple____

2. What is a computer case and why is it important?

   _____*A computer case is the sheet metal frame that provides structure for the computer components including motherboard, power supply and drives to properly mount to. On the external part of the Frame is the chassis cover. There is one side of the chassis cover which is a removable door for servicing. This removable panel connects to the rest of the case by pins that line up and they create a faraday cage to protect the internal components from ESD._____*

3. What is the most common style of motherboard for the home pc?

   _____*The Most common style of motherboards for case layouts is ATX in today home environment however BTX is also rapidly gaining in popularity._____*

4. What does the acronym CPU and RAM stand for?

   ___*CPU is the acronym for Central Processing Unit and RAM is the acronym for Random Access Memory._____*

5. Explain how RAM interacts with the CPU and chipset?

   _____*RAM interacts with the CPU by providing a logical environment for the software to live within. The RAM works in lock step fashion including operating at the same exact frequency as the CPU and the Chipset. The RAM provides an addressable memory pool for the cpu to issue reads and writes to and from which provides the environment for the software to operate from.____*

6. What is the FSB and why is it important?

   _____*The FSB stands for Front Side Bus and this bus is the main data path between the very fast function cpu, chipset and the Memory. All 3 of these items live on the front side bus____*

7. Why is RAM so important?

   _____*RAM is so important as it is what is responsible for the operating system to correctly function. Its main purpose is to create the logical environment for the operating system as well as applications to correctly* *operate. If you don't have enough RAM installed on your computer then there is a strong chance that performance issues will be observed._____*

8. What uses RAM?

    _____This is an interesting question in that the computer uses RAM. However I wanted you to dig a bit deeper and tell me that the software (OS, Apps, Drivers) directly uses RAM. The general concept here is that more RAM installed the better things will operate.___

9. What programs or applications use memory (a.k.a: RAM)?

    ___See answer 8 above_____

10. Can contiguous memory be reused between operating system and applications provided that the program was written correctly to release memory when done? <u>*Yes*</u>

What is a memory leak?

_____A memory leak is when software is not written correctly and during the usage of the software program the memory is consumed for normal operation how the program never releases the memory when done and instead it continues to consume more and more memory. In essence consuming all the available memory and leaving none left for any other applications nor operating system to use when needed. This will sometimes lead to either an application crash or operating system crash. This was common in earlier operating systems and or earlier versions of applications however in recent years the operating systems and application developers have become more aware of this and commonly write cleaner code resulting in less memory leaks

11. What does input and output mean in reference to the computer?

    ___Input and output refer the data that is being sent into the computer or being sent out of the computer. It's always referenced from the computer side. For example if you are using the keyboard to send data into the computer then that would be referred to as input. If you're sending data out to an external monitor or printer then that would be referred to as output.____

12. Why are so many devices generically called input and output (I/O)

    _____The reason so many devices are generically called input and output devices (also referred to as I/O) is because they are sending and receiving data into and out of the computer itself just as previously mentioned. Some of these devices are mouse, keyboard, hard drives, DVD-ROM and Blu-Ray, USB, Audio, networking, etc..._____

13. Classify the device as either input or output and Explain the details of the following I/O items:

a. *Mouse = (Input) - The mouse allows the end user to select items in the computer to perform given tasks.*

b. *Keyboard = (Input) – The keyboard allows the end user to use various keys to type and input data into the computer.*

c. *VGA =(Output) - The VGA adapter sends data out of the computer main compartment and to the external Monitor.*

d. *USB = (Input and Output). The USB adapter is a bi-directional serial bus that allows data to flow from various devices at a high rate of speed.*

e. *Hard drive = (Input and Output) A computers hard drive whether Pata or Sata connected are both bi-directional devices and allow data to flow at high rates of speed (Sata being even higher than Pata) and the data is stored in a non-volatile manor for safe keeping.*

f. *SATA = (Input and Output) Sata stands for Serial ATA and it is the new faster bus for connecting hard drives.*

g. *Video (PCI-e) = (Input and Output) There are multiple forms of PCI-e but for Video I'll refer to the x16 which is primarily used for high speed video data transfers and it comes directly off the cpu avoiding the chipset and the slower I/O bus.*

14. Why do we need I/O devices?

_____We need I/O devices in order to effectively communicate with the computer in many fashions. We need to issue commands to direct the computer and we need to be able to get feedback from the computer via output devices._____

15. What are the 3 different types of printers that exist?
    1. *_____Dot Matrix / aka: Impact Printers_____*
    2. *_____Ink Jet_____*
    3. *_____Laser_____*

16. What are the pros and cons for each printer type?

    _____Dot Matrix was good in that you could easily feed reams of paper into it without reloading and you could easily use it for multiple layered paper due to its impact abilities. Cons was it was slower and the ink cartridge was either a single color (black) or possibly a 2 tone cartridge (black and red)

    _____Ink Jet was the next version of printer to come out and it allowed for more colors to be printed but it lost the abilities that the impact printer provided.

    _____Laser was the next printer to come out and it was faster to print material and it could be both black or in color. The primary drawback here was the cost of the laser printer and the ink. _____

17. Which printer will you choose and why? *_____To be determined by reader. This is readers' Choice._____*

Page 87 learning check (MS Windows):

3. What is an operating system and why do I need it?

    _____An operating system is software that is first to be loaded after the hardware passes power on self-test. This first piece of software "called the operating system" is the primary foundation of the operating environment for applications to operate from. The OS also interacts with the computer equipment (aka: hardware) via smaller pieces of software called "drivers". These drivers allow the OS to interact with remote peripherals (devices) such as printers, monitors, keyboards, mice, etc. All of this is needed in order for you the end user to correctly do the tasks you are choosing to do with a computer such as surf the web, create a document or check email._____

4. Explain the history of Microsoft Operating systems:

    _____Answers will vary but please refer to page 75-77 for details. _____

3. List 3 of the new features of Windows 10 and their significance to each:
   A. Start Menu (with Tiles) = this menu combines the best of both worlds in my opinion. It has the standard 'start' menu we are use to from previous versions (excluding Windows 8 and 8.1). It also incorporates the tiles from Windows 8 and 8.1 to the right of the Start menu when it's opened. You can also customize both the start menu and the tile board as you see fit.

   B. Cortana = This is a new assistant Microsoft has incorporated into Windows 10 where you can speak to Cortana to issue commands, open programs, dictate, search for files, etc...

   C. Edge = This is the replacement web browser to Internet Explorer which has many good new features such as drawing on the page and exporting it. Newer security, etc. You also still have an option in the Edge tool bar to open up an older version of Internet Explorer if you need to.

4. What are hotkeys and provide an example of one?
   _____*A hot key is a keyboard shortcut where a user can press "CTRL+C" at the same time to issue the copy command. This really improves speed for the user when doing certain tasks in Windows. There are a number of HOTKEY's that are universal throughout windows operating systems and programs*_____

5. What is the difference between Microsoft Windows and Microsoft Office
   _____*The difference between MS Windows and MS Office is MS Windows is the base operating system. This is what loads when you start your computer. Without Microsoft Windows Operating system no programs could successfully load. (Excluding other operating systems). The point here is you have to have a base OS to boot the computer into. Conversely Microsoft Office is an office suite program which loads when you need to work on office documents. MS Office loads into (or on top of) the base installed OS which would be MS Windows. Please make absolute sure you understand this difference.*
   *Versions MS Windows 95, 98, 2000, Millennium, 7, 8, 2010 are all operating systems and versions MS Office 97, 2000, 2003, 2007, 2010, 2013, 2016 and Office 365 (Online version) are all Office suite applications which operate in the OS.*_____

Bonus: How do you Power On/Off/Restart the Windows OS?
   _____*You do this from the Start Menu from within the Windows Desktop which is from the operating system*_____

Page 95 learning check (Apple OS-X):

a. What is the difference between OS X and Windows?

_____*OS X is the operating system for the Apple/Macintosh environment whereas Microsoft Windows is the operating system for the PC world._____*

b. What hardware requirements are needed for OS X (10.10)?

____*The hardware requirements for OS X are at least a core2duo processor or above. This will not run on the older processors/platforms that previous apples ran on. _____*

c. Can OS X (10.10) be run on an i5 (greater) CPU in PC?

_____*Yes it can be run on I5 or greater due to the use of i5 with newer Mac OS'es an i5 will operate without problems._____*

Page 105 learning check (Linux):

8. What is Linux?

_____*Linux is an operating system much the same way as MS Windows and the Apple OS X are operating systems. Linux is a version of UNIX that will operate on the pc environment._____*

9. What is the history of Unix/Linux? .

_____*Linux was created by Linux Torvald and is created on the C-programming language. Linus licensed it under the GNU license which means the kernel is free to everyone in the world._____*

10. Why is Linux an important operating system in todays world.

_____*Linux is an important operating system in todays world due to its versatility and functionality it provides. With Linux being open source program it allows for many different instances to be used for various needs including private programming. Linux is used in the server environment, client operating system environment, Base OS'es, DVR's, video production, etc..._____*

11. What is open source code verses closed source or private code.

_____*Open source is a term that means the editable code for creating a program or operating system is open for anyone to download and modify as they want to without penalties This is referred to as 'open source code'. Whereas closed source means that the editable source code is held privately and not released for the public to view, download nor edit._____*

12. Who is the person who is responsible for starting the Linux movement?

_____*Linus Torvald _____*

13. Can you do the same thing in Windows as you can do in Linux? (If so explain to what degree, If not explain to what degree)

_____Yes for the most part you can do the same thing in Windows as you can in Linux and Vice-versa. Both of these are operating systems and excluding any specific customized features these 2 operating systems can do basically the same thing for the average user.

_____

14. What animal is associated with Linux? *_____Tux the penguin_____*

Page 106 summary check (Operating Systems):

- What did I learn from the Windows, Macintosh and Linux Operating systems?

  _____(This will vary based on the readers. There is no wrong concepts for this answer)_____

- What is the difference between OS X and Windows?

  _____OS X is the operating system for the Apple/Macintosh environment whereas Microsoft Windows is the operating system for the PC world._____

- What hardware requirements are needed for OS X (10.10)? _____

  _____The hardware requirements for OS X are at least a core2duo processor or above. This will not run on the older processors/platforms that previous apples ran on. _____

- Can OS X (10.10) be run on a i5 (greater) cpu in PC?

  _____Yes, due to the use of i5 with newer Mac OS'es an i5 will operate without problems.

- What is Linux?

  _____Linux is an operating system much the same way as MS Windows and the Apple OS X are operating systems. Linux is a version of UNIX that will operate on the pc environment._____

- What do I know about the history of Unix/Linux

  _____(This will vary based on the readers. There is no wrong concepts for this answer)_____

- Why is Linux an important operating system in todays world.

320

_____ *Linux is an important operating system in todays world due to its versatility and functionality it provides. With Linux being open source program it allows for many different instances to be used for various needs including private programming. Linux is used in the server environment, client operating system environment, Base OS'es, DVR's, video production, etc...*_____

- What is open source code verses closed source or private code?
  _____*Open source is a term that means the editable code for creating a program or operating system is open for anyone to download and modify as they want to without penalties   This is referred to as 'open source code'.   Whereas closed source means that the editable source code is held privately and not released for the public to view, download nor edit.*_____

- Who is responsible for starting the Linux movement?
  _____*Linus Torvald*_____

- Can you do the same thing in Windows as you can do in Linux? (If so explain to what degree, If not explain to what degree)
  _____*Yes for the most part you can do the same thing in Windows as you can in Linux and Vice-versa. Both of these are operating systems and excluding any specific customized features these 2 operating systems can do basically the same thing for the average user.*

- What animal is associated with Linux?
  _____*TUX the penguin*_____

Page 119: Learning Check: (binary

1. What numbers are used in binary?
   _____*There are only 2 numbers in the binary system and they are zero (0) and one (1). The location of these numbers refer to the value that's assigned to them. Then these values are added up for a total value that is needed.* _____

2. What is the msb and lsb of an octet?
   _____*The MSB is the most significant bit of the string of numbers. Conversely the LSB is the least significant bit of the string of numbers. How this relates to an octet the place values of the octet are 1,2,4,8,16,32,64,128. So the lowest number would be the LSB and the largest number would be 128.*_____

3. How many bits are in an octet?

_____*8 bits in an octet.*_____

4. How many octets are in an IPv4 address?

_____*There are 4 octets in an IPv4 address*___

5. What is the maximum number for an octet if all bits are enabled?

_____*255*_____

Page 135 learning check: (IP Version 4)

1. Q: What is an IPv4 address?

____*An IPv4 address is a logical numbering scheme that we use to identify a computer on a given network. It is 32 bits in length and we break that 32 bits in 4 groups called octets which are listed in decimal between 0 to 255. Each octet contains 8 bits and each bit can be either 0 or 1. Of the 4 octets the first part of the IPv4 address will be the network and the later part of the IP address be the host address.*____

2. *Q: What is a subnet and why is it important?*

_____*A subnet is another numbering scheme that can be applied to the ip address to divide up the network into smaller pieces. This will allow for more secure smaller networks or for increasing the number of nodes on the network. Depending on the end result needed, there are different subnet masks which can be applied such as class [a,b,c] subnet masks. The type of subnet mask to apply is typically determined by the first octet of the IP address* ____

3. Q: What are the different classes of IP Addresses (List all classes, number of networks and number of hosts)?

Class	IP Range	# of Networks	# of Hosts/Network
A	0.0.0.0-127.255.255.255	128	16,777,216
B	128.0.0.0-191.255.255.255	16,384	65,536
C	192.0.0.0-223.255.255.255	2,097,152	256

Q: What are the different sizes of a network? (Not classes)

_____*See above answer for details*_____

322

- Q: Which is best for home or small office use and why?

     _____Usually for the standard home or small office a class C network is sufficient. It allows for most standard home connections to properly connect to the small network and traverse to the internet._____

- Q: Is there a difference between a Wi-Fi-Lan (aka: WAN) and a wide area lan (aka: WAN)? If so explain:

     _____Even though both have the same acronym of WAN, there absolutely is a difference between the two and I've seen a handful of students who get these terms confused. Wi-Fi is a term reserved for local area networks Wireless Lan is a wireless connection to a given network whereas the acronym for WAN stands for Wide Area Network. Wide Area Networks cover a long physical distance such as connecting networks from city A (Seattle) to city B (San Diego) to city Z (New York)_____

- Q: Convert the following IP address (192.168.29.57) to binary:

     _____11000000.10101000.00011101.00111001 _____

- Q: Apply the correct subnet mask to the above IP address answer you provided to net out the correct IP address when the subnet mask is active.

     _____ 11111111.11111111.11111111.00000000 _____
     also known as
     _____255.255.255.0_____

- Q: Convert the following binary address to decimal:
  11000000.10101000.01100011.01101001

     _____192.168.99.105_____

Page 164 learning check: (IP Version 6)

8. What is IPv6 address?

     _____An IPv6 address is the next version of internet addressing to come out which is to replace IPv4 addressing. _____

9. What is an IPv6 address?

     _____As previously mentioned; an IPv6 address is the next version of internet addressing to come out which is to replace IPv4 addressing. There are many new items to IPv6 which allow it to be more beneficial into the future such as allowing for many more networks and many more hosts to exist on each network. IPv6 is also referred to as the Internet of Things (aka: IoT) due to there will be enough IPv6 addresses for everything on the earth____

10. How many devices can an IPv6 address support compared to IPv4 address scheme:

_____ *IPv6 is 128 bits long and is 2^{128} which equals 340,282,366,920,938,463,436,374,607,431,768,211,456 total addresses. Compared to IPv4 which is a 32bit addressing scheme (created in 1980) and allowed for 2^{32} which equals 4,294,967,295 total addresses (just under 4.3 billion addresses).* _____

11. Does IPv6 use subnet mask?

_____*Yes IPv6 does use subnet mask but not the same way that IPv4 uses a subnet mask. Please refer back to the IPv6 chapter for details.*_____

12. Does IPv6 use a gateway address?

_____*Yes IPv6 does use gateways. Please refer back to the IPv6 chapter for details.*_____

13. What is a link-local address?

_____*IPv6 uses what we call a Link-Local address which is what we would call a broadcast address in IPv4. Just like in IPv4 we could assign a broadcast address for that given network; in IPv6 we use what is called a link-local address which is basically the same concept.*____

14. What is an Any-cast address?

_____*An any-cast address is an address that is used for Wi-Fi and Cellphone connections. These devices like to use anycast as they are always reaching for a 'Any' connection to link to as they move around a neighborhood, city, etc... Since these devices are reaching for a 'any' connection to link up to they are the client devices. On the other side of the connection is the point where the many devices connect to. On this point there is a range of IPv6 addresses that would be predetermined to be a range for 'any' device connections and that would be determined by the local administrator.* _____

15. What is a multi-cast address and why is it important:

>_____ *A Multicast address is any address in the range* 224.0.0.0 *to* 224.0.0.255 *and can connect your one device to multiple other devices. Multicast addresses are supposed to be for a larger number of devices and allow for less network bus contention.*_____

16. How many Bytes are an IPv4 address compared to an IPv6 address?

>_____*There are 32 bits in an IPv4 address which correlate to 4 Bytes in an IPv4 address (32 divided by 8 = 4 Bytes). This is compared to IPv6 which has* 340,282,366,920,938,463,436,374,607,431,768,211,456 *bits which theoretically equals* 2^{128}, *or approximately* 3.4×10^{38} *(Thirty Four Undecillion) addresses. I don't know that trying to figure out the number of Bytes in this IPv6 number but instead I'll look to see how many Hextets there are. To do that, take this number (3.4x1038) and divide by 16 due to IPv6 uses Hextets and walla.. you have your answer.. the number of hextets in an IPv6 Address. I think this is where we could say a full boat load.* _____

17. Give an example of a link-local address in Hexadecimal notation:

>_____ *FE80::1/64*_____

18. Briefly explain what the IoT is and its importance:

>_____*With the IPv4 version of the internet it was coined the 'Internet of People" and it's purpose was to connect people. With the IPv6 version of the internet it is coined the 'Internet of Things (IoT) and its purpose is to connect all the things in the world such as computers, smart devices such as cars, thermostats, cameras, refrigerators, etc).*_____

Page 180 learning Check: (Troubleshooting Tools):

1. Q: What command will display your hardware (MAC) address and list the correct syntax in how you would use it:

>_____*ipconfig /all*_____

2. Q: What will Ping allow you to do?

>_____*Ping is a command line tool which when issued from a command prompt it will allow you to send ICMP packets from your current machine to a remote machine across a TCP/IP network to determine if the remote device is alive and responsive. This will also test the entire path between*

the 2 devices and give you percentage of successful ping requests or failures._____

3. Q: What does netstat allow you to see/check?
    _____Netstat is another command line tool that you can issue from a command prompt to see the network statistics information for that interface. There are many different results you can get from this command and you need to use the options via the /? Or help option._____

4. Q: To check a path a packet is taking what command will I issue?
    _____You would use the 'tracert' command line tool to test the path between your computer and a remote computer. _____

Page 181 Summary Check (Networking):

1. What numbers are used in binary?
    _____There are only 2 numbers in the binary system and they are zero (0) and one (1). The location of these numbers refer to the value that's assigned to them. Then these values are added up for a total value that is needed. _____

2. What is the msb and lsb of an octet?
    _____The MSB is the most significant bit of the string of numbers. Conversely the LSB is the least significant bit of the string of numbers. How this relates to an octet the place values of the octet are 1,2,4,8,16,32,64,128. So the lowest number would be the LSB and the largest number would be 128._____

3. How many bits are in an octet?
    _____8 bits in an octet._____

4. How many octets are in an IPv4 address?
    _____There are 4 octets in an IPv4 address____

5. What is the maximum number for an octet if all bits are enabled?
    _____255_____

326

6. Q: What is an IPv4 address:?

       _____An IPv4 address is a logical numbering scheme that we use to identify a computer on a given network. It is 32 bits in length and we break that 32 bits in 4 groups called octets which are listed in decimal between 0 to 255. Each octet contains 8 bits and each bit can be either 0 or 1. Of the 4 octets the first part of the IPv4 address will be the network and the later part of the IP address be the host address._____

7. Q: What is an IPv4 subnet and why is it important?

       _____A subnet is another numbering scheme that can be applied to the ip address to divide up the network into smaller pieces. This will allow for more secure smaller networks or for increasing the number of nodes on the network. Depending on the end result needed, there are different subnet masks which can be applied such as class [a,b,c] subnet masks. The type of subnet mask to apply is typically determined by the first octet of the IP address _____

8. Q: What are the different classes of IPv4 Addresses (List all classes, number of networks and number of hosts)?

Class	IP Range	# of Networks	# of Hosts/Network
A	0.0.0.0-127.255.255.255	128	16,777,216
B	128.0.0.0-191.255.255.255	16,384	65,536
C	192.0.0.0-223.255.255.255	2,097,152	256

9. Q: What are the different sizes of a IPv4 network? (Not classes)

      _____See above answer for details_____

10. Q: Which is best class of IPv4 addresses for home or small office use and why?

      _____Usually for the standard home or small office a class C network is sufficient. It allows for most standard home connections to properly connect to the small network and traverse to the internet._____

11. Q: Is there a difference between a Wi-Fi-Lan (aka: WAN) and a wide area lan (aka: WAN)? If so explain: *_____Even though both have the same acronym of WAN, there absolutely is a difference between the two and I've seen a handful of students who get these terms confused. Wi-Fi is a term reserved for local area networks Wireless Lan is a wireless connection to a given network whereas the acronym for WAN stands for Wide Area Network. Wide Area Networks cover a long physical distance such as connecting networks from city A (Seattle) to city B (San Diego) to city Z (New York)_____*

12. Q: Convert the following IPv4 address (192.168.29.57) to binary:
_____11000000.10101000.00011101.00111001_____

13. Q: Using your above answer; Apply the correct subnet mask to the above IP address answer (you provided) to net out the correct IP address when the subnet mask is active.
_____ 11111111.11111111.11111111.00000000 _____
also known as
_____255.255.255.0_____

14. Q: Convert the following binary address to decimal:
11000000.10101000.01100011.01101001
_____192.168.99.105_____

15. What is IPv6 address?
_____An IPv6 address is the next version of internet addressing to come out which is to replace IPv4 addressing. _____

16. What is an IPv6 address?
_____ As previously mentioned; an IPv6 address is the next version of internet addressing to come out which is to replace IPv4 addressing. There are many new items to IPv6 which allow it to be more beneficial into the future such as allowing for many more networks and many more hosts to exist on each network. IPv6 is also referred to as the Internet of Things (aka: IoT) due to there will be enough IPv6 addresses for everything on the earth____

17. How many devices can an IPv6 address support compared to IPv4 address scheme:
_____ IPv6 is 128 bits long and is 2^{128} which equals 340,282,366,920,938,463,436,374,607,431,768,211,456 total addresses. Compared to IPv4 which is a 32bit addressing scheme (created in 1980) and allowed for 2^{32} which equals 4,294,967,295 total addresses (just under 4.3 billion addresses). _____

18. Does IPv6 use subnet mask?
_____Yes IPv6 does use subnet mask but not the same way that IPv4 uses a subnet mask. Please refer back to the IPv6 chapter for details._____

19. Does IPv6 use a gateway address?

_____*Yes IPv6 does use gateways. Please refer back to the IPv6 chapter for details.*_____

20. What is a link-local address?

_____*IPv6 uses what we call a Link-Local address which is what we would call a broadcast address in IPv4. Just like in IPv4 we could assign a broadcast address for that given network; in IPv6 we use what is called a link-local address which is basically the same concept.*____

21. What is an Any-cast address?

_____*An any-cast address is an address that is used for Wi-Fi and Cellphone connections. These devices like to use anycast as they are always reaching for a 'Any' connection to link to as they move around a neighborhood, city, etc... Since these devices are reaching for a 'any' connection to link up to they are the client devices. On the other side of the connection is the point where the many devices connect to. On this point there is a range of IPv6 addresses that would be predetermined to be a range for 'any' device connections and that would be determined by the local administrator.* _____

22. What is a multi-cast address and why is it important:

_____*A Multicast address is any address in the range* 224.0.0.0 *to* 224.0.0.255 *and can connect your one device to multiple other devices. Multicast addresses are supposed to be for a larger number of devices and allow for less network bus contention.*_____

23. How many Bytes are an IPv4 address compared to an IPv6 address?

_____*There are 32 bits in an IPv4 address which correlate to 4 Bytes in an IPv4 address (32 divided by 8 = 4 Bytes). This is compared to IPv6 which has* 340,282,366,920,938,463,436,374,607,431,768,211,456 *bits which theoretically equals* 2^{128}, *or approximately* 3.4×10^{38} (Thirty Four *Undecillion) addresses. I don't know that trying to figure out the number of Bytes in this IPv6 number but instead I'll look to see how many Hextets there are. To do that, take this number (3.4x1038) and divide by 16 due to IPv6 uses Hextets and walla.. you have your answer.. the number of hextets in an IPv6 Address. I think this is where we could say a full boat load.* _____

—

24. Give an example of a link-local address in Hexadecimal notation:
_____ *FE80::1/64*_____

25. Briefly explain what the IoT is and its importance:
_____*With the IPv4 version of the internet it was coined the 'Internet of People" and it's purpose was to connect people. With the IPv6 version of the internet it is coined the 'Internet of Things (IoT) and its purpose is to connect all the things in the world such as computers, smart devices such as cars, thermostats, cameras, refrigerators, etc).*_____

26. Q: What command will display your hardware (MAC) address and list the correct syntax in how you would use it:
_____*ipconfig /all*_____

27. Q: What will Ping allow you to do?
_____*Ping is a command line tool which when issued from a command prompt it will allow you to send ICMP packets from your current machine to a remote machine across a TCP/IP network to determine if the remote device is alive and responsive. This will also test the entire path between the 2 devices and give you percentage of successful ping requests or failures.*_____

28. Q: What does netstat allow you to see/check?
_____*Netstat is another command line tool that you can issue from a command prompt to see the network statistics information for that interface. There are many different results you can get from this command and you need to use the options via the /? Or help option.*_____

29. Q: To check a path a packet is taking what command will I issue?
_____*You would use the 'tracert' command line tool to test the path between your computer and a remote computer.*_____

Page 194 learning check (Hard Drive):

1. Will your hard drive fail? When?

_____*Yes your hard drive will fail. In fact every hard drive will fail at some point. So the question is when will that failure point occur? My response to this is, "at the most inconvenient time". This is why I'm a strong advocate of doing backups._____*

2. Explain what a backup is and why it's important?

_____*A backup is nothing more than a copy of your existing data. The reason it's important is for when your original copy of your data is damaged, deleted, or upon hard drive failure you can still access your data from your backup copy. Remember a backup is only good to you if it is current. If you backup is old then you will only be able to restore data from that old time frame and everything you've made after that point will be lost._____*

3. Where is the average home users personal data kept in MS Windows Operating system?

__*C:\users\<username>\My[Documents, Pictures, Music, Videos, etc...]_*

4. Who needs to do backups?

_____*In my opinion I believe that every person who uses a computer and saves data needs to do backups. Here is the answer I give to my students when they ask me if they should be doing backups; Can you live with losing your data right this moment._____*

5. List and explain the 3 method (types) for backups:

_____*The 3 method types are Full, Incremental and Differential backups. A full backup is just as it sounds and it starts at the beginning of the drive and fully back up all the data on the drive. An Incremental backup is a partial backup of only the items that have changed since the last full backup occurred.. A differential backup is a cumulative of backups that have occurred since the last full back. In other words it only backs up what has changed since the last full backup occurred._____*

6. Can a backup device be internal or external to your pc/laptop and explain?

_____*A backup device can be either an internal or external device. What's important to remember is that every hard drive is going to fail. So it's best to have your backup drive (aka: medium) be another drive which can be mounted either internally inside your computer tower or you may have an external USB backup drive._____*

Page 196 Learning Check (Windows Managing Files):

1. Where does Microsoft keep your picture files inside of the operating system: _____*My Pictures folder*_____

2. Where does Microsoft keep your music files inside of the operating system: _____*My Music folder*_____

3. Where does Microsoft keep your document files inside of the operating system: ___My Documents folder_____

4. What is a library and why is it important?

   _____*A library is a virtual representation object which reflects multiple actual folders. For example you may have a pictures library however if you right click on the pictures library properties you will easily see there are multiple directories which make up that library. The same goes for Music and pictures libraries. In the properties window you can select one of the folders to be the primary folder for saving newer items into. Libraries are important as they give you a single point of reference to multiple pictures when the pictures reside in multiple different directories. This can really help the end user keep track of their pictures, documents, music, etc.*_____

Page 199 Learning Check (File and Disk Management):

1. What folders are best for checking for unneeded files in a computer?

   1. *Temporary folders (C:\temp, All installed Web-browsers)*
   2. *All users Desktops*
   3. *All users Downloads*
   4. *All users Documents*
   5. *All users Music*
   6. *All users Pictures*
   7. *All users Videos*
   8. *All users Personal Network Drives (i.e.: K:\, T:\, etc..)*

2. How do I delete a file or directory I no longer want? _____

   _____*When you find unwanted files; simply drag the items to the Recycle Bin on your Desktop or right click on them and select delete. When done with searching items 1-7 above you can empty your recycle bin.*___

3. If I empty the recycle bin what happens to the contents? __

   _____*When you delete a file or directory from its location in Windows it's moved to the recycle bin (aka: trash bin) until you empty the trash bin. When you empty the recycle bin then the contents in the recycle bin is truly deleted as far as windows is concerned. This is the same process as when a janitor comes into your office and takes the trace out of the recycle bin under your desk and takes it outside to the main trash/recycle bin. At that point; for the simplification of this book; it's gone*_____

4. What is the best practice method for keeping a clean computer operational?

_____ *The best practice method for keeping a computer clean is to keep it organized without much clutter. By this don't have a bunch of various programs installed as they all take up space and use RAM which can degrade your instance of Windows. Also run a cleanup utility such as ccleaner.exe to help clean up the unused data files, programs, program temporary files and probably the most important is the registry files._____*

Page 200 Summary Check (File and Disk Management):

1. Will your hard drive fail? When?

_____*Yes your hard drive will fail. In fact every hard drive will fail at some point. So the question is when will that failure point occur? My response to this is, "at the most inconvenient time". This is why I'm a strong advocate of doing backups._____*

2. Explain what a backup is and why it's important?

_____*A backup is nothing more than a copy of your existing data. The reason it's important is for when your original copy of your data is damaged, deleted, or upon hard drive failure you can still access your data from your backup copy. Remember a backup is only good to you if it is current. If you backup is old then you will only be able to restore data from that old time frame and everything you've made after that point will be lost._____*

3. Where is the average home users personal data kept in MS Windows Operating system? __

__*C:\users\<username>\My[Documents, Pictures, Music, Videos, etc...]_*

4. Who needs to do backups? _____*In my opinion I believe that every person who uses a computer and saves data needs to do backups. Here is the answer I give to my students when they ask me if they should be doing backups; Can you live with losing your data right this moment._____*

5. List and explain the 3 method (types) for backups:

_____*The 3 method types are Full, Incremental and Differential backups. A full backup is just as it sounds and it starts at the beginning of the drive and fully back up all the data on the drive. An Incremental backup is a partial backup of only the items that have changed since the last full backup occurred.. A differential backup is a cumulative of backups that have occurred since the last full back. In other words it only backs up what has changed since the last full backup occurred._____*

6. Can a backup device be internal or external to your pc/laptop and explain?

_____*A backup device can be either an internal or external device. What's important to remember is that every hard drive is going to fail. So it's best to have your backup drive (aka: medium) be another drive which can be mounted either internally inside your computer tower or you may have an external USB backup drive._____*

7. Where does Microsoft keep your picture files inside of the operating system:

_____*My Pictures folder*_____

8. Where does Microsoft keep your music files inside of the operating system:

_____*My Music folder*_____

9. Where does Microsoft keep your document files inside of the operating system:

_____*My Documents folder* _____

10. What is a library and why is it important?

_____*A library is a virtual representation object which reflects multiple actual folders. For example you may have a pictures library however if you right click on the pictures library properties you will easily see there are multiple directories which make up that library. The same goes for Music and pictures libraries. In the properties window you can select one of the folders to be the primary folder for saving newer items into. Libraries are important as they give you a single point of reference to multiple pictures when the pictures reside in multiple different directories. This can really help the end user keep track of their pictures, documents, music, etc._____*

11. In this section what folders are best for checking for unneeded files in a computer?

    1.   *Temporary folders (C:\temp, All installed Web-browsers)*
    2.   *All users Desktops*
    3.   *All users Downloads*
    4.   *All users Documents*
    5.   *All users Music*
    6.   *All users Pictures*
    7.   *All users Videos*
    8.   *All users Personal Network Drives (i.e.: K:\, T:\, etc..)*

12. How do I delete a file or directory I no longer want?

    _____ *When you find unwanted files; simply drag the items to the Recycle Bin on your Desktop or right click on them and select delete. When done with searching items 1-7 above you can empty your recycle bin.*___

13. If I empty the recycle bin what happens to the contents?

    ____*When you delete a file or directory from its location in Windows it's moved to the recycle bin (aka: trash bin) until you empty the trash bin. When you empty the recycle bin then the contents in the recycle bin is truly deleted as far as windows is concerned. This is the same process as when a janitor comes into your office and takes the trace out of the recycle bin under your desk and takes it outside to the main trash/recycle bin. At that point; for the simplification of this book; it's gone*_____

14. What is the best practice method for keeping a clean computer operational?

    _____*The best practice method for keeping a computer clean is to keep it organized without much clutter. By this don't have a bunch of various programs installed as they all take up space and use RAM which can degrade your instance of Windows. Also run a cleanup utility such as ccleaner.exe to help clean up the unused data files, programs, program temporary files and probably the most important is the registry files.*_____

Page 213: Learning Check (Internet):

1. List the reasons the internet is so successful in today world?

_____*There are many reasons the internet is so successful but mainly it's due to it successfully completed what it's setup to do and that is connect people to each other. The internet allows us humans to connect to each other and share information at lightning fast speed. You can now send emails, setup webpages, post pictures and comments on various internet platforms. All of this is due to the basis of what the internet was setup for and again that is to connect people._____*

2. How do you read a webpage address?

_____*To read a webpage URL address you start by reading from left to right. Start with the http:// followed by the www.websitenamehere.com/ Once you get to the first domain name after the name of the website there will be a forward slash (/). This is where you will stop reading from left to right. Now you will reverse the reading direction and read from right to left. This means that you are on the .com domain as compared to the .net, .org, .mil, etc... domains. Next you will see a website name and this is the true website of where you are (provided it's a legitimate name and not a spoof). If there is another name in front of your website name with a period (.) separating the 2 names then the name closest to the domain is the true website. _____*

3. Name some of the job search engines you can use to search for new jobs:

___ *www.monster.com, www.dice.com, www.edd.ca.gov, www.linkedin.com, www.jobs.com, www.facebook.com, etc.._____*

4. List some of the online email websites you can use for email:

_____ *www.gmail.com , www.mail.yahoo.com, www.hotmail.com* _____

5. Explain the process on how to log into your online email website?

_____*First start by opening your choice of browser and then go to the website where your email is housed. Example if I'm using Gmail as my email server then I would go to www.gmail.com. Once you get to www.gmail.com find the link at the top of the screen that says to login. Once there then type in your email address followed by your password. This will open your webmail._____*

6. How do you start an email?

_____*There are many different ways of how to start an email based on whether your using a standalone program writing email such as Outlook Express (legacy program), MS Mail, Apple Mail, Incredimail, Thunderbird, etc...Most of these programs will have an icon button where you can click on them to start drafting (writing) a new email. However if you're using an online email service such as www.gmail.com, www.hotmail.com, or www.mail.yahoo.com then you will start composing your email by clicking on a button that stays 'compose' or 'new' or it may just be a plus sign (+). Each company may vary slightly however the concepts are the same so please don't get caught up in the I can't do this mentality if the vocabulary is a bit different. You can do this and look around for something that appears to point in the direction of creating a new email. (Hint: you can always click on a button if you don't know what it does and if you don't like it click the undo button at the top of the screen or you can also use the Microsoft short-cut of 'CTRL+Z' for undo._____*

7. How do you send the email?

_____*You send the email after you draft is complete. To send the email make sure the To: address is correct (we don't want to be sending email to people it's not intended for). Then when you're ready you will click on the 'send' button or there might be an 'Arrow' button which also refers to sending._____*

8. In order to follow best practice; what should you always do when you are done with your online email session?

_____*You should always click on the link from within the page to exit the web session. This sends a message to the server that you want to close the session. The server will then close the connection from the server side and then you can close your webpage. If you close the webpage by clicking the red X in the top right corner or the red circle in Apple 'Safari' it will close the web browser however your session may not be closed. This is especially important for when you're traveling and at a remote location/computer (example: Hotel). If you don't close your web session correctly as I've noted above then after you leave the next person who comes along and opens the web browser may open the browser and have access to all your information._____*

9. Explain the process for your answer in step 8 above: __*See the answer given above in step 8* _

Page 242: Learning Check (Troubleshooting):

1. What are the CompTIA 6 steps to troubleshooting (explain in detail):
    1. *Identify the problem* _____
    2. *Establish a Theory of Probably cause* _____
    3. *Test the theory (If more than one test each)* _____
    4. *Take Action and implement corrective measures* _____
    5. *Verify the action corrected the problem* _____
    6. *Document the problem and solution.* _____

2. What is the purpose of Cpu-z?
    _____*CPU-Z is a aftermarket program which is good for troubleshooting the cpu itself.*_____

3. What is the name of a system stressor/tester program?
    _____*Memtest86, prime95 and there are many other good ones but I have found that just getting the operating system to load and be functional is always a good stress test in itself.* _____

4. What is the name of the memory tester program?
    _____*Memtest86*_____

5. What program helps network technician break down TCP/IP traffic?
    _____*Wireshark* _____

6. What does ESD stand for? _____*Electrostatic discharge*_____

7. Why is ESD so dangerous to computers?
    _____*ESD is so dangerous to computers due to it can be the silent killer of computers. It can damage computers by statically shocking all computer parts at voltages that are not even detectable by humans. By this I mean that humans cannot even feel the shock. However to the computer it could be very serious. ESD is one of those things that when it attacks the computer it may attack the computer just a little bit or very severely. That is why damage may be instantaneously or occur 5 months later or even 5 years later. This is why we always practice safe ESD procedures when working on computer equipment.*__

8. At what voltage do humans feel ESD compared to what voltage can damage occur to electronics?

_____*ESD is measured in volts and for us humans to feel the zap it has to increase into the thousands of volts range.* _____

9. What items can be used to combat ESD?
    A. _ESD wrist strap _____
    B. _ESD Grounding mat _____
    C. _ESD Jacket _____

10. To test a power supply for functionality without using a motherboard; what is the best way to do so? (Explain)

_____ *The best way is to use a power supply tester. This will plug into the main power connector (aka:P1) and then when you plug in the a/c power cord to the power supply you will be able to hit the test button on the power supply tester. This will tell you if the power supply is operational as well as each voltage rails' status such as +12Vdc, +5Vdc, +3.3Vdc, etc...*_____

11. When troubleshooting an operating system what do you want to make sure is updated?

___*The operating system itself. This can be done by running the windows update utility.*_____

12. List a few updates that you can do to verify the best performance for a computer?
    a. *Windows updates*
    b. *Java updates*
    c. *Web-browser updates*
    d. *Flash updates*
    e. *Specific applications updates (i.e.: office, antivirus, antimalware)*

13. List 4 command prompt commands that come with MS Windows to troubleshoot its network connectivity? (Explain each in detail)
    A. _Ping *= sends icmp connectivity checks to remote system.*
    B. _ipconfig /all *= Shows local IP address information for system.*
    C. _Netstat –a *= Shows network statistics*
    D. _Traceroute *= Shows router path including hop count to remote location.*

14. What output does ipconfig /all show you?

_____the command 'ipconfig /all' shows you the same output as ipconfig command which is the computers current IP address, mask and gateway for each network interface such as Ethernet, wireless, virtual interfaces, VPN's, etc. The difference between 'ipconfig' and 'ipconfig /all' is that the /all option also provides a lot more detail for the interfaces such as host name, Primary DNS, Node Type, IP routing, WINS Proxy enabled, and then each interfaces individual MAC addresses, DHCP configuration, NetBIOS (enabled/disabled)._____

15. What 2 websites can test your internet connectivity and quality of service for your internet connection?

_____ www.speedtest.net and www.pingtest.net _____

16. In regards to Wi-Fi; explain what a WAP is and does?

_____The term 'WAP' Stands for Wireless Access Point and it is a device on a network which converts a hard network connection (i.e.: network cable connection) into a wireless connection for remote mobile devices. This is very beneficial for wireless mobile devices that need mobility and still need to be connected to a network. _____

17. Explain how a WAP broadcasts its signal?

_____A Wireless Access Point (WAP) can have internal or external antennas. I'll refer to an external antenna for this answer but keep in mind an internal antenna does something very similar in nature (without going into the details of the internal). Using the example of the wireless antenna; the signal is broadcast out in an omni-direction from the antenna. Meaning that it broadcasts the Wi-Fi signal in 360 degree horizontal plane from the antenna. Again to better understand this concept think of the rock being thrown into a lake and what happens to the top of the water where the rock enters the water. There is a 360 degree ripple effect away from the point of entry. Same thing for Wi-Fi broadcast._____

18. What can cause a blockage in a Wi-Fi environment?

_____Basically anything that gets in between the sender and the receiver. In this case anything that gets between the wireless device and the antenna.

___

19. Are all Wi-Fi encryption levels the same?

_____No, As time passes the security and encryption levels get more and more complex which means they are also more and more secure. Conversely, the further back in time you go or another way of saying this is the older you get in wireless technology the less and less security features are available and that is mainly because the newer technologies were not created back then. _____

20. Is one encryption level better than another? (if so, why and if not, why)

_____This will depend on the administrator/owners choice for security for that given Wi-Fi network. If there is super-secret information that must be secured then the administrator/owner would want a higher level of encryption. However if the administrator/owner didn't feel as if a high level of encryption was needed then he/she might opt for a lower level of security. Also keep in mind that for average home networks have a general distance rule of thumb of 150ft (indoors) and 300ft (outdoors); So your surrounding areas are also a level of protection and having your Wi-Fi surrounded by unpopulated distances greater than the rule of thumbs (aka: nature) might also help in providing security. _____

21. List some steps you can do to test connectivity on a web-browser; when that web browser does not show you a website of your choice?

1. *Refresh the web browser*
2. *Try a different website or a website you don't go to often.*
3. *Try a different web-browser.*
4. *Try to access a different search engine.*
5. *Open command prompt and run ipconfig /all to see if you have a valid IP address on this computer.*
6. *In the command prompt window; ping the local IP address of the computer, it's router, it's DNS, and ping www.google.com to see if there is connectivity.*
7. *If items 1-5 fail then reboot the computer you're on and retest. This usually fixes most problems I've seen on windows client machines (which are what most versions of windows are for home users.).*

Page 277 Learning Check (Command Line):

8. How can you find a command you need to use in command prompt (DOS) if you forget the command?

_____*Simply type 'help' at the command prompt (cmd>).*_____

9. In command prompt (Dos), what does the . mean in a directory listing?

_____*it means the current directory that you reside in.*_____

10. In Dos, what does the .. mean in a directory listing?

_____*The first period (.) means the same thing as answered in question 9 above. However the second period (..) refers to the parent directory which is above the current directory. For example if the directory path is c:\dir1\dir2 and you're current location is in dir2 then if you issued the command 'cd ..' then you would move from dir2 up to dir1.*_____

11. Using Dos; how do you change directory into a folder called, 'my backyard projects'?

_____*you would issue the change directory command (cd) and then follow it with the 'my backyard projects' in quotes. This will tell the command prompt (dos) window what you are trying to do. (Example: cd 'my backyard projects' <enter>)*_____

12. In Dos (CLI) environment how would you map the U:\ drive letter to a remote computer shared folder called umbrella:

_____*This would be a 2 step process where you would need to use the windows features to map a remote system via its universal naming convention (UNC)path (\\remotecomputername\umbrella) and then map it to the U:\ drive letter. Dos could then cd to u:\ You could also use the netsh command to do this as well.*_____

13. What other programs are command line interface based:

*powershell, command prompt, and 3rd party CLI programs* __

14. *What is PowerShell:* __*Powershell is a program by Microsoft corporation that is a bit more powerful than just command prompt. It has the same feel as command prompt but it does a lot more and has more features which gives it the appearance of being more powerful.*__

Page 291 Learning Check (Applications):

15. How can you find a command you need to use in command prompt (DOS) if you forget the command?

_____*Simply type 'help' at the command prompt (cmd>).*_____

16. In Dos, what does the .. mean in a directory listing?

_____*The first period (.) means the same thing as answered in question 9 above. However the second period (..) refers to the parent directory which is above the current directory. For example if the directory path is c:\dir1\dir2 and you're current location is in dir2 then if you issued the command 'cd ..' then you would move from dir2 up to dir1.*_____

17. In Dos, what does the .. mean in a directory listing?

_____*The first period (.) means the same thing as answered in question 9 above. However the second period (..) refers to the parent directory which is above the current directory. For example if the directory path is c:\dir1\dir2 and you're current location is in dir2 then if you issued the command 'cd ..' then you would move from dir2 up to dir1.*_____

18. Using Dos; how do you change directory into a folder called, 'my backyard projects'?

_____*you would issue the change directory command (cd) and then follow it with the 'my backyard projects' in quotes. This will tell the command prompt (dos) window what you are trying to do. (Example: cd 'my backyard projects' <enter>)*_____

19. In Dos (CLI) environment how would you map the U:\ drive letter to a remote computer shared folder called umbrella:

_____*This would be a 2 step process where you would need to use the windows features to map a remote system via its universal resource locator path (\\remotecomputername\umbrella) and then map it to the U:\ drive letter. You could also use the netsh command to do this as well.*_____

20. What other programs are command line interface based:

_*powershell, command prompt, and 3rd party CLI programs*__

21. What is PowerShell:

__Powershell is a program by Microsoft corporation that is a bit more powerful than just command prompt. It has the same feel as command prompt but it does a lot more and has more features which gives it the appearance of being more powerful.__

22. What are the different products which make up the MS Office suite? \
_____*Microsoft Word, Excel, PowerPoint, Outlook, Access are the main programs and I refer to these 5 as the sister products due to they all have a common flair to them but they do different tasks. However there are some commonality between them. I have to also say there are additional products under the MS Office suite such as OneNote, OneDrive, Sway, Calendar, SharePoint, Yammer and many more...*_____

23. What is the term that we refer to these products as?
_____*Microsoft Office* _____

24. List all the primary file extensions for:
    a. *Word:* _____ *primary extensions are .doc and .docx* _____
    b. *Excel:* _____ *primary extensions are .xls and .xlsx* _____
    c. *PowerPoint:* *primary extensions are .ppt and .pptx* _____
    d. *Outlook:* _____ *primary extensions are .pst and .ost* _____
    e. *Access:*_____ *primary extensions are .accdb* _____

25. List 2 ways on how to open a new word document?
_____*The first option is to open Microsoft Word and then select NEW document when prompted. If Word is already open then you can go to backstage view (click on the File tab) and then select new and then choose the format you want for your new document. The other common way to open a new document from your desktop would be to right click on the desktop. This will provide a contextual menu (drop down menu) with an option to select new. Once you click new you will see an option for word document.*_____

26. List 4 ways on how to save a word document?
    a. *File > Save*
    b. *File > SaveAs*
    c. *CTRL + S*
    d. *Alt > f > s*

27. Can these 4 ways of saving a word document be used across other office products?

>_____Absolutely, This is one of the many benefits that are built into the operating system. The people of Microsoft were very smart when they decided to use common command features across operating system as well as within all their programs. It's also become common practice for these common features to be used within non-Microsoft products. Therefore one could even go as far as to say it's industry practice to use common features between operating systems and programs._____

28. In MS Word what is the dialog box and why would you use it?:

>_____A dialog box is any pop up window within MS Word that you can use to issue further commands/features. To access the dialog box from within the ribbon you would click on the little arrow in the bottom right corner of the subject box you are working with in. The arrow points to a 45 degree in the bottom right corner of that window. There is also another viewpoint of dialog boxes and that is for informational purposes. If MS Word or any of the office programs need to display a message to you they can display them in a dialog box which could be only information or may require your attention to take further action(s)._____

Thank you for reading this book.
I hope you enjoyed it and have learned a lot.
Please tell others about this book.

Sincerely,
Chris Anderson

www.ingramcontent.com/pod-product-compliance
Lightning Source LLC
Chambersburg PA
CBHW062033090426
42740CB00016B/2895